# OLAF STAPLEDON

# Science-Fiction Writers

# OLAF STAPLEDON
## A Man Divided

# Leslie A. Fiedler

**OXFORD UNIVERSITY PRESS**
Oxford  New York  Toronto  Melbourne
1983

OXFORD UNIVERSITY PRESS

Oxford London Glasgow
New York Toronto Melbourne Auckland
Delhi Bombay Calcutta Madras Karachi
Kuala Lumpur Singapore Hong Kong Tokyo
Nairobi Dar es Salaam Cape Town

*and associate companies in*
Beirut Berlin Ibadan Mexico City Nicosia

First published by Oxford University Press, New York, 1983

First issued as an Oxford University Press paperback, 1983


Library of Congress Cataloging in Publication Data

Fiedler, Leslie A.
  Olaf Stapledon, a man divided.

  (Science-fiction writers)
  Bibliography: p.
  Includes index.
  1. Stapledon, Olaf, 1886-1950. 2. Authors,
English—20th century—Biography. 3. Science
fiction, English—History and criticism. I. Title.
II. Series.
PR6037.T18Z66 1983     823'.912 [B]     82-8168
ISBN 0-19-503086-9          AACR2
ISBN 0-19-503087-7 (pbk.)

*Grateful acknowledgment is given for permission to reprint
from the following:*
  From "Spain 1937," copyright 1940 and renewed 1968 by
W. H. Auden. Reprinted from *The English Auden: Poems,
Essays and Dramatic Writings, 1927–1939,* by W. H.
Auden, edited by Edward Mendelson, by permission of
Random House, Inc., and Faber and Faber Ltd.
  From "Just a Smack at Auden" in *Collected Poems of
William Empson,* copyright 1949, 1977 by William
Empson. Reprinted by permission of Harcourt Brace
Jovanovich, Inc., the author, and Chatto & Windus Ltd.

Printing (last digit): 9 8 7 6 5 4 3 2 1

Printed in the United States of America

To my latest time travelers

ERIC SERGIO, WONDER, and TAIRA

# EDITOR'S FOREWORD

For the first eight decades of this century critics of fiction have reserved their highest praises for novels and stories that emphasize individual psychology in characterization, unique stylistic nuances in language, and plausibility in the events presented. It is an interesting feature of literary history that during this same period of time a body of fiction has flourished which privileges the type over the individual, the idea over the word, and the unexpected over the plausible event. This body of work, which has come to be called—with only partial appropriateness—"science" fiction, has had some recognition from serious critics but still hovers between genuine acceptance and total dismissal in literary circles.

Schools now offer courses in science fiction—either because one zealous teacher insists upon it or because "the kids read that stuff." But it is rare to hear of works of science fiction integrated into "regular" courses in modern literature. The major reason for this is that as long as the dominant criteria are believed to hold for all fiction, science fiction will be found inferior: deficient in psychological depth, in verbal nuance, and in plausibility of event. What is needed is a criticism serious in its standards and its concern for literary value but willing to take seriously a literature based on ideas, types, and events beyond ordinary experience.

The *Science-Fiction Writers* series of critical volumes is an attempt to provide that sort of criticism. In designing the series we have selected a number of authors whose body of work has proved substantial, durable, and influential, and we have asked an appropriate critic to make a book-length study of the work of each author selected, taking that author seriously enough to be critical and critically enough to be serious.

In each volume we will include a general view of the author's life and work, critical interpretations of his or her major contributions to the field of science fiction, and a biographical and bibliographical apparatus that will make these volumes useful as a reference tool. The format of each book will thus be similar. But because the writers to be considered have had careers of different shapes, and because our critics are all individuals who have earned the right to their own interpretive emphases, each book will take its own shape within the limits of the general format. Above all, each volume will express the critical views of its author rather than some predetermined party line.

In the present volume Leslie Fiedler has undertaken the study of one of the most influential writers ever to work in the field of science fiction, and one of the unlikeliest. A graduate of Oxford, Stapledon served in an ambulance unit in World War I and returned to Liverpool University to pursue graduate study in philosophy and become a teacher. He became a teacher, though an unorthodox one, lecturing on philosophy to working-class groups in the Liverpool area while writing philosophy and poetry. In 1930, when he was forty-four years old, he published his first "romance of the future," *Last and First Men.* Here is the way this volume struck the young Arthur C. Clarke:

> I came across this volume in the public library of my birthplace, Minehead, soon after its first appearance in 1930. With its multi-million-year vistas, and its roll call of great but doomed civilizations, the book produced an overwhelming impact upon me. I can still remember patiently copying Stapledon's "Time Scales"—up to the last one, where "Planets Formed" and "End of Man" lie only a fraction of an inch on either side of a moment marked "Today."
>
> *Science Fiction*, p. 33

Robert Heinlein learned from Stapledon, and so did many other American writers of science fiction's "Golden Age." Moreover, some of these writers brought to their work a popular touch in style and characterization that Stapledon could never manage. In his lively history of science fiction, *Billion Year Spree*, Brian Aldiss has praised Stapledon's sustained invention, "nourished by imagination," calling him "the great classical example, the cold pitch of perfection as he turns scientific concepts into vast ontological epic prose poems, the ultimate science fiction writer." Praising him for lucid prose as well as a "huge and frightening" imagination, Aldiss called his novel *Star Maker* "truly frightening," "almost unbearable," a "magnificent and neurasthenic vision."

Magnificent and neurasthenic. In those two shrewdly chosen adjectives we have perhaps the keys to an understanding of Stapledon. His vision of the cosmos is indeed magnificent: immense in scale and rich in detail. Distance is Stapledon's special quality, and it is his problem as well. He could only be familiar with aliens. His persistent treatment of the entire human race as one species among others, with no privileged claims on our sympathy or concern, gives all his books their eerie power. But it is a power bought at a terrible price in self-division and alienation. The sources of Stapledon's vision in his personal struggles for psychic wholeness, and in the irreparable divisions of his mind, are at the center of Leslie Fiedler's study of Stapledon in this volume. Fiedler brings to his task a genuine appreciation for popular modes of expression and a long-standing interest in psychoanalytic approaches to literary study. He has written science fiction himself as well as critical studies of modern American and British culture. His treatment of Stapledon is very much in the spirit of this enterprise: critical, provocative, and important.

*December 1982*                                                          R.S.

# CONTENTS

# OLAF STAPLEDON

# INTRODUCTION

It has been thirty or thirty-five years since I read Olaf Stapledon for the first time. I am not sure whether it was *Star Maker* or *Last and First Men* with which I began—one of the two surely. But I can clearly recall my sense of frustration verging on rage when I discovered that though the book I held in my hands purported to be a novel, it contained nothing like what is ordinarily called a "story" or indeed a proper "character" aside from the narrator; and that it was, moreover, almost utterly lacking in humor, pathos, and "love interest," whether sexual passion or romance. I have hesitated ever since, therefore (and feel obliged to be quite candid on this score at the outset of the study I am so improbably writing on so anomalous an author) to recommend Stapledon to the "general reader." Such readers read, as is their right, to laugh and to cry, to be kept in suspense, to be titillated and satisfied—to be *moved*. They are consequently more likely than not (and they are hereby duly warned) to find Stapledon's novels not merely sluggish, repetitive, abstract, and abstruse, but without charm: austere at best, icy cold at worst. Read him at your own risk then, I say to the unwary.

Even readers who think of themselves as science-fiction fans should be forewarned that they will not discover in his books the more obvious pleasures provided by best-sellers and cult favorites of the genre like, say, Robert Heinlein's *Stranger in a Strange Land* or the *Dune* trilogy of Frank Herbert. Yet it

3

was surely such a science-fiction fan who recommended Stapledon to me in the first place; though it must be confessed that most self-declared "lovers of science fiction" whom I have encountered since have not read him at all, and many of them do not even recognize his name. It is, however, as science fiction that his novels are catalogued by librarians and classified by those critics who pay attention to him at all. In fact, this generic placing is almost the only thing about him on which critics agree. Some of them consider him profoundly pessimistic, even nihilistic, while others assert that he is fundamentally an optimist. Similarly, some describe him as deeply religious, others as radically skeptical; some deem his politics progressive, intelligent, and still relevant, while others find him a muddled dupe of the Communists; some consider him eminently sane, and others classify his skewed vision as paranoic-schizophrenic.

Clearly, his work is ambiguous—though whether this is the result of the subtlety of his thought or deep confusion is a question on which critics again disagree. To understand him properly, I would argue, one has to read all of him; but this is by no means easy to do, since terseness is not one of his virtues and he seems absolutely convinced that any point worth making once is worth repeating over and over and over. Nonetheless, I have in fact read if not quite all of his work, fiction and non-fiction, at least as much of it as is available, and have loved a great deal of it, despite the fact that much of it seems contradictory and confused, not a little downright tedious. There is not, I am driven to confess, a single book of his (with the possible exception of his quite uncharacteristic *Sirius*) which I find interesting and alive from beginning to end. Yet there is none, I must also admit, which does not contain passages which move me deeply, not even so depressed and depressing a work as *Darkness and the Light*, or so pedestrian and labored an effort as *A Man Divided*. Others, flawed minor masterpieces like *Odd John, Last and First Men*, and especially, especially *Star Maker*, for all their occasional *longueurs* or almost forbidding density of texture, I return to again and again with real pleasure.

I find myself, therefore, in the teeth of everything I have thus far said, moved to urge others to read him—critics, science-fiction fans, yes, even the general reader. Alerted to what is not present in him, they will not waste their time looking for nor will they miss it, once they have experienced what *is* there: a unique vision of the breadth of the physical universe and the depth of the human psyche as revealed by modern science. What Stapledon renders better than any other writer I know is the awe, the wonder, the terror, and desperate exhilaration begotten as the tiny microcosm we once thought was all of us there was and the limited macrocosm we were long taught we inhabited have expanded and expanded—until the traditional boundaries between reality and illusion, sanity and madness, self and other blur to indistinction. Once the images in which Stapledon has embodied his vision possess us (he is a gifted image maker, whatever his limitations as a spinner of yarns), it is hard to exorcize them, though indeed they may disturb us profoundly. Certainly, since encountering him, I have never been able to stare up at the night sky with the same secure faith that either God exists or he does not; anymore than I have been able between sleeping and waking to be sure that the nighttime "I" preparing to dream is either identical with or totally different from the conscious "I" about to surrender its dominion.

Apologists for science fiction like to think of that genre as particularly suited to translating such insights into the mysterious nature of man and the universe out of the language of metaphysics and "mysticism" into a new tongue, more viable in a world whose technology has enabled us to see beyond the limits of "the Heavens."

It is, perhaps, because he first fully exploited those possibilities, that in-house critics of science fiction have hailed Olaf Stapledon not just as one of their own kind, but as one of the greatest among them. Sam Moskowitz, for instance, ranks him with Mary Shelley, Edgar Allan Poe, Jules Verne, and H. G. Wells as one of the five "immortals" of the genre, "authors whose impact is so tremendous that they belong in a class by themselves." Katherine MacLean narrows the list of contenders, calling him "a genius, one of the four greatest writers in science fiction"; while Brian Aldiss, who regards his *Star Maker* as "the one great grey holy book of science fiction," makes the final cut, insisting that Stapledon stands alone with

Wells as "an indisputable giant among science fiction writers past and present." Eric Rabkin and Robert Scholes concur, ranking him not only as "the most distinguished writer of science fiction in English in the period between the first and second World War," but also as "one of the most influential to write in any language."

It is hard, indeed, to think of anyone, with the possible exception of Wells himself, who has inspired so many later authors to the supreme tribute of imitation. Stapledon's vast cosmological point of view widened once and for all the scale and scope of science fiction, opening up for the imagination unlimited time and space—including realms hitherto reserved for the visionary and the mystic; and his unflagging invention created, in passing, plot material which has since been mined and quarried by writers, who turn episodes he dismisses in a paragraph or a phrase into whole novels and series of novels. Sam Moskowitz has listed among those so indebted to him: Eric Frank Russell, Clifford D. Simak, Robert Heinlein, Isaac Asimov, Arthur C. Clarke, and Kurt Vonnegut. I am inclined to add Philip José Farmer, Philip K. Dick, Ursula LeGuin, Stanislaw Lem, Samuel R. Delany—and especially, Poul Anderson, who in an essay called "Star-flights and Fantasies" (included in The Craft of Science Fiction edited by Reginald Bretnor) describes in some detail how he solved a fictional problem of his own by recourse to Stapledon:

> I was planning a yarn . . . about a spaceship which was trapped into traveling closer and closer to the speed of light. In consequence, the laws of relativity made time inboard pass ever more slowly with respect to the rest of the universe, until at last the stars aged by millions of years while a crewman drew a breath . . . . Now how could I hope to give a hint of the enormousness? Well, how had Stapledon done it? Studying him, I found he gets us used to one order of magnitude before moving on to the next . . . . In mathematical terms, his progress is logarithmic. I followed his lead . . . . Many readers have told me how well it works. But credit Stapledon . . . .

Even C. S. Lewis, whose Perelandra, Out of the Silent Planet, and That Hideous Strength were written to refute what he considered the theological heresies of Stapledon (and H. G. Wells), ended by borrowing from as well as travestying him;

so that in a preface to one of those science-fiction novels, in which he describes the creation of a disembodied brain much like the Fourth Men of *Last and First Men*, he feels obliged to acknowledge his possible indebtedness, writing, " . . . Mr. Stapledon is so rich in invention that he can well afford to lend, and I should feel no shame to borrow."

Nonetheless, Stapledon has generally been ignored by novelists and critics outside the science-fiction "family." The recent Nobel laureate Saul Bellow, it is true, evokes his name a couple of times in *Mr. Sammler's Planet*, whose protagonist boasts of having known him (along with Wells, Gerald Heard, and George Orwell) and at one point, meditating on the six billion years of futurity presumably still left to the earth, recalls that "Olaf Stapledon reckoned that each individual in future ages would be living thousands of years." He then goes on to develop at some length an image out of *Star Maker*: "The future person, a colossal figure, a beautiful green color, with a hand that had evolved into a kit of extraordinary instruments, tools, strong and subtle, thumb and forefinger capable of exerting thousands of pounds of pressure. Each mind belonging to a marvelous analytical collective. . . ." But Bellow's critics have not troubled to remark on this; nor do they share Mr. Sammler's enthusiasm for the author of *Star Maker*.

Indeed, few established critics of any persuasion have. During Stapledon's lifetime, for instance, no substantial overview of his work was published, though his individual books were reviewed—often favorably—as they appeared, usually, however, by undistinguished staff writers or journalists like Elmer Davis. At least two reputable critics, V. S. Pritchett in England and Alfred Kazin in America, early on wrote favorable reviews of his fiction, and certain aging British novelists including, of course, Wells but also J. B. Priestley, Hugh Walpole, and Arnold Bennett had kind words to say about him. But their own reputations were already beginning to decline before they went on record in his behalf, and these days they are considered by the literary establishment as little worthy of attention as Stapledon himself. Moreover, though in the years since Stapledon's death several loving and careful treatments of his work have been published, they have been produced largely by rather parochial apologists for science fiction, almost as removed as Stapledon from those centers where literary standards are set.

It was therefore possible, as late as 1973, for Brian Aldiss to observe (in his *Billion Year Spree: A True History of Science Fiction*) that "None of the standard literary references see fit to mention his name . . . "; and to cry out in baffled indignation: "How is it that the funeral masons and morticians who work their preserving processes on Eng. Lit. have rejected Stapledon entirely from their critical incantations is a matter before which speculation falls fainting away." It seems to me natural that an elitist like Cyril Connolly, who in the name of Modernism leaves out of his canon even the popular romances of Wells, should also ignore Olaf Stapledon. It is, however, a little surprising to discover that Connolly's list of distinguished thirties novels (in a little book published in 1965 and called *A Discussion of 100 Key Books from England, France and America 1880-1950*), though it excludes Stapledon's *Last and First Men* and *Star Maker*, does include—along with such expected avant-garde or elitist works as Virginia Woolf's *The Waves*, Nathanael West's *Miss Lonelyhearts*, Christopher Isherwood's *Goodbye to Berlin*, and James Joyce's *Finnegans Wake*—Aldous Huxley's futurist dystopia, *Brave New World*.

Even more astonishing and puzzling is the fact that in *The Novel Now* (1962), Anthony Burgess, who should know better, similarly ignores Stapledon and praises Huxley, as well as L. P. Hartley and George Orwell, under the rubric of "Utopias and Dystopias." Yet Burgess not only properly appreciates Wells, whom he calls "the only 'progressive' writer of the early modern age to have been both absorbed and reacted against" and describes as having been "absorbed as the Pioneer of science fiction—a productive, vigorous and popular form"; but he himself is the author of at least two novels, *A Clockwork Orange* and *The Wanting Seed*, classifiable as science fiction.

Here, in fact, is a clue to the special status of Stapledon on the literary scene; since quite clearly Huxley's *Brave New World* is taken more seriously than any of his novels not because it is a "better" book. It is, indeed, wittier and more immediately engaging, more on target in the sense of predicting more correctly what lies just ahead for Western society; but it is surely *not* more poetically resonant, imaginatively daring or at home in the vast universe science has opened around us. Moreover, reputable critics have also treated with the same respect Huxley's later utopia, *The Island* (1962), which is clumsy, banal, in fact, downright silly in a way Stapledon never is. No, Huxley is respectfully noticed rather than contemptuously ignored because, unlike Stapledon, he began his literary career by publishing recognizable "art novels," like *Crome Yellow* (1921), *Antic Hay* (1923), and *Point Counter Point* (1928), which is to say, by addressing a minority rather than a majority audience.

For this very reason, in fact, *Brave New World* was regarded suspiciously for a long time by the official spokesmen of the science-fiction community; though it quite quickly became a kind of "best-seller," whose readership included some who had never willingly read an "art novel" before, not even those of Huxley himself—preferring the unpretentious pulp fiction of Heinlein, A. E. Van Vogt, and Isaac Asimov. Yet without ever losing the approval of the elitist critics, *Brave New World* was eventually accepted as "hard-core science fiction" by so ultimate an insider as Heinlein himself. Indeed, more committed fans of the genre read Huxley now in the last decades of the twentieth century than read any of the novels of Olaf Stapledon.

This, then, is the final irony. Rejected by the guardians of high literature, on the one hand, Stapledon has, on the other, never won a mass following—not even in the ever-increasing audience for science fiction. He remained pretty much invisible, for instance, to the dissident young, who in the troubled sixties swelled the ranks of science-fiction readers, making Heinlein's *Stranger in a Strange Land* (1961) and Frank Herbert's *Dune* (1965) unforeseen best-sellers in paperback and turning the television series *Star Trek*, so short-lived in prime time, into a long-lived cult favorite in replays and animated cartoons. Though Stapledon has been reprinted in paperback editions, none of his books has succeeded in capturing the mass market—in this or any other form. Indeed, not a single one of them has ever been translated into the most widely available media.

None, for instance, has been adapted for the comic books, like the porno-science fiction of Philip José Farmer, or for tele-

vision, like the work of many old pros ranging from Richard
Matheson to Harlan Ellison. Nor has any of them made it into
the movies, whether as art films, like Stanislaw Lem's *Solaris*,
or box-office hits, like those Stanley Kubrick created out of
Burgess's *A Clockwork Orange* and Arthur C. Clarke's *2001*.
Apparently, Mrs. Stapledon has been teased for years by the
prospect of a movie being made posthumously from *Odd John*,
but nothing has ever come of it. Consequently, Stapledon remains unknown to the largest and most recent group of con-
verts to the genre, who respond not only to cinematic versions
of works on the leading edge of science fiction, like *Solaris*
and *2001*, but—with even greater fervor perhaps—to charming
but old-fashioned fairy tales in science-fiction guise like *Star
Wars*, *Close Encounters of the Third Kind*, or, for that matter,
the movies about Superman.

It seems clear to me, in any case, that Stapledon (though
he did at one point make for the BBC a radio script, alas, never
to be performed, based on *Last and First Men*) would have
been a little appalled if a film derived from his work had managed to please the mass audience, of whom he had observed
disapprovingly in *Youth and Tomorrow* (1946) that "In spite
of themselves, they drift into picture houses, or watch football
matches, or bet on dogs and horses." To understand, however,
the snobbism which limited his sympathy with the ordinary
pleasures of ordinary people, as well as that which excluded
him from the canon of o.k. literature, we must understand first
the sense in which he simultaneously belonged to and was
alienated from his own time and place.

Unfortunately, there exists no full-scale biography of Stapledon, and we must therefore depend for information about
when, where, and how he lived on rather scanty sources. Besides the entries in biographical dictionaries and a few recorded interviews, with Stapledon before his death and his
wife afterward, there is a brief "authorized" life by Sam Moskowitz, which serves as an introduction to his *Far Future
Calling: Uncollected Science Fiction and Fantasies by Olaf
Stapledon* (1979)—plus a couple of thumbnail autobiogra-
phies composed as jacket copy, and a more substantial piece
of a similar kind written for *Twentieth Century Authors* (1942),
edited by Stanley J. Kunitz and Howard Haycroft. Finally, there

is the longish reminiscence of his service with the Friends Ambulance Unit during World War I, which Stapledon contributed to *We Did Not Fight: Experiences of War Resisters*, a tribute to the pacifists of 1914 to 1918, edited in 1934 by Julian Bell, who, ironically enough, was to be killed just a few years later fighting in the Spanish Civil War.

I find it tempting to augment such scant and rather reticent sources by recourse to the two Stapledon novels that have struck everyone as being more "autobiographical" than his others: *Last Men in London* (1932), whose protagonist, Paul, lives through war experiences much like Stapledon's own, and *A Man Divided* (1950), in which both halves of the split personality, James Victor Cadogan-Smith/Victor Smith, work, as Stapledon did, first in a shipping office and then as a teacher of extension courses to workingmen. But in truth it would be hard to stop with these, since scarcely any of Stapledon's books are entirely free of references, direct or oblique, to his own life. The earthly frame story of *Star Maker*, for instance, in which is set the comic voyage that constitutes its main action, deals with a domestic crisis, a conjugal quarrel of great bitterness, which (I cannot help feeling) casts some light on Stapledon's complex relationship with his own wife.

Indeed, taken in conjunction with certain rather testy comments in the prefaces to his first two novels ("To my wife's devastating sanity I owe far more than she supposes . . . . I would thank my wife both for the hard labour, and for other help which she is apparently incapable of appreciating . . ."), it would seem to challenge radically Sam Moskowitz's bland assertion that "Fortunately for his wife he proved to be one of the most amiable of men, unflaggingly even-tempered . . . ." So too, seemingly, does the "Second Interlude" of the late fiction, *Death into Life*, in which an "I," apparently the author, says of a "you" described as his beloved lifelong mate, "you are sometimes perplexingly remote . . . sometimes we are at arm's length, or we break step, or we fly apart, cleft by some sudden discord . . . . Again and again our diversity hurts, it even infuriates . . . "; and alludes rather mysteriously to "that most sharp discordancy of all," which must be the one referred to at the beginning of *Star Maker*.

"Seems to," "seemingly"—it is all surmise finally, as are

the other intriguing deductions we can make from Stapledon's
fictional texts and the apparatus which surrounds them; the
indications especially that he suffered from an Oedipus complex so classic that it seems invented to fit the Freudian paradigm, yet which he could only confess fictionally. In *Odd John*,
for instance, the superhuman protagonist first separates himself from the rest of humankind by killing a kindly old cop, a
beloved authority figure, then by sleeping with his mother,
who alone in his family understands him. Typically, in almost
all of Stapledon's novels, mothers are portrayed sympatheti-
cally, while fathers tend to be rather insensitive, when not
downright obtuse. Yet consciously and for publication, Stapledon invariably spoke lovingly, indeed, admiringly of his
father but resentfully of his mother, who he insisted had tried
to smother him with affection, refusing to let him grow up.
His widow, in an interview with Harvey Satty, suggested that
the good maternal figures in Stapledon's fiction (referring in
particular to Pax in *Odd John*) were intended as portraits not
of the woman who bore him, but of *her*, whom, she suggested
with the gentlest of ironies, he thought of as "peaceful and
comfortable—and not very bright." In light of the fact, however, that theirs was a quasi-incestuous union, her father having been brother to Olaf's mother, this only further compli-
cates the situation.

     Other contradictions between what the public record as-
serts and what the fiction suggests cast doubt not just on some
of his avowed political beliefs but on his psychic health.
Though a believer in total non-violence up to the beginnings
of World War II and never an advocate of individual terror or
assassination, Stapledon in none of his scientific fantasies
imagines a world without war; and his two fictional supercreatures, the human, Odd John, and the dog, Sirius, are both
multiple murderers. They are, moreover, portrayed not merely
as lovable still after they have killed, but as fully lovable only
then, perhaps to their author as well as their fictional lovers.
There is in all this more than a hint of a streak of sado-
masochism in Stapledon, verging (it seems to me) on the pathological—as well as a suggestion that he, too, like certain of his
characters is a man divided against himself. His wife, when
asked by Harvey Satty whether, like Victor Smith, Olaf had

suffered from a "divine schizophrenia," did her best to down-play it: "Well, I don't think you would want to say that he suffered from it acutely. He was quite conscious of the fact that everybody suffers from it to a certain extent. And, of course, in order to make a good story, he had to exaggerate it."

Still and all, this advocate of sanity and a stoical acceptance of fate, who—as far as the record shows—never had a drastic breakdown or was confined to a mental institution and died of natural causes in the bosom of his family, seems obsessed in all of his novels with the threat of madness and the temptation of suicide. Why, for instance, does one of his most patently autobiographical characters end up in the madhouse, and another die by his own hand? And why, above all, does the representative in our time of the Eighteenth Men, who in *Last and First Men* represent the ultimate triumph of human evolution and are the theoretical inspirers of the book, finally reveal to us that in his own far-future world insanity is rampant and impulse to self-slaughter epidemic?

To these matters I shall return in my discussion of Stapledon's novels and their meanings; but, however reluctantly, I feel obliged to abandon them as reliable biographical evidence. It is not that I take seriously the kind of warning with which Stapledon prefaces *Last Men in London*: "The last section of the chapter on the War, though it makes use to some extent of personal experiences, is none the less fiction." Novelists are notorious liars, who in their fiction invent lies that tell the truth, but in what they say about it afterward are likely simply to lie; and we have it, moreover, on good authority that the critic's duty is to believe the work rather than the writer. But the relationship of fictional truth to historical truth is a tricky one, since fantasy operates in the realm of the unconscious, in which what might have been is quite as valid as what actually was, what we fear will happen as real as what we hope might or know will occur. I shall, therefore, attempt to reconstruct Stapledon's life and speculate about its meanings, by sticking as close as possible to the extra-literary documents.

# 1
# FROM WALLASEY
# TO THE WALDORF-ASTORIA

Stapledon was born in 1886 and christened William Olaf Stapledon, which he shortened, first by turning the "William" to
an initial (the title page of *A Modern Theory of Ethics* (1929)
reads "by W. Olaf Stapledon, M.A., Ph.D."), then by dropping
it entirely—though, or, perhaps, precisely because it had been
the given name of his father and grandfather. Escaping from
his antecedents (if that was what he really had in mind) was
not all that easy, however. He was born in Wallasey, now a
part of Merseyside, England. He had been conceived in Port
Said, where his father was then working in the family shipping business; but his mother returned to England for the delivery, to the place in and around which (though he was taken
back to Egypt as an infant and passed there his first six years)
he was to spend most of his adult life.

The importance to Stapledon of having been thus rooted
in a particular spot, however provincial, is attested by the fact
that he begins the account of his career in *Twentieth Century
Authors* by observing, "I was born in the Wirral, across the
river from Liverpool. The Wirral has always been my head-
quarters. I now live at the opposite corner of the peninsula,
across the water from Wales"; and only then adds, "Most of
my childhood, however, was spent on the Suez Canal, which
in a way still seems my home." It was, indeed, to be quite a
while before he settled back into his natal place. He was edu-
cated, as he goes on to say, "at Abbotsholme School and Balliol

College. Then for a year, with much nerve strain and little success, I taught at the Manchester Grammar School. Next I entered a shipping office in Liverpool, to deal ineffectively with manifestoes and bills of lading. A short period in a shipping agency at Port Said concluded my business career."

Though he confesses his sense of inadequacy over his first attempts to do a man's work in a man's world ("little success," "ineffectively"), Stapledon does not make it clear here, as he does elsewhere, that all of these early jobs—except for his brief attempt at being a schoolmaster—were performed in a firm founded by his grandfather, or under the watchful eye of his father. But what his father felt toward him at this low point of his life, and how he himself responded, we do not really know; though his mother, Sam Moskowitz assures us, was delighted whenever failure brought him back to the domestic nest. Olaf was, in any case, very much at a loose end in 1913, when, two years after his twenty-fifth birthday, he found himself jobless, a failure not only in the uncongenial family trade but even in his first attempt at teaching. Moreover, the academic position for which he had prepared (he had earned both a B.A. and a M.A. in history at Oxford), and surely all along desired, did not materialize. For a while, there seems to have been a glimmer of hope that he would be offered a post at the University of Wales, but this came to nothing.

He settled back into his family home, therefore, as a kind of belated adolescent, unmarried still, and, though not quite unemployed, working not quite full-time at the ill-paying and not very prestigious job of lecturing "to tutorial classes for the Workers Educational Association, under the University of Liverpool." Under their auspices, he imparted, he tells us self-deprecatingly once more, "my vague knowledge of history and English literature to a few workers of Northwestern England." He was, in fact, to teach such extramural classes for most of the remainder of his life, apparently without ever gaining much confidence in his own pedagogical skills—noting in another autobiographical snippet, that "Worthington miners, Barrow riveters, Crewe railwaymen, gave me a better education than I could give them." But his teaching career was interrupted by the coming of World War I, during the final three years of which he served in France in a motor convoy run by English Quakers, though attached to a division of the French Army.

Of all the events in a life otherwise unmarked by much drama, it is of this that he has left the fullest record: not only in the autobiographical piece he did for Julian Bell's 1934 gathering of essays, but in the quasi-autobiographical sections of his second novel, *Last Men in London* (1932), in which he attributes adventures much like his own to a character not unlike his young self. Anyone expecting an account of passionate and unequivocal pacifism in heroic action will be disappointed by Stapledon's reminiscences about his decision to neither go to jail with the hard-line war-resisters nor enlist for full military service, but to play a non-combatant role as close to the front lines as possible. His commitment to non-resistance was unequivocal, in fact, only in print and between wars; indeed, his pacifism disappeared completely with the outbreak of World War II.

The story of his activities in the Great War was, therefore, as he begins by telling us, one "of long and inconclusive heart-searching, of a deeply felt conflict of loyalties, and of a compromise which, though perhaps inglorious, was, I believe, at least an honest attempt to do justice to both claims as they were felt at that time by a thoroughly bewildered young man." Not all that young, we are moved to protest, since in 1915 when he came to his decision, he was nearly thirty; but he grew up, as we have already noted, very slowly indeed, and is writing from the vantage point of twenty years later. It is, moreover, typical of him to put the worst possible face on his own motives, so we are inclined to be wary when he talks about "sheer funk" and wanting "to have the cake and eat it." Sometimes, indeed, he puts himself in a better light, speaking of his "compromise" as "a sincere expression of two overmastering and wholesome impulses, the will to share in the common ordeal and the will to make some kind of protest against the common folly."

He portrays himself, in short, as "A Man Divided," a metaphor for his own plight and that of mankind in general which continued to intrigue him through his final novel, in which it becomes the title; and he finds in his experiences at the Front occasions for guilt and vision equally typical of his later work.

He is obsessed throughout, for instance, by a sense that in the Friends Ambulance Unit, he remains shamefully embusqué, sheltered from the total catastrophe confronted by the ordinary foot soldier; and he is haunted by memories of his own cowardice or inadvertence in driving past while under fire a presumably dead soldier, who turned out to be only wounded. Nonetheless, twice at least he suggests that in combat he was vouchsafed an ecstatic revelation—not fully articulated until the climax of *Star Maker*—of the ultimate rightness and beauty implicit in ultimate horror. "I began to wonder," he writes at one point, "how much more I could stand. Yet deep down in my mind, and difficult to introspect, was a strange quietness, an aloof delight"; and at another, "One seemed even to catch surprising glimpses of a kind of super-human beauty in the hideous disaster of war itself."

But a surprising amount of space is devoted to recounting the small pleasures of wartime camaraderie and that rather boyish delight which participants in foreign war, combatants and non-combatants alike, seem always to find in the opportunities it provides for tourism: "All the same, there were compensations. The town was unharmed and full of life. There were shops, historic palaces, and the ancient royal forest . . . . When we were off duty, we walked on the bare hills or through the forest, or gathered apples in deserted orchards, or ate 'gauffres' and honey . . . or bathed, or sat in one another's cars discussing the universe . . . ." His essay ends, in fact, with a joyous account of a frustrated raid on a wine cellar in quest of champagne with which to toast the Armistice; though, to be sure, he rather characteristically closes, even as he had begun, with an apology, this one to the Friends "for recording this significant little incident which crowned the long and strange career of S.S.A. 13."

By the end of 1917 his three-years' holiday from responsibility was over and Stapledon back on the Wirral again; though this time, in addition to picking up his teaching duties with the WEA, he returned to his university studies, still at his father's expense but much closer to home in Liverpool, where he finally earned a Ph.D. in philosophy. Still without a permanent academic post, he nonetheless took another step toward long-delayed maturity and independence by marrying in

1919 a woman whom he describes in *Twentieth Century Authors* as "Agnes Miller, an Australian," then adds a little mysteriously, "Thus was sealed an intermittent romance of twelve years' standing." Actually, Agnes Zena Miller was his first cousin, daughter of his mother's brother, whom he had known for close to twenty years, having first laid eyes on her in 1902, when she was a child, he an early adolescent, during one of her family's infrequent business trips to England. Their actual courting, however, had apparently been done while she, then seventeen or eighteen, was studying languages and music in Europe.

But their not-quite-incestuous betrothal and wedding had been arranged—rather oddly, it strikes me—at long distance by slow mail, and apparently with the blessings of the family. Once wed, they moved into the quite magnificent house of Olaf's parents, where, as might have been predicted, their situation proved to be more uncomfortable than cozy (largely, he claimed later, because of his overly possessive mother). Even when they moved once more, the newlyweds did not escape her completely; since Olaf's father obligingly bought them a place of their own quite nearby. Here they lived together for twenty years of their lifelong marriage, beginning in 1920; and here they raised a daughter, Mary, born in that same year, along with a son, John, who followed three years later. Though needing (if what he later advocates for all mankind in both his fiction and non-fiction can be applied to himself) occasional vacations from both, Stapledon was deeply committed to monogamy and domesticity; and devoted much of the next three decades to loving his wife, nurturing his children, helping with household chores, and puttering in the garden.

But this did not suffice to take up the slack of time, energy, and desire left over by his second-best vocation; nor was radical politics, with which he seems to have become more and more involved after the coming of the Great Depression and the mounting threat of a new war in the thirties, quite enough. He needed also to write, and more, to become a recognized writer. He had been a practicing poet from earliest youth, even publishing (apparently with the aid of a subsidy from his father) in 1914 a collection of poems called *Latter-Day Psalms*, and he would continue to versify to the day of his death; but his only prose which had made it into print before 1929 were contributions to scholarly journals, which culminated in that year with the appearance of *A Modern Theory of Ethics*, an ambitious philosophical essay.

Though it failed to win wide acclaim or even to establish his academic reputation, that book seems to have given Stapledon faith in his ability to complete a long project; and, especially in its concluding section, it opened up for him certain themes more appropriately treated in the freer and more mythic form with which he experimented a year later in *Last and First Men*. Unlike its predecessor, the latter was greeted by enthusiastic reviews and sold so well that Stapledon was emboldened to abandon the pursuit of academic tenure and to take up the life of a free-lance writer. Not that he ceased teaching ever; he continued to do extramural lecturing for most of the rest of his days and during World War II conducted classes for servicemen.

As it turned out, he could not have made it on his royalties alone; since his second novel, *Last Men in London*, was not nearly as successful as the first; and though occasionally he did as well again, Stapledon never reached a large audience anywhere outside of England, not even in America. He was, in fact, finally forced to confess that his combined income from books and teaching was not enough for him and his family. Indeed, the only thing that bought him time for writing at all was a considerable inheritance from his father, who died in 1932. Since he remained always a Socialist, his dependence on income for which he had not worked embarrassed him, though he tried to carry it all off with a certain amount of bravado, writing in *Waking World* (1934), "I live chiefly on dividends and other ill-gotten gains, even while I proclaim that the system on which I live must go. . . . Having failed to earn enough by honest toil . . . I fall back with due thankfulness on dividends, until such time as the community has the good sense to take to itself the ownership of the means of production . . . ."

In any case, he continued to write up to the day of his death (leaving behind a not-quite-completed manuscript, since edited and published by his wife), and producing finally ten volumes of fiction and seven more of non-fiction, some of the latter done on assignment, all of them didactic and hortatory. "Philosophy" he sometimes called those works or "sociology," though they also contained much theology, popular science, and political theory; preaching not only social revolution, pacifism, and educational reform, but reverent agnosticism and spiritual reawakening. Stapledon's reputation tended to fade, however, and his readership to shrink as he grew older—in part, because his most effective and moving work was produced early in his career; in part, because he repeated over and over the same unchanging phrases, until they began to seem not merely monotonous but irrelevant to a rapidly changing world.

Ironically, he achieved in 1949, as he began the last year of his life, a kind of renown bordering on notoriety: his name for the first time blazoned in the headlines of the daily press, and his picture reproduced on the pages of mass-circulation illustrated magazines, ordinarily devoted to shots of movie stars, champion athletes, and the rulers of the world. The reporters and caption writers were not quite sure who he was, sometimes giving his name as "Dr. Olaf Stapledon" or "William Stapledon," and describing him as a "psychologist" or a "scientist" more often than as a philosopher or novelist. But none of this mattered, since he had achieved transitory fame not for any past achievement, scholarly or artistic, imaginary or real, but simply as the only English representative at the Cultural and Scientific Conference for World Peace held at the Waldorf-Astoria Hotel in New York City, March 23-25, 1949, and organized—the pickets protesting it charged and the press agreed—by Communists.

Few Englishmen had been willing to lend their support or presence to begin with. Indeed, most really eminent "intellectuals," like Bertrand Russell, Alfred North Whitehead, and T. S. Eliot, had publicly declined to be a part of the proceedings; and though Dr. Hewlett John, the well-publicized "Red Dean" of Canterbury, gave his blessings at long distance, the only "celebrities" who agreed to go were J. D. Bernal, a distinguished physicist and long-term supporter of leftist causes, a rather obscure historian called J. G. Crowther, Patricia Burke, a stage and movie actress, and Louis Golding, author of some now forgotten best-sellers. Plus, of course, Olaf Stapledon.

Though apparently none of them was an actual member of the British Communist Party, and all of them were innocuous enough politically to have been initially granted visas, the first four were finally denied entry into the United States.

Stapledon was told at first that his visa, too, had been withdrawn, not learning until the very last moment that he was free to go. On arrival in New York, he was quizzed for nearly two hours by immigration officials, who—he told reporters afterward—asked him "where my mother and father were born and what not," as well as whether he had ever been a member of the Communist Party. "It was very friendly," he summed up in his typical self-deprecatory way. "My own feeling was that I was sorry to be such a bother." Nor did he trouble to say that the "friendly" officials had confiscated (only to release later) recorded greetings to the conference from the four colleagues he had left behind. When queried later about why he thought the others had been excluded and he admitted, he called the whole situation "fantastic," adding—once more with ironic humility—"I suppose they let me come in because they think I am harmless. Well, I am harmless. The trouble is too many people are not harmless, and that applies to both sides."

Meanwhile, back home in England, the Communist M.P., Willie Gallacher, was telling the House of Commons that information turned up by Scotland Yard had convinced the United States State Department that Bernal, Crowther, Burke, and Golding were undesirables. "A foreign government used Scotland Yard against our own citizens," Gallacher cried passionately, if a bit disingenuously. "What a shameful business! How is it that members of the house can glory in their shame and grovel before the dollar god?" But what precisely the Yard had been able to find out about the banned Britons he left as unclear as Stapledon had. Bernal and Golding were more candid, revealing that they had been queried about their participation in an earlier "peace conference," held during August of the previous year in Wroclaw, Poland, under similarly suspect French-Polish auspices. But neither Crowther nor Burke had been among the forty-two British delegates, while Stapledon *had*, turning out, indeed, to be one of only three would-be repeaters.

Why then did the American State Department not ban him?

And more mysteriously (perhaps the answer to the first question is implicit in that to the second), why did he go back for more of the same? To many less "innocent" than he, the Wroclaw conference had revealed that its organizers were primarily interested not in peace or mutual understanding between East and West, but in recruiting support for the Soviet Union in its propaganda war with America. The leaders of that country and the parties throughout the world who accepted its ideology were acutely aware of a need somehow to win back (or, at least, to create the semblance of having won back) to their side the "intellectuals" who had rallied behind them from the late twenties on—their numbers peaking in the era of the Spanish Civil War and the pre-World War II United Front Against War and Fascism. Such "intellectuals," however, had ceased flocking into Communist "front" organizations after Stalin's killing off of most of the Old Bolsheviks, the revelations about forced labor camps in Siberia, and the Hitler-Stalin Pact, which had made possible the quick conquest of Poland and the Second World War.

Yet as the forties drew to a close, the Soviet Union felt badly in need of influential friends in the West: not party members, suspect on the face of it, but "sympathizers," dedicated or naive enough to believe that the national interests of Russia were identical with those of the poor and oppressed masses in their own lands and that a nation desperately striving for atomic parity was a selfless advocate of world peace. The accords reached at Yalta after the defeat of Germany had served only as camouflage for a struggle over the hegemony of the conquered world; and as paranoia answered paranoia, fed by real threats and mutual fears but exaggerated by political exigencies and postbellum hysteria on both sides, the Cold War between Russia and the United States threatened to turn hot. To make matters worse from the viewpoint of the Soviet Union, America—with its capacity for massive Lease-Lend Aid to Europe, its forging of Mediterranean and Atlantic alliances, and especially its success in breaking the Berlin Blockade— seemed to be winning everywhere on the diplomatic front. Moreover, the United States alone possessed the Bomb.

To provide, therefore, an interval of uneasy peace until such time as espionage, their own developing technologies, and the know-how of German scientists who had gone east rather than west had given them the capability of atomic destruction; or, at the very least, to convince the opinion makers in England and Western Europe that America was the chief threat to peace: this was the task assigned by its Soviet organizers to the World Congress of Intellectuals in Wroclaw and its planned spin-offs in New York and elsewhere. But the meetings in Poland were so obviously manipulated by the delegation from Russia, so biased and so heavy-handed in their deliberations, that only the most gullible were taken in.

A correspondent from the London *Times*, for instance, filing a dispatch on August 26, 1948, reported that, despite the declared intent of the Congress "to find a road to peace," it had opened in "anything but a peaceful manner"; the keynoter from the Soviet Union, Alexander Fadayev, leading off with a blast at "American imperialism" and its "reactionary, aggressive culture." Indeed, before he was through, he had turned his righteous wrath against Western high culture in general, especially condemning the work of T. S. Eliot, Eugene O'Neill, Jean-Paul Sartre, and André Malraux. "If hyenas could type and jackals use a fountain pen," he proclaimed, "they would write such things." At this point, Olaf Stapledon (alone in his protest, as far as can be told from the newspaper accounts) rose to make what the *Times* correspondent described as "a temperate but firm reply"; defending Eliot as "an important figure in British poetry" and reminding Mr. Fadayev that "no side could lay claim to all the truth and that both sides, not just one, were guilty of using 'instruments which pervert the truth.' "

It was presumably for this dignified demurral that Stapledon was granted entry into the United States, and for their silence that his fellows were denied it; though we learn, reading further, that instead of withdrawing from so palpably stage-managed an event, Stapledon instead "arranged a private meeting . . . between the British and Russian delegates to enable them to get to know each other better." And, of course, less than a year later, he ended up as the sole representative of his country at another such conference, orchestrated by the same Alexander Fadayev and similarly dedicated to an unremitting attack on America and the Roman Catholic Church.

This time, things went more smoothly, and Fadayev was more discreet in his public utterances. But the very few invited participants unwise enough to insist, as Stapledon had in Poland, that "the other side" might also be in bad faith, were greeted with an embarrassed hush, cut through with a scattering of boos and hisses.

On this occasion, too, Stapledon mildly dissented, insisting in his address to a panel session on "Religion and Ethics" that "To avoid a savage religious war it is desperately urgent that each side make a serious attempt to understand and respect the most cherished values of the other and to see itself through the other's eyes." These were apparently his final remarks in New York, though he was to appear once more at a follow-up meeting across the Hudson River in Newark, New Jersey; but earlier he had spoken differently. He had, indeed, been one of the handful of featured speakers at the opening dinner of the conference; but on that occasion he had left the dissenting role to Norman Cousins, editor of the *Saturday Review of Literature*, who dismayed a carefully screened audience of two thousand by expressing some sympathy with the pickets carrying anti-Soviet placards and shouting anti-Soviet slogans, through whom the delegates and invitees had to pass on their way in.

Fadayev had been diplomatically kept off the dais but had laid down the line of the conference earlier that day at a press conference, in which he had announced that the chief threats to world peace were the North Atlantic Pact and America's atomic energy program. Most of the other dinner speakers had followed his cue: Lillian Hellman, the American playwright, for instance, mildly rebuked both Mr. Cousins and the unruly protestors he had sought to defend; a Puerto Rican professor called Cabrera more fiercely condemned such "irrational outbursts against peace"; a Yugoslav named Popovich identified the pickets with those "inciters of a new war," who were, he maintained, also "the enemies of culture." And Stapledon had concurred; apparently so disturbed by the hostile demonstration that he abandoned his prepared speech to deplore American war hysteria and to hint darkly that if a Third World War did break out, the British people would not be as "wholeheartedly against Russia" as they had been against Germany.

He did not quite say at that point that they would be "wholeheartedly against America"; but a few days later in Newark, he asserted toward the end of a long evening of tirades against the State Department and the Vatican that the British attitude (including, presumably, his own) was best summed up in the words of a London taxi driver who had taken him to the airport: "Tell those Yanks to stop putting it over on us. We don't want to sell our souls to the Americans." To be sure, he did not stop there, characteristically moderating into an appeal for mutual understanding and ending with the plea, "Let's all get together!" Clearly, he thought of himself still as a mediator between all hostile factions, secular and religious, communist and capitalist, the War Party and the Peace Party.

He was no longer as "pure" a pacifist as he had been from just before World War I, in which he had chosen non-combatant status, until just before World War II, in which his only son had served, indeed, almost died in combat, and he himself had helped to educate soldiers. "There was, I believe," he had written in 1945, in a pamphlet called *The Seven Pillars of Peace*, "a moment for absolute pacifism and unilateral disarmament . . . . But the moment was lost. Folly and harshness recreated hate. Hence Nazism . . . . Nazism has shown us the limits of non-violence . . . ." But he thought of himself as a peacemaker still, perhaps even dreamed of reestablishing his reputation, reentering the consciousness of the young with whom he had lost touch, in precisely that role. If there is a touch of vanity in all this, it is understandable in light of the fact that in 1948 not a single one of his books was in print.

But his belief that he could play such a role in the context of the Communist-sponsored meetings at the Waldorf-Astoria (particularly after his experiences in Wroclaw) is not fully explicable in terms of vestigial pacifism and desperate vanity. To understand it better we must first understand the deep roots of his lifelong political bias: on the one hand, his stubborn conviction as a revolutionary "socialist" that the Soviet Union still represented—for all its evident flaws—the last best hope of the world; and, on the other, his inveterate aversion (evident, as we shall see, in his fiction) to what he liked to call "the cruder sort of Americanism." How this deep-seated prej-

udice must have been reinforced by the jostling demonstrators
outside their meetingplace, the Catholic and Jewish war vet-
erans, the disaffected émigré Ukrainians and Lithuanians, the
native-born hardhats and rednecks yelling, "Death to the
Commie Rats!"

Nor can Stapledon have been reassured by the more edu-
cated and articulate Americans who joined them, the poets
and pundits banded together in an organization called "Americans for Intellectual Freedom"; since they, too, in their leaflets
and interventions from the floor, questioning the good faith of
the organizers and raising questions about jailed or executed
Soviet intellectuals, must have seemed to him not just shrill
and hysterical—but above all, wrong! He had no way of knowing that they included in their number many of the most
promising younger writers and thinkers in America, the best
of a generation which at that moment, in journals like the *Partisan Review* and *Commentary*, were establishing themselves
as leaders of the cultural movement that was to dominate the
high culture, not just of the United States but of much of the
world. Even as isolated as he had become from the mainstream of the arts, Stapledon doubtless recognized the names
of some of the elders, British and American, who supported
the AIF—John Dewey, for instance, and Bertrand Russell and
Arthur Koestler, perhaps even John Dos Passos, Max Eastman,
and James T. Farrell. But it seems hardly likely that he was
familiar with the work of Newton Arvin, Daniel Aaron, Robert
Lowell, Nicolas Nabokov, William Philips, Philip Rahv, Mary
McCarthy, Arthur Schlesinger, Jr., Harold Rosenberg, or Lio-
nel Trilling.

Stapledon was, moreover, almost certainly unaware of the
political tradition of dissent which had made those writers anti-
Stalinists rather than anti-Communists; opponents of the Soviet Union not because it represented the threat of revolution,
but because it had betrayed the Marxist-Leninist dream. To
not a few of them, the death of Leon Trotsky (murdered in
1940 by a Soviet agent) had seemed a major calamity, marking
the end of their illusions about Russia and the beginning of
their acceptance of America as a lesser evil, if not a force for
positive good on the world scene. Certain compatriots of Stapledon like George Orwell and Richard Crossman had already

come to similar conclusions; but Stapledon gives no evidence of having read Orwell's *Homage to Catalonia* (1939), an account of Communist perfidy in the Spanish Civil War, or *1984* (1948), a futurist fantasy about the death of the human spirit in a Bolshevized England. Nor does he seem to have been affected by Crossman's *The God That Failed*, a collection of essays by Arthur Koestler, Ignazio Silone, and Richard Wright, and another about André Gide, all recounting their loss of faith in the Soviet Union.

If, however, Stapledon was ignorant about such young American anti-Stalinists and what they read, they were equally ignorant about him and what he wrote. Reporting on the Waldorf conference, for instance, in *Partisan Review*, Irving Howe, a spokesman for the anti-Stalinist Left, says of the speakers at the opening session, who included Olaf Stapledon, "None . . . was either a prominent or a serious intellectual." And though William Barret, who commented on the proceedings in *Commentary*, felt obliged, being a philosopher himself, to acknowledge Stapledon's existence, he dismissed him as "a run-of-the-mill pedagogue of very little reputation."

The only contemporary account of the Cultural and Scientific Congress for World Peace by someone who knew and respected Stapledon as novelist is an essay by Sam Moskowitz, then a young aficionado of science fiction; and typically it made its first appearance in 1949 as a pamphlet called *Peace and Olaf Stapledon*, clearly intended only for a handful of science-fiction initiates, its total press run being 112. It has, however, been reprinted since for a somewhat larger audience as an appendix to an anthology of Stapledon's hitherto uncollected fiction and drama, in the introduction to which Moskowitz retells the story from the vantage point of 1979. Together the essays constitute a valuable study, confronting head-on, as criticism of his work seldom does, Stapledon's ambiguous and unfashionable politics; and setting, as no journalist was willing or able to do, his remarks at the Waldorf-Astoria in the context of his total *oeuvre*.

Moskowitz is especially useful in filling in our knowledge about Stapledon's farewell performance in Newark, since he is a native of that city and actually endured enough of the dreary session at the Mosque Theatre to hear him speak. He

records, in fact, not just the kind of statements Stapledon seems
to have felt obliged to make in his role of public man in a
public place ("I am not a Communist. I am not a Christian. I
am just me. I am, however, a socialist . . . "), but the *obiter
dicta*—some asides from the platform, some revelations in personal telephone calls and letters—which reveal the private man
behind the public face. From the latter we learn, for instance,
that Stapledon did not like meetings or travel or big cities,
that he "felt helpless without his wife to take care of him,"
that he was deeply troubled by his books having gone out of
print, and that he despaired finally of being able to "survive
the wild rush of America."

It was on such grounds that he asked to be excused from
attending a meeting in New Jersey of science-fiction writers to
which Moskowitz had invited him, even when it was suggested that there might be in the group some people influential enough to get him republished in America. But he had, as
he apparently did not tell Moskowitz, already attended a similar gathering in New York; though even there he had confined himself to polite chitchat, feeling no doubt (as his earlier
remarks to the editor of *Scientifiction* would seem to indicate)
as alienated from the kind of pulp fiction written by most local authors of science fiction, who embarrassingly hailed him
as one of their own, as he did from their pro-American Cold
War politics.

Moskowitz apparently felt that a chance to talk candidly
with his transatlantic colleagues might have tempered Stapledon's view of the United States as totally possessed by war
hysteria. But though Stapledon had, as it turns out, been given
that chance, it seems to have made no difference; since he told
the press on his return to England that "there may be a war at
any moment . . . ," the clear implication being that if and
when it came, the Americans would have triggered it. Nor had
his faith in the Communist-inspired "peace movement" been
shaken by his experiences in New York, as Moskowitz would
also like to have us believe, writing, "Stapledon had been taken
and knew it." After all, the Waldorf-Astoria had represented
his second encounter with the ubiquitous Fadayev, and even
Wroclaw had been preceded by twenty years of involvement
with the Communist Party and its front organizations, includ-

ing the Left Book Club, at one of whose earlier meetings in the thirties he had spoken. If, then, he had been duped, he had in some sense willed it—choosing to be used in what he continued stubbornly to consider a good cause.

Worn out by his troubled journey and haunted by intimations of approaching death, Stapledon completed *A Man Divided*, a novel whose protagonist commits suicide in despair, and began *The Opening of the Eyes*, an experiment with a new genre, in the midst of which he asks, "Yet how can I not look questioningly beyond the world, being already rather old and tired, and soon perhaps to die?" He did, indeed, die before a year was out, leaving unfinished a strange book addressed not to the world but to a not-quite-believed-in "God," seen in a flash of illumination. Beginning with a stuttering attempt to re-create the ineffable vision, he moves on to theodicy: a meditation on the place of suffering in the perhaps-created universe. Though initially more concerned with the private than the public (its immediate occasion was the death in agony of a beloved female friend), the book deals finally with the "comrades" once more, in light of the role Stapledon thinks of them as playing on the post-World War II international scene. He has criticized them earlier for their Machiavellianism, and even disavowed them as an obstacle between him and salvation. But he feels forced to grant that "Tyranny is triumphant"—meaning by "tyranny" the capitalist democracies of the West—and that ". . . alone the comrades, whom I chose to reject, are enlisted against it . . . those who love peace must fight for peace, and against those who plot war as a means to strengthen tyranny."

I have little doubt, therefore, that had he lived, Stapledon would have appeared on the rostrum again when next the Communist Party called. Certainly, his widow seems to have thought so, two years after his death making a pilgrimage to the Soviet Union, which Olaf had never found time to do but which she assumed he still was planning at the end of his life. To the international press, too, Stapledon remained always a pro-Soviet Cold Warrior. Consequently, it was in those terms that they wrote of him when on September 6, 1950, he died of a coronary occlusion; though in fact it was in his role of sexagenarian suburban grandfather that he made his exit, collaps-

ing on the kitchen floor with a pile of dirty dishes in his arms,
after having earlier strained his heart perhaps chopping wood.

The lead of the *New York Times* read, "William Olaf Stapledon, author and philosopher, who took part in recent
Communist-organized conferences of intellectuals, died last
night in his home in Cheshire." Though it went on to say that
"The books that brought him the widest repute were boldly
speculative and scientific fantasies," it named only one, *Last
and First Men*, devoting most of its remaining space to an account of "the controversial Cultural and Scientific Conference
for World Peace." The little squib under "Milestones" in *Time*
did somewhat better, mentioning his first novel, too, then adding *Odd John* and *Sirius* to the list of "early-Wellsian fantasies," before getting to the heart of the matter with the snide
observation that "Stapledon achieved a measure of distinction
in March 1949 as the only British delegate" at that conference.
As was to be expected, however, the London *Times* did best
of all, mentioning almost everything Stapledon had published
up to 1946, when apparently their files ran out. But their lead,
too, concentrated on the one newsworthy event in his life, beginning: "Dr. Olaf Stapledon . . . a left-wing liberal thinker
who in recent years had taken a prominent part in various
Communist-organized international conferences of intellectuals, died at his home in Cheshire . . . ." Yet however su-
perficially ironic, this emphasis is, in a deeper sense, just; since
Stapledon's supra-temporal fantasies, to be properly understood, must be seen in the context of his time-bound politics—
his attempt to carry with him into the fifties attitudes toward
"the coming struggle for power" born in the thirties and long
since abandoned by most other writers and thinkers in the
Western world.

# 2
# LOST IN THE THIRTIES

Stapledon was essentially a thirties novelist. His first novel, *Last and First Men*, appeared in 1930, *Last Men in London* in 1932, *Odd John: A Story Between Jest and Earnest* in 1935, and *Star Maker*, his greatest achievement in the genre, in 1937; after which he published nothing but non-fiction for five years, apparently having decided to give up the novel completely. But, for whatever reason, he did return to fiction with *Darkness and the Light* (1942), *Old Man in New World* (1944), *Sirius: A Fantasy of Love and Discord* (1944), *Death into Life* (1946), *The Flames: A Fantasy* (1947), and *A Man Divided* (1950). But of these, only *Sirius* ranks with the works produced before 1940—and all are reworkings of themes established in the earlier books. It is scarcely surprising, then, that his whole oeuvre turns out to be as typical a product of the crisis of conscience endured in the 1930s by the Oxbridge-educated sons of the English upper classes as the novels of the young George Orwell, Christopher Isherwood, and Graham Greene, the early poetry of W. H. Auden, Stephen Spender, and C. Day Lewis, the popularized science of J.B.S. Haldane and J. D. Bernal, or, for that matter, the politics of pro-Soviet "moles" in British Intelligence like Kim Philby, Guy Burgess, and Donald McLean.

It reflects, that is to say, the same loss of faith in capitalism and parliamentary democracy, the same Oedipal contempt for Christian humanism, the same queasy fascination with revo-

31

lutionary violence (oddly combined with theoretical pacifism), the same faintly condescending adulation of the working class, the same ambivalent commitment to the Soviet Union
and the English Communist Party, the same odd mingling of
hope and despair in the face of the future. The apocalyptic
vision he shared with his contemporaries, Stapledon, like them,
felt obliged to deny was more religious than political; convinced that the Judeo-Christian God was as dead as the
churches in which the hypocritical bourgeoisie gathered to in-
voke His blessings on their profit-making and their imperialist
wars. Yet, as was the case with so many of the other radicals
of his time, his language continually betrayed his bondage to
presumably defunct pieties.

Finally, however, Stapledon was a thirties writer with a
difference, in large part because of his age. Born in 1886, which
is to say, two decades before Stephen Spender or Graham
Greene, he was a belated convert to the beliefs of that troubled
decade, bringing to it an obsession with the atrocities and fu-
tility of World War I more characteristic of the generation of
the twenties, writers like E. E. Cummings and Ernest Hemingway, Wilfrid Owen and Siegfried Sassoon. It is that war and
its aftermath which haunts him rather than the Civil War in
Spain, which he tends to ignore—his first extended reference
to it appearing in *Youth and Tomorrow*, which was not published until 1946.

Yet for most writers on the Left in thirties England (as in
America), it was the desperate battle between Franco and the
Loyalists, ending in their defeat by the Fascists from without
and their betrayal by the Communists from within, which
seemed the central event of the age: the "Last Great Cause,"
while there was still hope, and an eternal "Wound in the
Heart" (the phrase is André Malraux's), when all hope was
lost. A sizable number of such young English writers, among
them George Orwell, actually went to Spain as combatants,
and some of them died fighting against the Fascists, including
Julian Bell, John Cornford, Ralph Fox, Esmond Romilly, and
Christopher St. John Sprigg, better known by his pen name
Christopher Caudwell. Others from all parts of the Western
world went to the front as observers, and returned home to
bear witness in prose and verse: Ernest Hemingway from

America, André Malraux from France, Stephen Spender and W. H. Auden from England being perhaps the most notable.

And while the fighting still raged, it was Auden's poem "Spain 1937" which seemed most to possess the imagination of the young; indeed, nearly half a century later, it evokes still the otherwise irrecoverable mood of the times.

Tomorrow the rediscovery of romantic love;
The photographing of ravens, all the fun under
    Liberty's masterful shadow;
Tomorrow the hour of the pageant-master and the musician.

Tomorrow, for the young, the poets exploding like bombs,
The walks by the lake, the winter of perfect communion;
    Tomorrow the bicycle races
Through the suburbs on summer evenings: but today the struggle.

Today the deliberate increase in the chances of death;
The conscious acceptance of guilt in the necessary murder;
    Today the expending of powers
On the flat ephemeral pamphlet and the boring meeting.

Today the makeshift consolations; the shared cigarette;
The cards in the candle-lit barn and the scraping concert,
    The masculine jokes; today the
Fumbled and unsatisfactory embrace before hurting . . . .

Auden's poem is more typical than personal, memorializing not just his own passage but that of a whole generation from a vision of the Old World dying "not with a bang but a whimper" to that of a New World burning in hope; and by the same token, from a disavowal of military force as dehumanizing and self-defeating to a celebration of justified violence, a Final Conflict that would usher in forever a peaceful Communist utopia.

Certain writers on the Right saw that limited peninsular war in much the same grandiose way, though it was of course Franco with his allies, Hitler, and Mussolini whom they supported, hailing them precisely for their defense of the Old World, in which they had not lost faith; the world of hierarchy, order, and an established Roman Catholic Church. The most eminent members of this much smaller contingent were, perhaps, the poet Roy Campbell and the novelist Wyndham Lewis, whose *Revenge for Love*, a vitriolic attack on the pro-Loyalist intellectuals, remains still a moving and disturbing

book even to those convinced that doctrinally it is a perverse
and wicked one. Certain old-time rightists, however, including T. S. Eliot and Ezra Pound, refused to take sides—con-
founding both their conservative allies and their liberal or radical adversaries.

On the Left, there were many fewer neutrals, though in
their number were two aging literary giants, those veteran
Victorian Socialists, George Bernard Shaw and H. G. Wells—
and, of course, Olaf Stapledon. "In Spain," declared the first,
"both the Right and the Left so thoroughly disgraced themselves . . . before the Right revolted, that it is impossible to
say which of them is more incompetent . . . "; "The enemy
of mankind," announced the second, "is not the Fascists but
the Ignorant Fool." But Stapledon, that odd hybrid born before the death of Victoria but converted to socialism only after
the October Revolution, said very little. In a sense, his silence
about what was going on in Spain is consistent with the oddly
abstract nature of his politics, his refusal, even in his polemical prose, to refer to particular events. He avoids, for instance,
alluding specifically to the Moscow Trials, the Hitler-Stalin
Pact, or the War of Abyssinia; or mentioning the name of Stalin only once—and those of Trotsky, Bukharin, Kamenev, or
Zinoviev never—in his many discussions of Russian communism.

To be sure, he evokes the name of Lenin from time to time
as a kind of departed saint, and of Hitler as an opposite and
almost equal force of evil—but only after he, too, is dead. Yet,
for reasons best known to himself, Stapledon rarely alludes to
such long-departed pioneers of socialism as Marx and Engels.
And the names of British politicians, Labour, Liberal, or Tory,
living or dead, are almost totally absent from his pages. But
the Spanish Civil War seems to have been for him not merely
hard to name but to confront. He pretended (it seems to me)
that it simply wasn't there; in part, perhaps, because recogniz-
ing it would have challenged his pacifist opposition to all war,
but surely also because of his more fundamental blindness to
the threat of Hitler and Mussolini. "Certainly I, who entirely
failed to foresee the advent of Fascism," he was to write in
1941 in the preface to *Darkness and the Light*, "cannot lay
claim to describe the next phase of European change." Espe-

cially in respect to Nazism, he appears almost willfully to have chosen not to see what lay just outside his range of vision, blinkered as he was by an admiration for Germany and its intellectual traditions.

He would have much preferred it if America, instead of remaining neutral in Spain quite like him, had been clearly on the "Wrong Side," since America had always been for him the mythological Enemy, the foe of all he most prized in both Western culture and evolutionary socialism. In fiction, he was able to imagine it in that role, as, for instance, in the opening chapters of *Last and First Men*. But actual history refused for a long time to conform to his scenario; the United States ending up as the ally of both England and Russia in World War II—the savior, in fact (as he never quite confessed) of both Europe and the "Worker's Homeland." Only after 1945, did the developing Cold War, in which America was pitted against the Soviet Union, provide for Stapledon a mythologically satisfactory Final Conflict; and he took sides then, as he had not in the mid-thirties. By doing so, however, he once more separated himself from the generation of English writers who had come of age during the Spanish Civil War; most of whom, including Auden, Isherwood, Spender, and George Orwell, had long ceased to identify the hope of mankind with the Bolshevik Revolution.

If Stapledon was aware of this final irony, he has left no record of it. Indeed, just as he had ignored such younger English writers in the early thirties, when they were first making their reputation, he continued to ignore them in the late forties, when their standing was considerably higher than his own. He was not much given, in fact, to discussing contemporary literature except in the most general terms; and when he refers at all to living British authors, it is usually to certain older ones, more nearly his actual contemporaries, like Eliot, Joyce, and D. H. Lawrence. But though, like him, the latter had lived as adults through World War I, they had little else in common; since Stapledon remained oddly untouched by the whole adventure of Modernism, the subversion of the traditional concepts of character, narrative, and coherence.

He seems in this respect not merely old-fashioned but provincial, as, indeed, befits one who avoided the metropolitan centers in which the literary coteries of his time flourished. He did not, like most of the thirties writers whose class origins resembled his own and whose politics he shared, gravitate toward London, Paris, or Berlin, New York or Los Angeles—not even Moscow, which he left for his wife to visit in 1952, as she said, "for both of us." Though his early childhood had been spent in the vicinity of the Suez Canal, and his schooling had taken him to Oxford, his war service to France, and his first job experiences to Manchester as well as back to Egypt, his life *as a writer* was, as we have seen, spent in and around Liverpool—far enough from its urban center, however, and close enough to the sea so that he could indulge in birdwatching, "rough walking with a very small spot of rock climbing . . . swimming . . . ," then return home to "arduous and brainless gardening," his chief pleasures of life, he wrote in *Twentieth Century Authors*. In all this he was sustained, of course, by inherited money, which endowed him simultaneously with freedom and guilt: the space and time to write what he would, and the need to prove himself by being, as his wife indicates he aspired to become, "a really successful writer."

Stapledon's situation was ambiguous in other senses as well. Relieved, on the one hand, from the economic pressures which beset the penniless professional, he was, on the other, alienated from the community of writers most highly prized by the critical establishment of his time. His closest personal relations seem to have been with family friends, old comrades from the Quaker Ambulance Unit and the shadowy other women in his life, whom we must surmise from ambiguous indications in his books. His professional contacts were chiefly with his academic not-quite-colleagues at the University of Liverpool—chiefly in philosophy, the social sciences, biology, and physics, however, rather than literature. Even when he corresponded with his more eminent contemporaries in the great world beyond the Merseyside, it was largely with scholars in such extra-literary fields, like J.B.S. Haldane, with the notable exception of E. V. Rieu, an editor for two of Stapledon's publishers, Methuen and Penguin. We are likely to remember

Rieu these days chiefly for his eminently readable prose trans-
lations of Homer's *Odyssey* and *Iliad* in the Penguin Classics
series, of which he was the general editor. But some ten years
before the publication of the first, Stapledon had turned to him
for help in revising and organizing the novel-in-process which
was finally to appear as *Star Maker.*

Also involved in that revision and duly thanked along with
Rieu in the preface, is the only contemporary novelist with
whom Stapledon seems to have carried on an extended literary correspondence, L. H. Myers. Though his first novel, *The
Orissers*, appeared in 1922, the bulk of Myers's work came out
at the same moment as Stapledon's early fiction, beginning
with *The Near and the Far* (1929), *Prince Jali* (1931), and *The
Root and the Flower* (1935), which combined the first two with
a sequel called *Rajah Amar.* In 1936, Myers produced a third
work, *Strange Glory* and in 1940 a second and last sequel, *The
Pool of Vishnu.* He committed suicide in 1944, after having
struggled vainly to complete a non-fictional work, half sociology and half autobiography; leaving instructions to destroy
that manuscript, and a plea to his friends to do the same with
his letters. But Stapledon, at least, did not accede to his request, making his correspondence with Myers available before
his own death in 1950 to C. H. Bantock, who drew heavily on
it in a book published in 1956 under the title of *L. H. Myers:
A Critical Study.*

Myers's novels have, at this point, been even more completely forgotten than Stapledon's, perhaps deservedly, since
their rather uninspired prose seldom does justice to their not
uninteresting themes. Indeed, when they first appeared, most
of the English literary establishment greeted them much more
coolly than they did *Last and First Men* or *Star Maker;* though
Myers was—unlike Stapledon—much touted in the most influential of all anti-establishment critical journals, *Scrutiny*,
whose editors D. W. Harding, F. R. Leavis, Q. D. Leavis, and
L. C. Knights were then engaged in a valiant effort to redefine
the canon of English literature. They succeeded in fact, in establishing the reputations of many of their favorite authors and
books, but not of L. H. Myers, despite a laudatory review of
*The Root and the Flower* by D. W. Harding in Volume II,

No. 1 for 1935, and Leavis's own point-blank assertion of 1940 that in the previous decade, "In the novel, there was *The Root and the Flower*; but what else is there to mention . . . ."

Stapledon and Myers, in any case, recognized each other immediately as being, in their very outsiderness, kindred spirits. Indeed, so extravagant was Myers's enthusiasm for Stapledon, whose *Last and First Men* he read over and over, sending copies to all his friends, that Bantock is driven to object, arguing that Myers's tendency to judge fiction by "the application from the *outside* of moral standards, ideas, already formed . . . led him to overvalue the works of writers such as Olaf Stapledon . . . ." In fact, however, what Myers thought he had discovered in *Last and First Men* and *Star Maker* is something connected, perhaps, to "moral standards" and "ideas," but finally quite different—as he reveals in a letter to Stapledon dated 28 May 1941: "When I come across a *live* book, I am so surprised and pleased that I just don't think about its patches of weakness. By a *live* book I mean one that (i) expresses a burst of vision and enlightenment in the author, and (ii) is the expression of a true enlightenment, i.e., the vision of a truth." Clearly, this describes what Myers was attempting to do in his own novels as well as what he, quite correctly, thought Stapledon was after in his.

But they had much in common besides their shared dedication to the writing of "philosophical fiction," in which "vision" was more central than plot, and the evocation of the "whole" more important than mimetic specification of character or setting. Both were born in the next-to-last decade of the nineteenth century and did not begin publishing until they reached their forties; and for that reason among others, both remained always hostile to Modernism—distrusting not just such founding fathers of the movement as Marcel Proust, but its latter-day heirs like the poetic circle around W. H. Auden. Both, moreover, hated with especial virulence "Bloomsbury": the congeries of rather overbred writers, so close as to constitute a "clan" or a "family," though it ranged from the philosopher Bertrand Russell to the economist Maynard Keynes and the novelists E. M. Forster and Virginia Woolf.

Unlike Stapledon, Myers grew up in the social world of Bloomsbury and for a while, flattered by the attention of its acolytes, participated in their salons. But he soon grew disaffected, and ended by savagely travestying their effete estheticism, fraudulent humanism, homosexual chic, and especially their inverted conventionality in *Prince Jali*, where Bloomsbury appears thinly disguised as the "Pleasance" or "The Camp":

> The Camp taught that thinking for oneself consisted in nothing more than in reversing established opinions, that the newest thing was necessarily superior to one that came before and that the ultimate test of the worth of an idea was its capacity to startle the Philistine and annoy him. They depended basically upon a solid, shockable world of decorum and common sense.

The words could just as easily have come from the mouth of Stapledon's Paul in *Last Men in London*, after he has fallen first in then out with the intellectual elite of that city.

Myers and Stapledon are, moreover, joined not merely by what they abhorred in the English high culture of their time. They share also certain allegiances: an anti-clerical, post-Christian religiosity, for instance, which speaks much of the "spirit" but avoids the word "God," while flirting with the occult, particularly those "paranormal" phenomena on the border between magic and science. Their politics also were much alike, combining an instinctive and only half-confessed elitism with an avowed espousal of the Bolshevik Revolution. In both cases, their Stalinoid leftism (Myers actually once headed a letter "Stalin's Birthday; God bless him") was based less on knowledge of what was actually happening in the Soviet Union, of which they were careful not to learn too much, than on hatred of the class into which they were born and guilt for living on inherited wealth.

Most important, perhaps, was their temperamental similarity. Not only were they both manic-depressive types, but their cycles of elation and despair seem to have been uncannily synchronous; so that the moment of utter terror which culminated in Myers's suicide seems to have coincided—judging by the nightmare quality of *Darkness and the Light*—with a low-point in Stapledon's own spiritual life. Myers's death must, in any case, have been a real blow to the survivor, since no other writer had so sustained and supported Stapledon in his otherwise lonely enterprise. Not only did they read each other's work, exchanging lengthy criticisms, which, even when they found themselves in disagreement, must surely have helped to focus and define their deep intent, but they seem also to have introduced to each other, or mutually discovered, other sympathetic authors, ranging from L. H. Myers's father, the psychic researcher F. W. H. Myers (inventor of the term "telepathy"), to Carl Jung and Martin Buber.

Two years after Myers's suicide, H. G. Wells, the only other novelist of distinction with whom Stapledon ever corresponded at length, died, too. To Wells, however, Stapledon seemed less a colleague and peer than another aspiring young man, whose first book, after all, had made its appearance more than thirty years after his own *Time Machine*. He admired some things about Stapledon's work, and was willing to say so; but always a shade condescendingly, like an old pro commending a neophyte, gifted, perhaps, but maybe not quite gifted enough. He was, Mrs. Stapledon reported years later, "very frank and he was very friendly towards Olaf, but he never buttered him up and told him he could write well. Wells knew he himself could write much more readable books than Olaf's books; and he told him so in quite plain words. But at the same time he said, 'I can't hold a candle to you in imagination . . . .' "

To Stapledon, on the other hand, Wells seemed a contemporary; and in a sense he was right. Not only did their lives largely overlap (Stapledon was ten years old when Wells' first fantasies appeared, old enough, that is to say, to have read them); but even as Wells remained, despite his pursuit of new fashions in politics and morality, esthetically an unreconstructed Victorian, so also did Stapledon. Both wrote as if neither the Modernist "revolution of the word" nor the consequent splitting of literature into high and low, popular and elite had ever occurred. And both, therefore, were able to produce what we now think of as science fiction without being aware that they had thereby separated themselves from the "mainstream" of polite letters; and that they were doomed, consequently, for a while at least, to be ignored, despised, or condescended to by the official guardians of literary standards, while being adulated by a group of parochial fanatics who thought of themselves as despising all fiction except that disreputable new sub-genre of the novel.

That Wells wrote "science fiction" without knowing it was understandable enough in the last decades of the nineteenth century; for the genre which he was unwittingly giving its classic formulation had as yet no name and no definition and could therefore be considered still nothing more than another form of the traditional romance, i.e., fantastic rather than mimetic fiction. "*Scientific* romances" Wells called his "stories of space and time," and though his hostile critics amended the adjective to "pseudo-scientific," they accepted the generic designation. But Hugo Gernsback, that émigré American enamored of New World technology, had launched in the twenties, *Amazing Stories*, the first magazine entirely devoted to what he first perceived as a new and separate genre, and called tentatively "scientifiction," then "science fiction." It was under that rubric that he reprinted as models for aspiring writers some thirty of Wells's tales. He also anthologized for their benefit and delight stories by Jules Verne and Edgar Allan Poe. But Wells was represented by twice as many selections as the other two combined, and it was apparently chiefly from his example that Gernsback derived the earliest definition of the new genre: "A charming romance intermingled with scientific fact and prophetic vision."

By the time Stapledon was writing *Star Maker*, both the name and the definition were firmly established, and a whole stable of writers was producing such fiction for a small but growing audience of devotees, largely American but English as well. The first "fanzine," which is to say, an amateur journal solely by and for such devotees, had in fact appeared in 1930; and the first convention of science-fiction writers and fans was held some time before the beginning of World War II. The institutionalization and consequent "ghettoization" of science fiction did not occur in England as quickly, nor was it ever as total as in the United States; so that certain British writers from Huxley and Orwell to William Golding and Anthony Burgess have been able to produce futurist fantasies, chiefly dystopias, without surrendering their claim to membership in the literary mainstream. Not a few others, however, from Eric Frank Russell to Arthur C. Clarke have committed themselves totally to the Gernsbackian mode, risking critical excommunication.

Clarke, indeed, is considered at this point one of the founding fathers of the genre—a surviving hero of its Golden Age, like the Americans Robert Heinlein and Isaac Asimov. It is, therefore, significant that he has paid loving tribute to Stapledon as Huxley, Burgess, Golding, and Orwell, oddly enough, have not; writing of *Last and First Men* in the introduction to his own *The Lion of Comarre*, and *Against the Fall of Night*, "I came across this volume in the public library of my birthplace, Minehead, soon after its appearance in 1930 . . . the book produced an overwhelming impact upon me." In later years, Clarke prevailed upon Stapledon to give one of his few public addresses to an audience composed in large part of science-fiction enthusiasts, for whose delectation he launched into his last free flight of fantasy on the themes of interplanetary travel and the controlled adaptation of man to extraterrestrial environments—though insisting in return that they listen to a rehash of his by-then rather tired social and metaphysical theories.

It had been Russell, however, who in 1937 introduced Stapledon to hard-core commercial science fiction by putting in his hands American pulp magazines like *Astounding Stories*, in which his own first published story had just appeared, and perhaps also the brand-new British journal, *Tales of Wonder*. It was to the editor of the latter, Walter Gillings, that Stapledon confessed publicly his considerably less than enthusiastic response, telling him that despite some "very striking ideas vividly treated," most of the stories had "too much padding . . . in proportion to the genuine imaginative interest," and that "the human side was terribly crude, particularly the love interest." One suspects that Stapledon was also put off by the naively technocratic politics of a good deal of such fiction— and even more by its chauvinism and blatant anti-communism. But characteristically diplomatic and polite, he did not say so.

In any case, he never referred to his own work as "science fiction," even after encountering the term. A "romance of the future" he had called *Last and First Men*, though also more grandiloquently a "myth"; and looking back much later on all his work, he spoke of it as "fantastic fiction of a semi-philosophical kind," or alternatively, "fantastic fiction dealing with the career of mankind." Occasionally, Stapledon warns his readers in a prefatory note that the book before them is, in the ordinary sense of the word, "not a novel"; and in *Waking World* (1934), his first attempt at popular philosophy, he confesses, "Now I am no highbrow, or only an imperfect one."

Yet he seems to have remained finally unaware that by spinning yarns about the future in a narrative mode which eschewed the example of Henry James and James Joyce, cofounders—in the view of real highbrows—of the modern English art novel, he was producing what they would have classified as lowbrow or pop literature, quite like the pulp science fiction which had so dismayed him. Part of his problem seems to have been that he did not think of himself as writing literature at all, high or low—but philosophy disguised as literature. Nonetheless, insofar as his "disguise" was novelistic, it was based on certain models, which turn out to be pre-Gernsbackian science fiction, quite as blissfully vulgar and politically regressive as anything in *Amazing Stories*, though in a distinctly old-fashioned way. In *Sirius*, Stapledon refers several times, for instance, to J. D. Beresford's *The Hampdenshire Wonder* (1911), one of the very earliest stories of a superhuman mutant. Moreover, as Sam Moskowitz convincingly argues, he seems to have learned something, too, from William Hope Hodgson's *The House on the Borderland* (1908) and S. Fowler Wright's *The Amphibians*; and perhaps also from the Barsoom novels of Edgar Rice Burroughs, whose specific influence on his work is hard to demonstrate, though Stapledon kept his books in his library to the end of his life. Nor could he have read them as a boy, since *Dejah Thoris, Princess of Mars*, the first of the series, did not appear until 1911, when Stapledon was twenty-five.

But Stapledon was most influenced, of course, by the "scientific romances" of H. G. Wells, works now considered to define the borderline between art and pop. Stapledon was, indeed, so steeped in the fiction of H. G. Wells that he thought

of them more as the medium in which he wrote than as prototypes for what he wrote; responding, therefore, when challenged for not having acknowledged his indebtedness, "A man
does not record his debt to the air he breathes." Nonetheless,
he did rise for the defense whenever Wells's ideology was attacked from the Left or the Right. "To belittle his achievement
as mere bourgeois blundering, or more plebian blundering,
silly . . ." he protested in *Waking World*. "The world's chief
outliner is Mr. H. G. Wells . . . . Mr. Wells is in his own
sphere beyond criticism." But he nowhere talks specifically of
what he had derived from Wells's strange kind of fiction, which
offers simultaneously the ecstatic release of fantasy and the
reassuring illusion of verisimilitude.

Yet this doubleness verging on duplicity, this capacity for
retelling ancient myth and fable in terms acceptable to those
whose definition of reality is based on positive science is what
chiefly characterizes modern science fiction, distinguishing it
from those neighboring genres, allegory and fantasy. It was
Wells's realization of this that made him the founder of the
genre, even more than his perception that its proper tense is
future and its ideal narrative form the "hook" or hypothesis,
which reimagines the world in light of a single "what if." All
three of these basic strategies of science fiction, Stapledon
learned from the master (though in narrative technique he
never satisfied him); but his debt is greater than that, since he
picked up from Wells most of his major themes as well.

*Food of the Gods* (1909), for instance, seems to have provided Stapledon with hints, even before he had encountered
Beresford's superman, for *Odd John*, in which a race of superhuman mutants confronts the hostility and incomprehension
of "normals"; *The War of the Worlds* (1898) with the notion
of interplanetary conflict with Mars, reworked in his account
of a failed Martian invasion in *Last and First Men*; and *The
Island of Dr. Moreau* with the conception of science taking
over from nature the process of organic evolution—as well as
the perception of man as an imperfectly evolved animal so
central to *Sirius*. But it was chiefly *The Time Machine* (1895)
which possessed Stapledon's imagination; and more particularly, that "one peep into the deeper abysm of time" which
follows the Time Traveller's escape from the doomed world of

the Eloi and Morlocks: his second chronological voyage, which climaxes in a vision of the End of Man, the End of Earth, the End of Life, the End of Everything, that has ever since constituted one of the major myths of science fiction.

In Wells, that myth (which later in his career he dismissed as mere "youthful pessimism") represents the negative aspect of the enlightened Victorian response to the "Death of God," news of which had been moving toward England from the Continent for over a hundred years. The vision of the vastness of space without a center, a cosmos without a creator, and humanity bereft of the promise of eternal life seems simultaneously to have exhilarated and depressed English intellectuals at the end of the nineteenth century. On the one hand, it suggested to them that men, relieved of traditional fears and restraints, could now create in place of the no-longer-believed-in Christian Paradise, a heaven here on earth—or, for that matter, wherever in the universe spaceflight took them; and that there they could become "as gods," living if not quite forever, at least longer and longer, as their power over the environment and their own bodies continued to grow. But, at the same time, they knew that when they did die—of natural causes, meaningless accidents, or the slow cooling of the universe—they would die forever, that eventually all intelligent life in whatever form would die, leaving nothing behind. Nothing.

Between such utopianism and nihilism, Stapledon, belated Victorian that he was, vacillated, too; but for him the dark side of the ambivalence was reinforced by the bleak mood of the Depression times in which he began to write. Even to the Marxists of the era, the prospect ahead seemed doubtful: the long lines of unemployed marching through a landscape of closed factories and rotting crops toward a bloody Apocalypse which might possibly mark the beginning of something new and hopeful, but surely meant the end of a world which however grim was at least familiar and in some sense loved. William Empson has travestied the chiliastic expectations of the era in a wicked little poem which runs in part:

> Shall I send a wire, boys? Where is there to send?
> All are under fire, boys, waiting for the end,

Knowing it is near boys, boys, trying to pretend,
Sitting in cold fear, boys, waiting for the end?

Shall we send a cable, boys, accurately penned,
Knowing we are able, boys, waiting for the end,
Via the Tower of Babel, boys? Christ will not ascend.
He's hiding in the stable, boys, waiting for the end.

. . .

What was said by Marx, boys, what did he perpend?
No good being sparks, boys, waiting for the end.
Treason of the clerks, boys, curtains that descend,
Lights becoming darks, boys, waiting for the end.

It is W. H. Auden, however, that less equivocal child of the thirties against whom Empson's satire (called, indeed, "Just a Smack at Auden") is directed. But Auden's images of the imminent End were conceived in the Berlin of the Weimar Republic and confirmed by the bombing of Guernica; while Stapledon's more remote and cosmic sense of an ending, with its aura of nausea and horror, comes not out of *any* history, lived or observed, but—it seems to me—out of literature, chiefly the coda to the fourteenth chapter of Wells's *The Time Machine*:

So I traveled, stopping ever and again, in great strides of a thousand years or more, drawn on by the mystery of the earth's fate, watching with a strange fascination the sun grow larger and duller in the westward sky, and the life of the old earth ebb away. At last, more than thirty million years hence, the huge red-hot dome of the sun had come to obscure nearly a tenth part of the darkling heavens . . . .
I looked about me to see if any traces of animal life remained. A certain indefinable apprehension still kept me in the saddle of the machine. But I saw nothing moving in earth or sky or sea . . . .
The darkness grew apace; a cold wind began to blow in freshening gusts from the east, and the showering white flakes in the air increased in number. From the edge of the sea came a ripple and whisper. Beyond these lifeless sounds the world was silent. Silent? It would be hard to convey the stillness of it. All the sounds of man, the bleating of sheep, the cries of birds, the hum of insects, the stir that makes the background of our lives—all that was over. As the darkness thickened, the eddying flakes grew more abundant, dancing before my eyes, and the cold of the air more intense. At last, one by one, swiftly, one after the other, the white peaks of the distant hills vanished into blackness. The breeze rose to a moaning wind. I saw the black central shadow of the eclipse sweeping toward

me. In another moment the pale stars alone were visible. All else was rayless obscurity. The sky was absolutely black.
A horror of this great darkness came to me. The cold, that smote me to my marrow, and the pain I felt in breathing overcame me. I shivered, and a deadly nausea seized me . . . .

Yet though Stapledon never quite lost the Wellsian sense that everything will end in nothingness, that "even if men do succeed at last in making the really splendid human world which at present we can only dimly imagine, that world will almost certainly be destroyed," and that "the universe is doomed to final quiescence and death," finally he does not, like the Time Traveller, regard that prospect with queasiness and terror; finding instead occasions for desperate joy and admiration in its rightness and beauty. Here then, "with diffidence, but also with firmness," he leaves Wells behind—posing questions unanswerable in terms of the older novelist's naive materialism and "the superficiality of his view of human nature."

All the phrases I have quoted from Stapledon's defense and criticism of Wells come from *Waking World*, a popular didactic work written in the early thirties, after *Last and First Men* but before *Odd John* and *Star Maker*. Fully to understand Stapledon's sense of the beauty and rightness of the cosmos, however, we must turn back to its first formulation in a rigorous and systematic book published before any of his fiction. Called *A Modern Theory of Ethics: A Study of the Relations of Ethics and Psychology*, it appeared in 1929; and though most of it turns out to be the kind of sober academic essay which its title promises, the three final chapters, numbered XIII, XIV, and XV, contain insights and images which strain the limits of philosophical discourse. Stapledon is uneasily aware of the problem, apologizing at the close of Chapter XII for "the very speculative inquiry on which I shall now venture"; confessing as he begins the conclusion to Chapter X that "We have been indulging in very vague and doubtful speculation"; then suggesting as he ends it, that it "seems all too likely" that "the wild speculations of these last three chapters are wholly mistaken."

Stapledon, as I have pointed out, is much given to such ambiguous apologies, which, in this case at least, I refuse to take at face value. True enough, for the next five years he does indeed present his "vague and doubtful" hypothesis only in imaginative works, where it asks of us not the philosopher's full belief but only a poetic suspension of disbelief. Still, he repeats in every one of his novels, at greater or less length but often in the same words, the thesis of the last chapters of *A Modern Theory of Ethics*. Moreover, when he returns to non-fiction after *Star Maker*, he recurs to it again and again until it seems not so much a *leitmotif* as an obsession. In any case, despite his modest disclaimers, he did not excise it even from his first book, aware surely that it constitutes the most moving section of an otherwise tedious and unoriginal study, read fifty years later not by students interested in modern ethical theories but by lovers of his fiction searching for clues to his *Weltanschauung*.

It takes Stapledon almost all of Chapter XII and part of the next to reach the mythical heart of his thesis. But when he describes in a discussion of "moral zeal," a mood in which "The universe is regarded single mindedly in relation to . . . the great struggle between the powers of light and the powers of darkness, or between life and death, or spirit's activity and the inertia of matter . . . ," then tells us that to one in such a mood "If the stars are indifferent to this vast crusade for the good, so much for them . . . . If, as some believe, the great enterprise of life on this planet must sooner or later end in defeat, then the universe is contemptible . . . ," we realize that he is returning to the apocalyptic vision of *The Time Machine*. And he remains faithful to the bleak tone of that vision when he continues: "From this zealous mood we may fall into disillusion . . . . No longer is the world a theatre . . . of the cosmic epic of good and evil; it is just a tedious and chaotic accident . . . ."

But when he moves to the third mood or spiritual moment which he calls "ecstasy," Stapledon has gone beyond early Wellsian pessimism to something vastly different, though, as he himself confesses, hard to distinguish from disillusion of the more tortured type, or even sheer masochism. Unlike disillusion, however, Stapledon argues, the ecstatic mood "comes to us with an enjoyment of . . . a kind of unusual wide-awakeness." Then, lest the word "enjoyment" mislead us, he quickly adds that the most usual occasion for "ecstasy" is "grave personal danger, or conviction of final defeat in some most cherished enterprise"; or especially (once more we remember the Time Traveller) the contemplation of "the possibility that the whole enterprise of mind will fail." Nonetheless, to Stapledon such a realization entails not terror but a "cold fervor of acquiescence . . . For in this mood not only victory but also defeat, even final catastrophe is experienced as a good . . . whatever befalls is good. We *admire* the issue of fate; we are not indifferent to it."

Aware that the state he describes resembles the "mystical" visions of saints and gurus, Stapledon warns us that it is "a mood which may happen to very many of us if not to all" and is therefore "not properly called super-normal." Not just in *A Modern Theory of Ethics* but in all his didactic non-fiction, he insists on the normality and almost universal accessibility of this kind of *ekstasis*; yet in his novels he invariably presents the "cold fervor of acquiescence" as a mood achieved only by more-than-human species and individuals—or if by ordinary humans, only at moments when they are "possessed" by fully awakened beings from another time or mode of existence. Moreover, returning to normal consciousness, they can render only approximately, misleadingly, like the "human author" of *Last and First Men*, what it is like to see supra-temporally in the icy light of eternity the total extinction of man and to find it "good."

# 3
# ECSTASY, *AMOR FATI,* AND THE END OF EVERYTHING

*Last and First Men* is a two-billion-year-long mytho-history which imagines eighteen succeeding species of mankind, rising and falling, making and unmaking themselves in an effort to achieve total communion with each other and the indifferent universe before their inevitable end. Beginning at a rather leisurely pace in the year 1930, the action speeds up as it goes, moving faster and faster, until aeons seem to pass in an instant, civilizations to crumble in the blink of an eye; while whole races blur to indistinction, or are lost in a hiatus scarcely long enough for the drawing of a breath. At no point, however, does Stapledon allow us to forget what is for him the central issue: will humanity attain before its inevitable extinction enough lucidity to accept and "admire" its fate.

"This book has two authors," its first paragraph begins, "one contemporary with its readers, the other an inhabitant of an age which they would call the distant future." The contemporary author, however, speaks in his own voice only once, in a "Preface" signed "O.S." and dated from West Kirby, July 1930, in which he explains the function of his collaborator ("I have pretended that he has the power of partially controlling the operations of minds now living, and that this book is the product of such influence . . ."). Then that collaborator, in an "Introduction" which immediately follows, explains *his:* "The actual writer thinks he is contriving a fiction . . . he neither believes it himself, nor expects others to believe it"; then pleads

These remnants of the second human species were not beasts but innocents, simples, children of nature . . . . In many ways their state was idyllic and enviable. But such was their dimmed mentality that they were never clearly aware . . . of the loftier experiences which had kindled and tortured their ancestors.

Nor were these "loftier experiences" recaptured until the emergence of the Fifth Men; though a vague perception of them had flickered fitfully among the Third Men, lovers of music and madness and creators of monstrous new life forms, culminating in the abortive Fourth Men, the Great Brains. These almost bodiless instruments of intellection proved even less capable of pity or ecstasy than their predecessors; yet before their demise, they managed to breed a New Adam and Eve, from whom descended the Fifth Men: the crown of controlled evolution. Beautiful, percipient, and socially adaptable, the Fifth Men developed a society in which material wealth and an eternally rising standard of living entailed neither class conflict nor international war.

Moreover, they had quite early come to terms with personal mortality; and when they came to suspect that *all* mind would eventually cease in the universe, they perceived "that even in this tragic brevity of mind's course there was a quality of beauty . . . ." Nor was their faith shaken, when entering the consciousness of past men, they discovered the omnipresence of horror; insisting, indeed, "that the very irrevocability of the past dignified the cosmos, as a tragic work of art is dignified by the irrevocability of disaster."

But in the universe as imagined by Olaf Stapledon, no triumph, material or spiritual, is forever. For the Fifth Men, the beginning of the end was a narrowing of the moon's orbit, which their scientists were able to predict would within ten million years render the surface of the earth uninhabitable. Knowing themselves to be the Last Terrestrials, the Fifth Men prepared for a mass migration to Venus; where the readjustment of the atmosphere necessary to make life possible for them threatened death to the sub-oceanic native sentients, whom they therefore decided "to put . . . out of their misery as quickly as possible." Stapledon's omniscient narrator uses the cliché without irony, then goes on to tell us:

As for the murder of Venerian life, it was, indeed, terrible, but right . . . . For as the navy proceeded with its relentless work, it . . . had learned to admire, even in a sense to love, while it killed. This mood, of inexorable yet not ruthless will, intensified the spiritual sensibility of the species . . . and revealed to it tones and themes in the universal music which were hitherto obscure.

But the music to which Stapledon's prose marches at this point is disconcertingly Wagnerian, Nietzschean—or more precisely, perhaps, Imperial British. There are, moreover, passages elsewhere in his work which reflect the same marriage of sadism (deplored in the Third and Fourth Men, but applauded in the Fifth) and chauvinism. Sensing this, C. S. Lewis in *Out of the Silent Planet* (1938), a work of Christian apologetics disguised as science fiction, includes Stapledon among those responsible for circulating

in obscure works of scientification, in little Inter-planetary Societies and Rocketry Clubs, and between the covers of monstrous magazines, ignored or mocked by the intellectuals, [the idea] that humanity, having now sufficiently corrupted the planet where it arose, must at all costs contrive to send itself over a larger area . . . a dream begotten by the hatred of death upon the fear of true immortality, fondled in secret by thousands of ignorant men . . . . The destruction or enslavement of other species in the universe, if such there are, is to these minds a welcome corollary.

Regrettably—from Stapledon's point of view—the genocidal Fifth Men became more and more subject to "the deep-seated, unreasoning sense of guilt produced by the extermination of the Venerians," and as a result, began to develop "symptoms of derangement," which even after recovery, left them without telepathic powers. They had always been genetically unstable and now—under stress—they began to mutate into the multiformed Sixth Men, some seal-like, some more like birds, but none capable of deep spiritual insight.

From an avian sub-variety of the Sixth Men, however, evolved the Seventh, pygmies in size but capable of true flight; and of all human species "probably the most carefree," which is to say, "completely without interest in the universal and the unseen." They were, in effect, artists rather than complete men; artists, moreover, dedicated to a kind of art for art's sake, ephemeral and sensuous, in which their bodies were the medium. Yet in the midst of flight, they were able to achieve "a genuine and ecstatic, though limited spiritual experience."

> So long as the individual was in the air, whether in lonely struggle with the storm, or in the ceremonial ballet with the sky-darkening hosts of his fellows . . . whether his enterprise was fortunate, or he found himself . . . crashing to death; always the gay and tragic fortunes of his own person were regarded equally with the detached aesthetic delight. Even when his dearest companion was mutilated or destroyed by some aerial disaster, he exulted . . . . But soon after he had returned to the ground he would be overwhelmed with grief, would strive vainly to recapture the lost vision, and would perhaps die of heart failure.

After nearly a hundred million years, however, a marine salt essential to the Seventh Men's diet became exhausted, so that more and more of their children were born incapable of flight. And when their winged progenitors ceased to weed them out by infanticide (a Draconian eugenic device of which Stapledon seems to approve), those brilliant but tortured "cripples" took over, converting their world to an industrial society in which the older feckless fliers were excluded and scorned, the winged newborn strangled to death. Finally driven to rebellion, the last generation of true avians proved no match for the planes of their oppressors, flying en masse, in a last elegant aerial maneuver, into the mouth of a volcano.

The descendants of the victors, the Eighth Men, gigantic and big-brained but pedestrian and hopelessly "philistine," were once more confronted by the threat of total extinction. Learning first that the sun was shrinking to a white dwarf, they prepared to move to Mercury; but even as plans for migration were underway, they became aware that "A volume of non-luminous gas" from outer space was on a collision course with that diminishing star and, on impact, would make life on any planet closer than Neptune intolerable. The sheer bulk of the Eighth Men, however, made them unviable in Neptune's strong gravitational field; nor could most of the miniature Ninth Men they then artificially bred survive long enough to adapt to its unstable crust and turbulent atmosphere.

The few who did survive begot mindless and bestialized offspring, who ended by crawling on all fours, bellies to the

ground, and inarticulate muzzles raised uncomprehendingly
to the stars. When the long process of evolution began once
more, as a rabbit-like sub-species of the Tenth Men rose to its
hind legs and acquired the skills of handedness, it was by slow,
random selection. Even the Fifteenth Men (Stapledon dismisses the Eleventh, Twelfth, Thirteenth, and Fourteenth,
along with the more than million years needed for their rise
and fall, in a few sentences—as he hastens breathlessly toward
the end), "awakened" enough to abolish the "five great evils"
of the past, disease, suffocating toil, senility, misunderstanding, and ill will and to create their own successors, the Sixteenth Men, as physically prepotent and psychically advanced
as the Fifth.

Not only were they telepathic; but "the ordination of the
nervous system was in them so finely tuned" that they were
able to abolish the sixth and greatest of the ancient evils, "selfishness." Yet the Sixteenth Men were still haunted by the
mystery of time, the problem of "mind's relation to the world,"
and, above all, "the need somehow to reconcile their confirmed loyalty to life . . . with their ever-strengthening impulse to rise above the battle and admire it dispassionately."
They artificially produced, therefore, the more advanced but
still imperfect Seventeenth Men, who, though they too failed
to achieve total illumination, were able to design the Eighteenth and, as it turned out, last human species.

In that species, to which the Neptunian narrator belongs,
all aspirations of mankind on three planets and over two billion years seem at last fulfilled. Not only has life been prolonged almost indefinitely, so that the continuity of the race
no longer depends on begetting; but sexuality, freed from its
ancient obligations, can be reinstitutionalized in the form of
ever-changing multisexual unions (ninety-six is for Stapledon
the optimum number of partners), which respect both the necessity of lifelong, loving monogamy and the need for casual
or recreational intercourse. Moreover, the problem of personality in community has been solved, the conflicting claims of
the individual and his society reconciled in a policy at once
utterly democratic—though not representative—and totally
bureaucratic. What binds together with duress this ultimate
utopia is the telepathic communion not merely between single

persons and within the psychosexual groups, but of each with all in a quasi-mystical experience which Stapledon calls "the waking of individuals together."

Out of such communal awakening is created "the mind of the race," which the narrator attempts to describe through the human author of *Last and First Men:*

> We who, in our familiar individual sphere are able to regard all conceivable tragedy not merely with fortitude but with exultation, are obscurely conscious that as the racial mind we have looked into an abyss of evil such as we cannot now conceive, and could not endure to conceive. Yet even this hell we know to have been acceptable as an organic member in the austere form of the universe. We remember obscurely, and yet with a strange conviction, that all the age-long striving of the human spirit . . . was seen as a fair component of something far more admirable than itself; and that man ultimately defeated, no less than man for a while triumphant, contributes to this higher excellence.

Not very different from what had already been perceived by the Fifth Men, and in a somewhat more limited way, by the Second, the Seventh, and even the First, this seems rather an anti-climax. Our Time Traveller, however, hastens to inform us that the Last Men, unlike their predecessors, can maintain "the ecstasy which admires the real as it is, and accepts its dark-bright form with joy," not intermittently and without full comprehension but "at all times" and "moreover, intelligently."

Once more, however, Stapledon's euphoric fantasy debouches in nightmare. The sun, subject to a mysterious bombardment of radiation from a "deranged star," threatens to disintegrate as the Eighteenth Men had always been aware it would. They had thought, however, that long before the end they would have managed to migrate to another planet, or perhaps would even have moved the one they inhabited into orbit around some younger sun. Moreover, there would be, they assured themselves, millions of years ahead for exploring the past; as well as for meditating upon the nature of time, which they had begun to perceive "is boundless, though finite . . . cyclic, yet not repetitive . . . . Everywhere within time's cycle, there is endless passage of events. In a continuous flux,

they occur and vanish . . . . Yet each one of them is eternal."
But what they had chiefly hoped for was the opportunity to
perfect at leisure their "relentless admiration of fate," so that
finally they could confront "with piety even the possibility of
cosmical defeat."

In light of their impending extinction, however, they were
forced to suspend all meditation in favor of action. For the
sake of the future, they dedicated themselves to the "forlorn
task of disseminating among the stars the seeds of a new humanity"; and for the sake of the past they attempted not merely
to observe, as they had hitherto, but to *influence* the working
of past minds. Stapledon examines at some length the para-
doxes implicit in such tampering with time: "The past event
would never have been as it actually was (and is eternally), if
there had not been going to be a certain event, which though
. . . ," etc. etc. But he manages to say little not already familiar to readers of subsequent time-travel science fiction; or, for
that matter, to readers of the thirties who had encountered an
immensely popular work, on which Stapledon clearly draws,
J. W. Dunne's *An Experiment with Time* (1927). Beginning
with an exploration of seemingly predictive dreams, Dunne
had concluded that we can and do (in deep sleep) see ahead
as well as backward; and his exploration on the border between scientific "fact" and the occult became a kind of best-
seller in the thirties.

The interventions of the Eighteenth Men in the past produced chiefly disastrous or ludicrous results; feeding supersti-
tions about ghosts and bogies, or creating such literary abor-
tions as *Last and First Men*, which (its inspirer from the Far
Future tells us) "has issued from the brain of the writer, your
contemporary, in such disorder as to be mostly rubbish." Nor
did they prevent either the final destruction or the penultimate degeneration of the Eighteenth Men. Everywhere during
their last days madness threatens, and only the ever more
hopeless project of the Scattering of the Seed keeps them from
suicide:

> In the early stages of our trouble lunatic asylums were founded,
> but they soon became over-crowded and a burden on a stricken
> community. The insane were then killed. But it became clear
> that by former standards we were all insane . . . .

Riots and revolutions follow, with the consequent reimposition of restrictive force and the drift toward war; and, as the economy breaks down and transport fails, starvation and trade reappear hand in hand. But worst of all, the "cold ecstasy" is no longer even believed in:

> We look back now at our former selves, with wonder, but also with incomprehension and misgiving. We try to recall the glory that seemed to be revealed to each of us in the racial mind, but we remember almost nothing of it. . . . It is not only impossible but inconceivable. We now see our private distresses and the public calamity as merely hideous. That after so long a struggle into maturity man should be roasted alive like a trapped mouse, for the entertainment of a lunatic! How can any beauty lie in that?

It is toward just so inglorious a conclusion, we realize at this point, that *Last and First Men* has been all along tending, since in Stapledon's initial vision of the end of humanity, there was implicit always a presentiment of man's final failure to redeem that end.

But this is not the book's last word; for Stapledon, like the Eighteenth Men, at the last moment fails his vision, too, tempering the bleak nihilism to which his deep imagination has led him by rebutting the last words of his Far Future narrator. To do this, however, he is forced to introduce—a little awkwardly, a little unconvincingly—a brand-new voice, the voice of one of his somewhat Sunday-Schoolish Christ figures, this time known as "the last born of the Last Men," or "the youngest brother." "Let his words, not mine, close the story," says the Neptunian teller of the rest of the tale and they do, beginning a little grandiloquently:

> Great are the stars, and man is of no account to them. But man is a fair spirit, whom a star conceived and a star kills . . . . Man was winged hopefully. He had it in him to go further than this short flight, now ending . . . . Instead he is to be destroyed . . . . The music of the spheres passes over him, through him, and is not heard.
> Yet it has used him. And now it uses his destruction. Great and terrible, and very beautiful is the Whole; and for man the best is that the Whole should use him.

Once more we have returned to ecstasy and admiration; and once more doubt enters:

But does it really use him? Is the beauty of the Whole really
enhanced by our agony? And is the Whole really beautiful?
. . . . Throughout all his existence man has been striving to
hear the music of the spheres, and has seemed to himself once
and again to catch some phrase of it . . . . Yet he can never
be sure that he has truly heard it, not even that there is such
perfect music at all to be heard . . . .

But even as Stapledon reestablished his characteristic, almost
intolerable, tension between desperate agnosticism and even
more desperate faith, it is all dissolved in a blander, easier
kind of reassurance—a last-minute "inspirational" Happy
Ending, whose pulpit rhetoric though much admired by some
critics of Stapledon, has always rung for me just a little false.

But one thing is certain. Man himself, at the very least, is music, a brave theme that makes music also of its vast accompa-
niment, its matrix of storms and stars. Man himself in his degree is eternally a beauty in the eternal form of things. It is
very good to have been man. And so we may go forward together with laughter in our hearts, and peace, thankful for the
past, and for our own courage. For we shall make after all a
fair conclusion to this brief music that is man.

# 4

# FUTURES FAR AND NEAR

If I have emphasized in my analysis of *Last and First Men* what seems to me to be its major theme, this is because it not only constitutes that novel's essential unity, but connects it with the whole body of Stapledon's other work. Such thematic unity, however, serves to make his novels repetitive, even monotonous, in a way that puts many readers off; and for that reason, perhaps, many critics have ignored it in favor of its scope, its grandeur, the vastness of its time scale, unprecedented in earlier utopias and seldom matched in later ones. It was, as I have suggested, the coda to H. G. Wells's *The Time Machine* which first showed Stapledon how to capture for the imagination a future immensely further from us than the remote moment at which human life began. But how timid and tentative Wells's foray into time seems when compared to Stapledon's.

Science had extended the history of man backward far, far beyond the six thousand years or so which biblical tradition had taught lay between the creation of Adam and the modern world. But it took fiction, more specifically the "scientific romances" of Wells, to open up what lay ahead in an analogous way, as well as to provide in its description of the Time Traveller's second chronic voyage, a model for speeding up traditional narrative in order to give a panoramic view of time's dazzling vistas:

For an indefinite time I clung to the machine as it swayed and vibrated, quite unheeding how I went, and when I brought myself to look at the dials again I was amazed to find where I had arrived. One dial records days, another thousands of days, another millions of days, and another thousands of millions. Now, instead of reversing the levers, I had pulled them over so as to go forward with them, and when I came to look at these indicators I found that the thousands hand was sweeping round as fast as the seconds hand of a watch—into futurity.

As I drove on, a peculiar change crept over the appearance of things . . . then—though I was still travelling with prodigious velocity—the blinking succession of day and night, which was usually indicative of a slower pace, returned . . . . The alternations of night and day grew slower and slower, and so did the passage of the sun across the sky, until they seemed to stretch through centuries . . . . I perceived by this slowing down of its rising and setting that the work of the tidal drag was done. The earth had come to rest with one face to the sun, even as in our own time the moon faces the earth . . . .

For Wells, however, the total span of man's existence was a mere thirty million years; and J.B.S. Haldane in a strange piece of fiction called "The Last Judgment," which appeared in America in *Harper's Magazine* and was reprinted as a kind of afterword to the English edition of *Possible Worlds* (1927), raised the ante only to forty million. At least, this is as far as he ventures into the future of mankind in his 7500-word piece; though, unlike Stapledon or Wells, he euphorically assumes (more faithful than they in this regard to the optimistic perspectives of Marxism) that there will be *no* End of Man. His final word, in fact—after tracing humanity's migrations from earth to Venus and back to earth again, and projecting its plans to colonize first Jupiter, then the remoter planets of our solar system, then those that orbit the most distant stars in our galaxy—is: "And there are other galaxies."

Even before this conclusion, Haldane had opened up his time scale, speaking of events 150 million years ahead and more—but leaving them for someone else to explore. That someone else proved to be Olaf Stapledon. There seems to me, indeed, little doubt that, however different in mood, Haldane's little essay was the immediate source of *Last and First Men*; though both works, of course, stem ultimately from Wells.

Nor did Stapledon hesitate to acknowledge his indebtedness; listing *Possible Worlds*, for instance, in the bibliography to his *Waking World* (1934), a non-fictional restatement of certain themes from his first novel, particularly those he was later to expand in *Star Maker*. But he owes more to Haldane in terms of plot than theme; though, to be sure, notions which inform both their works about the exhaustion of fossil fuels and the consequent use of tidal power, as well as predictions of alterations in the sun necessitating migration first to the inner planets, then to the outer, were already in the public domain.

They had, in fact, been transmitted to a large audience, not so much (before 1930) by novelists as by scientists, who had read Wells before they had encountered Einstein and Niels Bohr, Marx and Engels, or Jung and Freud. Indeed, as is seldom noticed but eminently worth pointing out, science fiction—insofar as it represents the reintroduction of wonder into a world neutralized by science, without the betrayal of scientific method or "materialism"—was, in its earlier phases at least, the work of fictionizing scientists as well as of scientizing fictionists. In the time of Stapledon, the former were represented not only by Haldane and his imitators, like Samuel Alexander; but especially by investigators on the border line of the paranormal, like J. W. Dunne, to whose work on seeing forward in time I have alluded, and J. B. Rhine, the parapsychologist, whose studies of extrasensory perception seem also to have influenced Stapledon.

In our time, too, qualified scientists and technicians insist on mingling fact and fancy; either producing for popular consumption—like Buckminster Fuller, for instance, Emanuel Velikovsky, and Carl Sagan—essays so extravagantly speculative that they afford to many the escapist pleasures of fiction; or by abandoning research and taking up the writing of novels, either intermittently like Fred Hoyle or full-time like Stanislaw Lem. Quite understandably in light of all this, when Haldane discovered *Last and First Men*, he assumed that its author, too, was a scientist. "It was because he kept within the bounds of the plausible at the same time as being wildly imaginative, that he managed to fool J.B.S. Haldane," Mrs. Stapledon told an interviewer. But though, indeed, her husband may have believed this himself, it seems to me that Haldane may have thought of Stapledon as "one of us" less because of his "plausibility" than because of his talent for (some would say his addiction to) high-level abstraction.

To literary critics, Stapledon's avoidance of the particular suggests that he may, indeed, be on the other side of our split culture; since despite all his disclaimers ("Though this is a work of fiction," he writes in the introduction to his next book, *Last Men in London*, "it does not pretend to be a novel . . . "). Both books were packaged and marketed as novels; and it is as novels that they continue to be read even now. The novel, however, has been traditionally considered of all literary forms the one most pledged to the presentation not of a macroscopic overview *sub specie aeternitatis* of mankind in general, but to a microscopic analysis in time of individual men and women, and more especially of their individual psyches.

Only thus, can that essentially psychological genre fulfill what Diderot believed he had learned from Samuel Richardson was its especial function: "to carry the torch to the back of the cave"; which is to say, to reveal in all their singularity the wishes and fears which inhabit the unconscious of each of us, and which we otherwise find so difficult to share. But there are, of course, two quite different ways in which the novel has always performed this function: by deep analysis, on the one hand, and by broad projection on the other. The former represents all mental processes, including unconscious ones, *as* mental processes; while the latter embodies them in symbolic figures performing symbolic actions in symbolic landscapes. Consequently, the first method tends to be used in mimetic or "realistic" fiction, and eventuates in the "stream of consciousness" techniques, variously employed by James Joyce, Marcel Proust, Dorothy Richardson, and Virginia Woolf; while the second characteristically appears in fantastic fiction or romance, from the early Gothic tales of M. G. Lewis and Charles Maturin to such contemporary fantasies as the Ring trilogy of J.R.R. Tolkien.

Science fiction, however, is ambiguously suspended between the two modes, allowing its duplicitous authors to have the best of both worlds, sometimes simultaneously. Perhaps, then, what Stapledon means when he warns us that his work though fictional is not fully novelistic is that it is largely projective rather than mimetic: figuring forth in what purports to be apocalyptic cosmic drama, his personal fear of death; and in its accounts of telepathy, group mindedness, and "possession" by persons from the Far Future, his own ambivalent attitude toward the tyranny of the ego and the reigning theories of his time about what separates sanity from madness. But Stapledon possesses mimetic skills as well; and, though his high-speed astronomical survey of human development over two billion years does not permit him to linger long over individual lives, he specifies with an hallucinatory vividness, which makes them seem more real than ordinary reality, the races of men that he imagines succeeding our own.

Indeed, such surreal figures remain in my memory when much else in *Last and First Men* has faded or blurred, including the detailed histories of incredibly long-lived civilizations, the involved metaphysics, even the most haunting themes. Incorporated into my own deepest fantasies, after a while they begin to seem oddly familiar, not like the faces of old friends or relatives, perhaps, but like grotesque visages seen in a recurrent dream or glimpsed once in a crowd and never forgotten. Some are themselves grotesque, like that of the Fourth Men, who consist of

a brain twelve-feet across, and a body most of which was reduced to a mere vestige upon the under surface of the brain. The only parts of the body which were allowed to attain the natural size were the arms and hands . . . induced to key themselves at the shoulders into the solid masonry which formed the creature's house . . . . The optic nerves were induced to grow out along two flexible probosces, five feet long, each of which bore a huge eye at the end . . . . The ears could also be projected upon stalks . . . ."

Some, however, are beautiful, like the miniature, streamlined Seventh Men, with their covering of feathery wool and their pseudo-wings: "A leathery membrane spread from the foot to the tip of the immensely elongated and strengthened 'middle finger' . . . . On the ground the Seventh Men walked much as other human beings, for the flight-membranes were folded close to the legs and body, and hung from the arms like exaggerated sleeves. In flight the legs were held extended as a flattened tail, with the feet locked together by the big toes."

Still others straddle the line between beauty and ugliness, inspiring both admiration and horror, like the colossal, multi-sexed Eighteenth Men, in whom the human raised to its ultimate power suggests both the bestial and the divine; though physically they vary very much among themselves and, in the aggregate, very little from humanity as we know it—apart from size, a certain enigmatic cast of countenance, and a few freakish excrescences. "In all of us," explains the spokesman for these Last Men, who is also, of course, the narrator of the book, "the outermost finger bears at its tip three minute organs of manipulation . . . . These excrescences would doubtless revolt our visitor. The pair of occipital eyes, too, would shock him; so would the upward-looking astronomical eye on the crown . . . ."

All this, however, is finally mere verisimilitude, seeming realism in service of the fantastic. Closer to what Northrop Frye would call the true "low mimetic mode" is the depiction, with which Stapledon's first novel begins, of events much closer to his own present. The original subtitle of *Last and First Men* was, after all, *A Story of the Near and Far Future*; which turns out to mean a relatively brief future dominated by men like us and a much vaster one in which the succeeding seventeen species of men evolve. Chapters I through IV cover the "less than five thousand years after the life of Newton"; while Chapter V traces their decline over one hundred and fifteen thousand. Only in Chapter VI, which spans ten million years, do we move into a time scale that allows Stapledon room enough for the free play of invention. Everything that comes before seems to me not merely pedestrian and labored, but, in effect, a false start, unconnected in any organic way with what follows.

Even what later proves to be the *leitmotif* of the whole, *amor fati*, the ice-cold worship of whatever is, is mentioned only in passing: as a not-quite-conscious "sentiment" in the minds of the French and English during the century after World War I and, some five hundred years later, as a flickering intuition in the minds of the Chinese. But in the former instance, it is cancelled out by "insane emotionalism," and in the latter, soon degenerates into "supine complacency." It is not so much a matter, I suspect, of these European and Oriental peoples not being ready to entertain a "detached yet fervent salutation of existence," as of Stapledon's being so enmeshed at this point in satire and allegory that he is not yet prepared to deal with it himself.

But even as satire or allegory, these early chapters strike me as dull and forced; so that I must confess I sympathize with Basil Davenport, who in *To the End of Time* (1953), a single volume edition of five of Stapledon's books, omits from *Last and First Men* three-quarters of Chapter I, all of Chapter II, and the last section of Chapter III. He was apparently motivated in part by political considerations, since many of the excised pages are embarrassingly anti-American and the Cold War was then still at its height; but he is also aware that they reveal Stapledon's inadequacies both as artist and as prophet. It is hard to resist comparing from the vantage point of the 1980s the falseness of his projection of our present plight with Huxley's *Brave New World* and Orwell's *1984*, each of which in quite different ways—complementary rather than contradictory—have been proved true by time.

Stapledon's forecasts, on the other hand, betray not just a perhaps pardonable inability to scent out what was to come, but a surely unforgivable ignorance of what was already happening. To write, for instance, of Italian fascism in 1930, nearly ten years after Mussolini's *coup d'état*, "Subsequently a flamboyant but sincere national party gained control of the state and afforded the Italians a new self-respect, based on the reform of social services, trains became punctual, streets clean, morals puritanical. Aviation records were won . . . "; or to say flatly after Hitler's Beerhall *Putsch* and the growth of the Nazi Party that "After the European War the defeated nation, formerly no less militaristic than the others, now became the most pacific, and a stronghold of enlightenment. Almost everywhere, indeed, there had occurred a profound change of heart, but chiefly in Germany . . . "—seems not just naive beyond belief, but willfully obtuse.

It is not merely a matter of being blind to fascism in particular, as Stapledon was to suggest he had been in the introduction to *Darkness and the Light* (1942); but of a failure to see *any* historical event in its full particularity, or, indeed, any nation, people, or ethnic group except in terms of generalizing

clichés. He seems especially fond of paired stereotypes, re-
marking of the French and English, for instance, " . . . these
two peoples were yet alike in being on the whole more scep-
tical, and . . . more capable of dispassionate yet creative intelligence than any other Western people. This very character
produced their distinctive faults, namely, in the English a cau-
tion that amounted often to moral cowardice, and in the French
a certain myopic complacency and cunning, which masquer-
aded as realism." Similarly, though even more rapidly, he observes of the Chinese and Indians, "The Chinese were interested in appearances, in the sensory, the urbane, the practical;
while the Indians inclined to seek behind appearances for some
ultimate reality . . . ." Finally, of the Germans and Russians
he is moved to say, " . . . the Germans, in spite of their practical genius, their scholarly contributions to history, their brilliant science and austere philosophy, were at heart romantic.
This inclination was their strength and their weakness . . . .
Beyond Germany, Russia. Here was a people whose genius
needed, even more than that of the Germans, discipline under
the critical intelligence . . . "; yet, he hastens to add, not just
since the Bolshevik Revolution, but always they have glimpsed
"man's littleness and irrelevance when regarded as an alien
among the stars . . . intuitively, by direct perception, instead
of after an arduous intellectual pilgrimage. . . . But because
of this independence of intellect, the experience was confused, erratic, frequently misinterpreted; and its effect on conduct was rather explosive than directive."

Such observations are not just commonplace, but depress-
ingly predictable for one of his time, place, and class; and he
is similarly the victim of his own racial stereotypes, character-
izing the Jews, whom he imagines persisting like an unassi-
milable surd to the year A.D. 6000, as "Though capable to some
extent of criticising the practical means by which ends should
be realized . . . by now incapable of criticising the major ends
[largely the acquisition of wealth] which had dominated their
race for thousands of years. In them intelligence had become
utterly subservient to tribalism. There was thus some excuse
for the universal hate and even the physical repulsion with
which they were regarded . . . ." If these anti-Semitic platitudes, in both tone and content, remind us uncomfortably of

Hitler and the Holocaust, we should be aware that they have more in common with the politer Anglo-Saxon varieties of Jew-hatred, which typically eventuated in snubs, scorn, and social exclusion rather than imprisonment, torture, and extermination, and which are, moreover, present everywhere in early-twentieth-century literature in English, from E. E. Cummings, T. S. Eliot, and Ezra Pound to Theodore Dreiser, Ernest Hemingway, F. Scott Fitzgerald, D. H. Lawrence, and Graham Greene.

It was anti-Americanism which most passionately obsessed Olaf Stapledon, distorting his view of history, past and future, as anti-Semitism had distorted Hitler's in *Mein Kampf*. There is, in fact, no anti-American cliché too gross or banal for him to repeat:

> Universally feared and envied, universally respected for their enterprise, yet for their complacency widely despised, the Americans were rapidly changing the whole character of man's existence . . . every human being throughout the planet made use of American products, and there was no region where American capital did not support local labour. Moreover the American press, gramophone, radio, cinematograph, and televisor ceaselessly drenched the planet with American thought . . . this was essentially a race of bright, but arrested, adolescents. Something lacked which should have enabled them to grow up . . . . Direct tragic experience might have opened the hearts of this people. Intercourse with a more mature culture might have refined their intelligence. But the very success which intoxicated them rendered them also too complacent to learn from their less prosperous competitors . . . .

In a foreword to the original American edition of *Last and First Men*, Stapledon makes a kind of apology for all of this, writing, "In the earlier chapters of this book America is given a not very attractive part. I have imagined the triumph of the cruder sort of Americanism over all that is best and most promising in American culture. May this not occur in the real world!" But he has already made it clear in the text which follows that he really desires what he pretends he wishes will not occur: "This, perhaps, would not have mattered, had America been able to give of her very rare best. But inevitably only her worst could be propagated . . . . For the best of America was too weak to withstand the worst."

It seems doubtful, moreover, that Stapledon knew very much about "the very rare best" of American culture. He pays his respects, to be sure, to the American contribution to modern philosophy, the American achievement in astronomy (largely due, he somewhat mean-spiritedly explains, to "costly instruments and clear atmosphere"); and he even manages to say a good word for the makers of American literature, who conceived new modes of expression, "but often behaved as barbarians." He alludes to no specific names, however, leaving the impression that the only distinguished American author of his time whom he has read is the expatriate T. S. Eliot, and him he insists on considering English. Even taken all together, such philosophers, astronomers, and poets constitute for him "a minority in a huge wilderness of opinionated self-deceivers": capitalists, militarists, fundamentalist preachers, howling lynch mobs—and, most dangerous of all, perhaps, the masters of the media.

His hatred, envy, and condescension toward the culture of the United States is, moreover, typically combined with a sense of impotence in the face of its political power; an almost masochistic relish at the prospect of its destroying both the heritage of the European past and the promise of the Bolshevik Revolution. Fascinatingly, he cannot imagine socialism triumphing over capitalism anywhere in the world immediately ahead, though he remained, of course, a Socialist to the end of his life. In this respect, he resembles that earlier Socialist and utopian fantasist H. G. Wells, whose Time Traveller found in the future not a classless society but one in which class conflict has become so exaggerated and indurated that it can only be solved by total destruction.

But though Stapledon lived after the establishment in the Soviet Union of a viable socialist state, he was able to conceive no more than his predecessor the emergence of world socialism among the First Men. In his bad dream of the Near Future, Russia goes down to defeat—"Americanized" from within and, therefore, incapable of resisting American aggression from without. Nor is the revolution rekindled elsewhere, not even among the Chinese, who seemed for a while the most likely of all peoples to take up where the Russians had stopped. Rather they, too, yielded to American cultural pressure, giving up joss sticks and opium for chewing gum and cigarettes; and, in any case, Stapledon assures us, in complete contempt of historical evidence, "communism was alien to China." He foresees then neither the alliance against fascism of the Soviet Union and the Western democracies nor the Cold War which followed it. He projects instead—in the interval between 1930 and A.D. 2500—a series of limited wars between France and Italy, France and England, Russia and Germany, culminating in an all-out confrontation of Europe and America, which ends in the "murder" of Europe and is followed by the final conflict in which America defeats China.

Just before the Euro-American War, but more than a century after the date at which it actually occurred, Stapledon imagines the invention of an atomic weapon, which in his scenario is used once, then destroyed by its creator, who commits suicide, taking with him the secret formula for its creation; so that it plays no subsequent role in the history of the First Men. His failure to predict the key role which that ultimate weapon was to play in fact is due in part to the fact that Stapledon is as poor a prophet in the realm of technology as in that of social change (he foresees neither computers, robots, and automation nor extra-uterine conception and cloning); but also to the fact that an atomic Holocaust is alien to the nightmare which possesses him: the grim vision of a *Pax Americana*, and a World State in which science has become the sole religion, even as material development has been confused with civilization. Moreover, though at its height, no one of its citizens lacks a "sufficiency of goods," everyone is in effect "a slave. His work and leisure consisted of feverish activity, punctuated by moments of listless idleness which he regarded as sinful and unpleasant."

To mitigate boredom and allay guilt, however, ever wider areas of sexual experimentation were legalized; and (in a system where whatever is not forbidden is required) flying, athletics, and dancing were elevated to the status of sacred occupations. Dancing, indeed, became the basis for annual rituals, in which a Negro symbolically raped a white woman, then actually knifed her, and was pursued by the "exultant mob" of spectators who if they caught him, tore him to pieces or burned him alive. Implicit in such rites was an "adoration of instinct" that implied also a contempt for intelligence, which began in fact to decline; so that when mindless routine could no longer maintain the instruments of production and natural resources had reached the point of exhaustion, no solutions were forthcoming.

What followed instead was panic among the rulers and rebellion among the ruled; and when the rebellions had become full-scale civil and international wars, those rulers, in a desperate attempt to restore law and order:

> . . . made the mistake of using not merely gas, but microbes; and such was the decayed state of medical science that no one could invent a means of restraining their ravages. The whole American continent succumbed to a plague of pulmonary and nervous diseases. The ancient "American Madness," which long ago had been used against China, now devastated America. The great stations of water-power and wind-power were wrecked by lunatic mobs who sought vengeance upon anything associated with authority. Whole populations vanished in an orgy of cannibalism . . . .

It is typical of Stapledon that the end of the First Men (like that of the Eighteenth, their last successors) is insanity. But in the Near Future, as opposed to the Far, that ultimate horror is triggered not by an astronomical catastrophe, but by America: a culture which he cannot help imagining triumphant, but whose triumph he can conceive only as the ultimate disaster.

# 5
# THEME AND VARIATIONS

Olaf Stapledon was to produce before the end of his life a long series of spin-offs from *Last and First Men*; since just as later writers of science fiction, when invention flagged, turned for help to him, so he himself returned time after time to the first of his novels. It was as if the vision which informs his most authentic fiction had been given him once and once only— along with the plots and images to embody them. *The Flames* (1947), for instance, the last piece of true science fiction he ever wrote, represents the fleshing out of half a sentence in a summary account of the cosmology of the Eighteenth Men, which closes Chapter XV of *Last and First Men*; while *Sirius* (1944) was suggested by a couple of phrases that appear in Chapter X in the midst of a discussion of the Third Men's experiments with beasts. Even the embryo of *Star Maker* (1937), which eventually grew so immense that it encapsulated all the events of his first novel in a few words, was initially contained in three or four of its pages. Moreover, *Odd John* (1935), which is *not* present in miniature on any of these pages, descends from it at a second remove; actually being forecast in the final chapter of *Last Men in London* (1932), an avowed sequel to *Last and First Men* and long considered its first off-shoot.

In 1977, however, the Olaf Stapledon Society published under the editorship of Harvey Satty a hitherto unknown and never performed (though it was clearly intended for the BBC)

radio drama; which became more widely available two years
later in a volume of uncollected pieces, edited by Sam Moskowitz and called by its title, *Far Future Calling*. Clearly, this
little skit represents the first recension of a book which, in a
real sense, Stapledon never ceased rewriting, though he could
not yet have been aware of that fact. What he apparently still
had on his mind when he sat down to compose it in 1931 was
his unfinished quarrel with America and its imperial culture.
The opening speech of the play is therefore, not surprisingly,
delivered with an "American accent," and written in Stapledon's rather unconvincing version of colloquial American
speech in the year A.D. 2500:

> . . . I'll start right in by saying that everything with us is just
> about 200% better than with you. We're more intelligent, and
> far more vital. We gotta be, to stand the racket. And we're
> 163% more spiritual, too, let me tell you. Every one of our
> churches is nearly twice as beautiful . . . as your Saint Paul's
> Cathedral. In fact everything of ours is much bigger and faster
> than everything of yours . . . . And—Gosh, Here's one of my
> wives butting in . . . .

What is surprising, however (to me at least), is that the
British actor, who is trying to summarize in "American" the
"Americanization" of the world in the Near Future, precisely
as Stapledon had in the initial four or five chapters of *Last
and First Men*, is interrupted by an Eighteenth Man, time-
traveling from the Far Future. He has earlier paralyzed the
pseudo-American actor and the actress who plays his wife;
and he tells them now: " . . . Your play-acting is over for
tonight. England is going to have something else, instead of
that cheap fantasy of five hundred years hence . . . the actual
voice of a future incomparably more remote." It is as if in 1931
Stapledon had come to realize that only his projection of the
Far Future in the novel published a year earlier had transcended "cheap fantasy," enabling him to achieve—or more
precisely, perhaps, to be "possessed" by—a truly prophetic
voice.

His little radio play, I am suggesting, is not simply, as
Harvey Satty would have it, "a précis of his great book LAST
AND FIRST MEN": it is also a piece of self-criticism (though
how conscious Stapledon was of this, I have no way of know-

ing), an attempt to winnow out what is central and essential from what is peripheral or merely optional. Of its many images, for instance, of man in his evolutionary adaptations to life over two billion years, only three are reevoked for the audience of the BBC—the same three, I am pleased to note, which especially impressed me: those flying pygmies, the Seventh Men; those monstrous Great Brains, the Fourth; and, of course, the gigantic, ugly-beautiful Eighteenth Men, whose superhumanity merges with both the bestial and the divine.

Similarly, of the many themes, major and minor, which tempted Stapledon into extended editorializing in *Last and First Men* only three survive in this hour-long script: the problem of time, the inevitability of humanity's ultimate end, and the possibility of its ecstatic acceptance. "I am not imprisoned in a single fleeting moment of time, as you are," the visitor from Neptune explains to his earthbound audience. "I have the freedom of eternity. It is from eternity, not from the future merely, that I influence you." Of man, he tells them from that supra-temporal vantage point: "Again and again he begins even to remake his own nature for more glorious life. But always the venture ends in disaster . . . some unforeseeable catastrophe wrecks him . . . ." Yet finally, he assures them, he and his people are capable of "the supreme act of the spirit, an ecstatic but intellectual love of the cosmos"; "The destruction of our world we have learnt to accept. We even exult in it, as the fitting climax to the brief music that is Man."

There are indications in *Far Future Calling*, moreover, that Stapledon may have felt he had not sufficiently fleshed out some of the scenes in *Last and First Men*; so that occasionally he expands rather than abbreviates material from that earlier book. This is particularly true of his account of the gathering of the Eighteenth Men in an attempt to achieve telepathically "the mind of the race." Though he describes briefly in his first novel how the individual at such moment of total communion, "savours in a single intuition all bodily contacts . . . Through the myriad feet of all men and women he enfolds his world in a single grasp . . . ," he does not *visualize* the moment of assembly: the swarming together in flying boats and individual flying suits of the myriad host that will become one; or their departure, which, viewed from above, resembles "the dusty surface of a road on a windy day, or steam from hot water . . . A vast smoke of men and women . . . Like an immense flock of birds. Like boiling clouds . . . ."

All of these metaphors appear again in *Last Men in London*, as they had not in the original version. Only the haunting image of the feet grasping the world is repeated in all three: becoming in the play, " . . . he discovers that he is embracing the whole planet through the feet of all men and women. He finds himself *holding* it, so to speak, as you might hold a ball in hand"; and in the later novel, "Through the feet of all individuals I grasped my planet, as a man may hold a ball in his hand." Regarded from this perspective, *Far Future Calling* comes to seem not so much a brief adaptation of *Last and First Men* as a transition between it and *Last Men in London*, particularly its Neptunian frame.

Both the second novel and the play, moreover, represent in varying ways Stapledon's attempt to introduce into the imagined world of the Far Future eros: an area of human experience he had scanted in the first, though it is one demanded by ordinary readers of all fiction. In this demand even so resolutely highbrow a contemporary of Stapledon's as James Joyce would have concurred; writing in *Finnegans Wake*, "Do you know or don't you ken it, every telling has a taling and that's the he and she of it." But there are no real he's and she's in *Last and First Men*; though sex appears in its pages more frequently than we tend to remember, actually determining the course of history at several crisis points of the Near Future. A war between England and France, for instance, is triggered by a "sexual outrage committed by a French African soldier upon an English woman"; and the "actual occasion" for the outbreak of the final conflict of China and America is America's moral indignation over the fact that in certain factories in India "Boys and girls under twelve were being badly sweated, and in their abject state their only adventure was precocious sex."

The closest thing, however, to a fully realized erotic scene comes at the end of Chapter III, when a representative from America and one from China meet on a Pacific island in a last desperate attempt to restore peace before all mankind is destroyed. As they conduct their negotiations on the beach, there emerges from the ocean "A bronze young smiling woman, completely nude, with breasts heaving after her long swim . . . ." Though the repressed American, offended by her nakedness, berates her for wantonness, while the gallant Chinese, dazzled by her beauty, flatters and flirts, she is drawn to the former, who seems to her finally "more of a real man." What decides her, however, is not his sexuality but his ideology— or more precisely, perhaps, the strength of his convictions; since the god he devoutly worships is "energy," while the divinity his Chinese counterpart somewhat cynically serves is "love." In any case, as the scene closes, she draws off with her into the sheltering palms the emissary from America, who "though he was a strict monogamist with a better half waiting for him in New York, longed to crush her sun-clad body to his Puritan cloth . . . ."

For all the superficial sensuality of the scene, it is too flatly, insistently allegorical (the woman from the sea is, we are told, "the Daughter of Man," her chosen lover "the Master of the World") to flutter a pulse; so that Basil Davenport understandably excised it, along with much other dull and tendentiously anti-American stuff, from his bowdlerized text of 1953. But his decision was in this case finally wrong, I think; since the episode is the climactic restatement of Stapledon's view that sexual repression is not only responsible for personal neurosis, but is an aggravating factor, if not the root cause, of man's inability to create a just society. There is little new, certainly, in what he has to say on this score, some three or four decades after the first publications of Sigmund Freud; indeed, he seems to be fighting, in his typically belated way, the good fight against a long-defunct Victorian ethos.

Still, until we have come to terms with his diagnosis of our present dilemma, we cannot understand his utopian projections of sexuality in the Far Future; the first of which is included in his description of love among the Second Men:

> Not only were both men and women encouraged to have as much casual sexual intercourse as they need for their enrichment, but also, on the higher plane of spiritual union, strict monogamy was deprecated. . . . The union, it was felt, was more pregnant the more each party could contribute from previous sexual and spiritual intimacy with others. Yet, though

as a principle monogamy was not applauded, the higher kind
of union would in practise sometimes result in a life-long
partnership. But since the average life was so much longer
. . . such fortuitously perennial unions were often deliberately interrupted for a while. . . . . Sometimes, on the other
hand, a group of persons of both sexes would maintain a com-
posite and permanent marriage together. In one form or another, this "marriage of groups" was much prized. Among the
First Men the brevity of life made these novel forms of union
impossible; for obviously no sexual, and no spiritual relation
can be developed with any richness in less than thirty years
of close intimacy . . . .

The ritual life-style of the Second Men, however, could not
survive the multiple Martian invasions; and with their deca-
dence the secret of liberated communal sex was lost for millions of years.

Indeed, it was not fully recovered until the telepathic Eighteenth Men reinstituted psychosexual groups, their number
now fixed at ninety-six, as the basic societal units. Though
their membership could change with time, all male members
at any given moment were expected to have intercourse with
all female ones; and, on rarer occasions, males and females
alike with the opposite sexes of some other specially selected
group. It would appear, however, that in two respects, at least,
Stapledon considers the sexual taboos of his time and place
unchangeable. On the one hand, he never imagines homosex-
uality as normative or even permissible; and, on the other, he
manages always to preserve something much like traditional
marriage. Even among the Eighteenth Men, whose lifelong
heterosexual unions are considered "as the ideal state"—
though to be sure "even in monogamy, each partner must be
periodically refreshed by intercourse with other members of
the group . . . ."

Nowhere, however, in Last and First Men is any heterosexual couple, whether bonded for life or casually joined for re-
freshment, portrayed close up. Ironically, the sole merging of
spirit to spirit which we are permitted to observe at length
and in detail is homosexual though fleshless; the intellectual
union of the two authors of the book we are reading, the First
Man who takes it for fiction and the Last Man who knows it
is truth. And what an odd couple they are: one so underde-

veloped, so imperfectly "awakened" that he never fully understands his violation, even when what begins as a kind of rape or seduction has turned into something very like love; the other fully aware but contemptuous of, more than half-repulsed by the inferior creature he has chosen to "possess." Yet that relationship is the prototype of many others in Stapledon's later fiction. Some of these are also homosexual, like that of narrator to superman in *Odd John*, or of madman to the flame he calls "he" in *The Flames*; while others are heterosexual but interspecific, like that of the girl Plaxy to the mutated sheepdog in *Sirius*. But in every case, they suggest that there can be no sexual union between full equals, no love free of the hint of shameful miscegenation, or untinged, on one side or the other, by a masochistic delight in self-abasement.

In *Far Future Calling*, however, Stapledon seems for the first time to be quite consciously trying (perhaps in hope of reaching a broader audience) to write love scenes of a more conventional kind. He, therefore, brings on his main characters, male and female, two by two, like passengers entering the Ark. We first meet an actor and actress, contemporary "First Men" who only pretend to be married, then a "Future Man" and "Future Woman," really bonded for life. For his first few moments on scene, the representative Eighteenth Man seems—like his equivalent in *Last and First Men*—without a mate, a solitary stranger in a strange land. But shortly he reveals the Future Woman who accompanies him, protesting to the actor and actress who finds her repulsive, "To me her whole form is eloquent. Every curve sings. She is the perfection of lithe grace." A third couple, moreover, doomed members of the flying Seventh human species, becomes briefly audible though never visible as the others; and as the male (always "offstage," as it were) tenderly kills his wounded mate to save her "from losing the aerial ecstasy" before death, they sing a *Liebestod* duet: "Farewell—best-loved one! . . . Dear beautiful one. I praise the stars for the song's end."

Stapledon had at first planned to have a "Second Future Man" and "Second Future Woman" enter: "Very close together . . . Spooning, in fact," as the embarrassed actress puts it; and they were to speak to each other lines like "Don't.

You're hurting, you old python . . . " and "How many times,
in all ages, in all the worlds, has this thing happened! She
and He, alone!" But aware, perhaps, of how close he had come
to sheer silliness, Stapledon finally struck out the whole scene;
though he saved some of its speeches for *Last Men in London*,
in which the Neptunian narrator has at his side from the start
his beloved, whom he describes, echoing the language of the
play:

> To me she is lovely, exquisite, the very embodiment of beauty;
> to you she would seem a strange half-human monster. To me,
> as she lay there with her breasts against the rock and one arm
> reaching down into the water, her whole form expressed the
> lightness and suppleness of a panther . . . .

She is called, in fact, Panther; which is to say, is individuated
by being named, as no denizen of the future has been before.

It would seem, indeed, as if in some sense Panther is intended to be a kind of portrait of or tribute to Olaf Stapledon's
wife. Though the odd erotic fantasy to which most of the first
chapter is devoted begins as a reworking of the abandoned
scene from *Far Future Calling*, it soon turns into a kind of
encoded reconstruction—displaced two billion years into the
future, and relocated from earth to Neptune—of an especially
tender moment in their life to which both Olaf and Agnes Stapledon inevitably referred in interviews. Perhaps the fullest
account of it comes in Mrs. Stapledon's recollection during an
interview with Harvey Satty:

> . . . we were on holiday in Wales together, and we were sit-
> ting on a hillside on the Welsh coast, looking down into the
> sea. The tide was evidently coming up, but below us at the
> foot of the cliffs there were some rocks, flat rocks that the lower
> tide would expose to the sun. And we were just lazing and
> lying in the heather, and enjoying the warmth of the sun, when
> we heard some curious noises coming up from down below.
> We got up and had a look and we found that there were a lot
> of seals that were basking in the sun on the dry rock, you see,
> which was above the tide . . . .

It is into such a rock-rimmed sea pool that Stapledon imagines his Far Future lovers gazing from a Neptunian cliff. "It is
a corner," his narrator tells us, "where the land juts out into
the sea as a confusion of split rocks"; among which "lies a

network of tiny fjords, whose walls and floors are embossed with varigated life" and through which swim creatures rather like the seals Mrs. Stapledon remembers.

> . . . very remote cousins of my own human species . . . fantastically degenerated . . . in one, whose name in our language you might translate "Homunculus," nature has achieved a minute and exquisite caricature of humanity. Two splay feet glued him to the rock. From these rises an erect and bulbous belly, wearing on its summit an upturned face. The unpleasantly human mouth keeps opening and shutting . . . . The ears, deaf but mobile, have become two broad waving fans, that direct a current of water to the mouth . . . .

In Agnes Stapledon's memory their watching of the scurrying subhuman creatures below them ended not in sex but art; or at least she reports of her husband that:

> . . . the idea of those seals, who were so nearly human . . . behaving in such a human way, lying in the sun on the rocks like that, set up a train of thought in his mind about the differences between human beings of one sort or another . . . it seemed to start him off on the idea of the possibility of human beings changing through the years and the centuries, and of life being lived in the sea, perhaps, or life being lived in the air, and quite different kinds of life still almost human or almost human as we know it . . . .

And this vision turned insight, she goes on to suggest, became the seminal "myth" of *Last and First Men*. In *Last Men in London*, however, it is the watching female who is inspired to cry out, "What a world this pond is! Like the world you are about to plunge into so soon." She is referring to the fictional journey into the past which her mate is about to undertake; but it can be understood also in terms of the no less fictional trip into the future which his collaborator, Olaf Stapledon, must make.

A more striking difference lies in the erotic tone of *Last Men in London*, in which the general reference to the seals' "behaving in such a human way" is specified in a description of Homunculus's successful wooing of his mate. "Quick! Come see!" Panther cries. "He's loose, he's moved an inch. He's waddling at breakneck speed. Now he's got her, and she's willing." Only then does she exclaim over the similarities between their world and that of the First Men, and yield to the importunities of her beloved. "This has been the best of all our matings," he says afterward, and she assents. Whereupon the scene turns domestic, as bedded down in the sun-warmed heather, they talk like some early-twentieth-century bourgeois couple about "the perplexing but lovely nature of their son," then rise to prepare and eat an evening meal, and end by singing together in darkness a song which, incredibly, turns out to be "Old Man River."

If this is absurd (and I must confess I find it so), obviously Stapledon does not realize it, anymore than he realizes the ridiculousness of the liberal clichés about race relations in long-defunct America into which it leads him: "With difficulty we called up in imagination the dark confusion that gave it birth, the harshness of man to man, and the yearning for a better world." People who knew Stapledon personally report that he was a witty man; but as a writer he seems essentially humorless, not only in the sense that he is seldom funny on purpose, but even more because he is unaware when—as here—he is inadvertently so. Fortunately, he is not often betrayed into such unwitting self-parody, though he appears to run that risk whenever he tries to write about love rather than death. On such occasions, he tends to lapse into autobiography, and his consequent desire to tell what "really happened" undercuts the fidelity to fictional consistency which makes possible "the poetic suspension of disbelief." And we laugh.

In all fairness, however, it must be said that once at least in *Sirius* he was able to stay inside an imagined erotic fable, which remains therefore both moving and convincing throughout. But in the erotic sections of *Last Men in London* the confessional impulse continually subverts the fable; and it only makes matters worse when Stapledon attempts to salvage its credibility by having his Neptunian explain that "Old Man River" is one of the many "rude chants which we explorers had discovered in extinct worlds." Nor does it really help when he reminds the reader and himself that the holiday couple from the Far Future alternate conjugal bliss with telepathic group sex, and seaside picnics with ritual "awakenings of the Racial Mind." Indeed, his Neptunian seems to have forgotten all this by the close of this episode, which finds him crying out: "Hideous! That such a world as ours should be burnt, wasted such a world of spirit and sweet flesh!" And when his beloved asks, "Even in the fire?" he answers, "Who knows? But we see it now." These are responses based not on icy detachment and *amor fati*, but on a desperate espousal of Romantic Love.

Indeed, this same love, tempered by aging, survives even in the final moments before the Holocaust which will destroy the last men in the universe. Most of the Neptunian survivors have at this point not just lost the ultimate insight into cosmic reality and the capacity for disinterested worship of the Whole; but even sexual passion "had already so far degenerated that neither sex could interest the other save in the crudest manner." Only a "scattered and dwindling aristocracy, were still capable, at least intermittently, of personal love," among them the book's extraterrestrial narrator, who has been driven by the intolerable heat into the sea—but not alone. Panther is with him still, or again, as at the beginning; and of her he talks with his last breath:

> She lies motionless in the shallow water. The waves, fingering the hot sand, recoil steaming. Her flesh, translucent formerly, now is filmed and grey, blind like her filmed eyes. We have taken of each other very deeply. The heat tricks us sometimes into intolerance of the other's unyouthful body, unpliant mind; yet each is the other's needed air for breathing. We have ranged in our work very far apart . . . . But now we will remain together to the end . . . .

The frame story I have been discussing up to this point constitutes somewhat less than a fifth of *Last Men in London*. The rest deals with twentieth-century Europeans in the midst of the post-World War I crisis, as experienced by a young man called by the Neptunian narrator, "Paul," though that is not his real name, lest he or his relatives "recognize the portrait, or setting, which I must give in some detail." It is tempting to believe that "Paul" is, in fact, Olaf Stapledon, since much of what we learn about the former resembles much of what biographical sources tell us about the latter.

Paul, for instance, has a relationship with his father like Stapledon's with his, a dog like Stapledon's childhood pet "Rip," and an impossible first teaching job in a grammar school like the one in which Stapledon spent an uncomfortable year.

He reads, moreover, many of the books which most influenced
Stapledon, including Abbott's *Flatland* and J. W.
Dunne's *An Experiment with Time*; and most importantly of all, perhaps,
he has wartime experiences with a Quaker Ambulance Unit
almost indistinguishable from those described by Stapledon
in his contribution to *We Did Not Fight*. But there are also
ways in which his protagonist is very different from the author. He lives, for instance, in a suburb south of London and
continues to teach at a boys' school in that city, finally becoming its headmaster; travels to Russia at one point, as Stapledon
had not; joins the Communist Party, of which Stapledon
claimed he was never a member; and is confined for a while
in a madhouse, a fate which evidently Stapledon never shared.

These represent perhaps alternative life histories close
enough to his own for Stapledon to have imagined living them
without undue strain. But he clearly distinguished Paul's des-
tiny from his own when he made him a reader in manuscript,
but *not* the author of *Last and First Men*—or, by the same token, of the book in which he appears. That author, indeed,
becomes a character in Paul's story, where he is portrayed as
a "timid and comfort-loving creature," who, when Paul seeks
in vain to enlist in a crusade for "a new social and spiritual
order," dismisses him as a lunatic. If Stapledon distrusted in
himself two opposite tendencies—one toward cowardly con-
formity and the other toward non-conformity verging on madness—the splitting of "Paul" from the author of *Last and First
Men* gives him the privilege of hating himself simultaneously
for both.

Despite such indications to the contrary, however, most
critics have felt *Last Men in London* to be—with the possible
exception of *A Man Divided*—the most autobiographical of all
Stapledon's fictions. It seems on the face of it, indeed, a standard *Bildungsroman*: the kind of portrait of the artist as a
young man, usually published as a first novel, which permits
its author simultaneously to learn his craft and to exorcise his
obsession with what happens to have happened to him on the
way to authorship. More often than not such books are centrally concerned with the sexual initiation of their artist-pro-
tagonists—describing in detail their delivery from frustration
and nympholeptic fantasy to fulfillment and real knowledge

of the opposite sex. But though Paul is from the first tormented by passionate longings, he does not actually make love to a woman until some time after the end of World War I (which Stapledon prefers to call "The European War"); which means, if we assume him to have been an exact contemporary of his author, he remained a virgin, writhing in his bed and crying, "God, give me a woman!," to the age of thirty-three or thirty-four—the age, that is to say, at which Stapledon finally married.

Indeed, by the time Paul has persuaded Catherine (a "tenderly maternal" girl, somewhat older than himself, whom he had tried for years to seduce but could not until she had become a real mother) to sleep with him, not only is his life half over, but the book is three-quarters done. When, in fact, Stapledon finally does get to their mating, which occurs, we are not surprised to discover, on a "rocky and seal-haunted coast," he gives it very little space.

Earlier he had devoted considerably more to Paul's most nearly successful attempt at getting Catherine into bed, which begins promisingly with his caressing her bare breast, but ends abortively when she bites his lip. Even the scene recounting his failure at making it with a prostitute (a standard feature of the genre) is rendered in greater detail: "On the way with her he was like a starved dog ready to eat anything," he writes; though once in her room, "he saw himself through her eyes. He felt his own body as she would feel it, clinging, repugnant. Stammering that he was ill, he put down his money and fled."

Insofar, then, as it is a sexual initiation story at all, Paul's is a *failed* initiation story; since even the long-deferred affair with Catherine turns out to be inconclusive and without issue. "I should hate you for a husband," she tells him finally, "you'd be too tiring and no good with children. Paul, if I have a baby, it will count as Richard's." His Neptunian overseer, however, seems convinced that even so perfunctory a relationship was sufficient, leaving Paul "henceforth in respect of woman at peace"; and we are told toward the book's close that he was to marry and beget children. But it is as a lonely bachelor that we leave him, and as a failed lover that we remember him. Finally, therefore, his story seems another exemplary account of the effects of repressive upbringing and the introjection of outmoded taboos—in this respect more like such Victorian novels as Samuel Butler's *The Way of All Flesh* (not published until 1903 but begun in 1872) than such Modernist *Bildungsromane* as Thomas Mann's *Buddenbrooks*, James Joyce's *A Portrait of the Artist as a Young Man*, or even Flaubert's *L'Education Sentimentale*, the prototype of them all.

In fact, Butler's name appears in *Last Men in London* as none of the others do, reminding us that in addition to *The Way of All Flesh* he wrote *Erewhon*, thereby providing a model for Stapledon's utopian frame story as well as the realistic narrative it encloses. It was, however, Stapledon's own idea—his greatest technical innovation—to combine both in a single work with two protagonists: one the embodiment of the present inhibited by the persistence of a dead past; the other a symbol of the same present liberated by the intrusion of a not-yet-born future. It is the Neptunian representative of that future who, unlike Paul, comes to know woman fully through extended conjugal bonding and is able, unlike him once more, not merely to sire but to claim as his own a son; while Paul remains effectively impotent and sterile.

Stapledon, however, though he must have felt himself, especially while still young and virgin, trapped in the plight of Paul, was, after all, for three decades a happy husband and father; and, as he constantly hints, presumably also a successful extramarital lover. If, then, in this most autobiographical of books he embodies this aspect of himself in a man from the Far Future, it is to make a polemical point: Only if mankind is radically altered—or better, radically alters itself—over the millennia ahead, can we be delivered from the effects of sexual repression. To be sure, a few truly "advanced" individuals, "possessed," as it were, by the spirit of things to come (it is hard to know just how literally Stapledon believed in such "possession"), can for a little while achieve full sexuality, and through it a perception of ultimate reality. But soon, soon, psychosis and senility threaten that delicate balance from within, and war menaces it from without.

War not love turns out to be the central topic of the book; or, more particularly, what was for Stapledon *the* War, the European War of 1914 to 1919, the War To End All Wars. Not only does the experience of combat precede for Paul the experience of sex; but the occasion for the invasion of his mind by a Neptunian, the conceit on which all that follows depends, is his tormented indecision about whether or not to join in that conflict—and if so, in what capacity. Many Last Men have, it would seem, telepathically leaped two billion years into what is for them the past, in order to participate in this "great crisis" of the First Men. What is being tested from their point of view is the ability of our species to transcend the "archaic" values of nationalism and patriotism, in the service of what Stapledon calls "loyalty to the spirit of man"—meaning, in this historical context, absolute pacifism.

But *Last Men in London* appeared in 1932, thirteen years after the end of World War I and only seven before the outbreak of World War II, so that its conclusion is long foregone: "the archaic position was victorious." Moreover, even Paul (in this respect quite undistinguishable from his author) did not manage to resist war totally; or, indeed, ever quite decide whether his decision to become a participatory non-combatant was the product of cowardice, confusion, and self-deceit or of a valid though imperfect perception of what "loyalty to the dawning spirit" required. In any case, he finally succeeded in having his cake and eating it; which is to say, he allied himself neither with the "happy warriors" to whom war was fulfillment nor with the "more pugnacious" anti-warriors who "refused absolutely to have any part in the great madness, and were therefore persecuted, imprisoned, or even shot." He cast his lot instead with those "others . . . less heroic, less confident of their own opinion . . . ," who chose "to help the wounded . . . to accept so far as possible on the one hand the great common agony, and on the other the private loneliness of those who cannot share the deepest passions of their fellows."

Stapledon insists (in what I find an uncomfortably self-congratulatory tone) that for Neptunian observers what made Paul and his ilk especially interesting was precisely their divided loyalties: "in them the balance between the archaic and the modern was most delicate. The conflict which in most had been violently solved, in one way or the other, was in these ever present and insoluble." Moreover, Stapledon apparently

hoped that his readers, too, would find Paul's perplexity interesting, as I must confess I do not.

All war reminiscences tend to be boring and pacifist ones
no less so; though this is not necessarily the case when they
have been turned into fiction. Indeed, of all the novels based
on their author's experiences in the European War, some of
the most fascinating were written by authors who had the same
equivocal pacifist-participant relation to that conflict as Stapledon. I think, for instance, of E. E. Cummings's *The Enor-
mous Room* and Ernest Hemingway's *A Farewell to Arms. Last
Men in London*, however, insofar as it is concerned with war
turns into yet another dull *non*-initiation story, this time thanatic rather than erotic: an account of one who in the midst of
killing neither kills nor is killed—and whose most traumatic
experience is driving in fear and under fire past a presumably
dead soldier, only to discover later that he was all the time
alive and in need of help.

Nor does Stapledon succeed in making Paul's semi-fictional
plight seem more significant by buttressing it with an entirely
fictional tale of a front-line German infantryman called Hans,
who does kill and die; a parable about a doomed race of "philosophical lemurs," who before their inevitable end attain "a
level of self-knowledge and mutual loyalty which the first human species was to seek in vain . . . "; plus page after endless
page of encapsulated world history, pacifist editorial, and
popular philosophy. Such long essayistic asides, with their inevitable references to "piety toward fate" and their evocation
of Gautama, Socrates, and Jesus, seem less an integral part of
the fiction in whose midst they appear than an anticipation of
*Waking World*, that lay sermon on metaphysics, theology,
biology, education, and the "need for revolution," which Stapledon was to publish two years later.

They remain, in any case, inert filler—a way of padding
out a book which Stapledon apparently did not really want to
write *("Last Men in London . . . "* Mrs. Stapledon told Harvey
Satty, "was a response to demand . . . and I think he felt it
hadn't got the real spontaneous response to impulse that *Last
and First Men* had . . . ")* and which consequently he had
difficulty in making long enough to pass muster as a full-blown

novel. It turned out to be, therefore, what Henry James would have called "a loose and baggy monster": an anthology of poetry, fiction, and non-fiction in poetry and prose, unified chiefly by the fact that Stapledon happened to have written it all. At least once he is led into discussing a topic which simply will not stay inside the structure; and he settles for tacking on as a postscript or addendum—the essay on "Submerged Supermen" which constitutes the first two sections of his final chapter.

More typically, however, he tries to pass off even the most tangential of his digressions as Paul's response to actual encounters in a life, which Stapledon imagines (not without some strain on our credulity) as having taken him into every area of contemporary culture. It is a device which permits him through Paul to comment not just on institutions, men, and movements which Stapledon knew from the inside, but on those with which he had only an outsider's relationship. Though what he says is not particularly original, it is at least credible when he who had spent almost all of his life in classrooms tells us of a schoolboy: " . . . he learned about England and the Empire, and became a patriot. The English were the only people who played fair in games, and were kind to animals, and could govern black people . . . ."

But it is hard to take seriously his amateur's indictment of a whole society which he knew chiefly from newspapers and books; and even harder to take it (as the fiction asks us to do) for wisdom inspired in an imperfect prophet by an omniscient telepath from the Far Future. Why should one, we are inclined to protest, able to see the entire cosmos and our place in it from the vantage point of eternity, end up with a handful of Lib-Lab or downright philistine clichés—however well turned: the clergy "had settled down to become a huge proliferating parasite . . . "; scientists "were imprisoned in deep galleries, isolated from each other in their thousand labs"; journalists "made their living from the sale of habit-forming drugs . . ."; many artists (clearly he is thinking of Bloomsbury) were "microcosmic creatures for whom love and hate and life itself were but the matter of art . . . the whole meaning of human existence seemed to lie solely in the apprehension of forms

intrinsically 'significant' . . . "; while other "half-artists . . .
novelists, playwrights, even poets" were pathological cripples, "Some . . . so tangled in the love of mother, and the discord of mother and mate, that they received from woman not
nourishment . . . but a sweet and torturing poison . . . ."

Though he despised the sterile aesthetics of the art-for-art's-
sakers and the even more sterile lusts of the decadents, Paul
was himself a poet as well as a prophet; and the poet in him
continued to make verses out of his quarrel with himself, even
as the prophet made sermons out of his quarrel with the world.
Unfortunately, the poems attributed to him (there are nine in
the text) are quite undistinguished: stuff salvaged—it would
appear—from old notebooks, and written by Stapledon, perhaps in the early and later twenties, before he had ever imagined Paul or the novel in which he appears. Indeed, Stapledon's first published work was, as we have already had
occasion to remark, a volume of poetry called *Latter-Day
Psalms*, with an epigraph from Thomas Carlyle which begins,
"There must be a new world if there is to be any world at all!"
Whatever the revolutionary political implications of this,
however, there is esthetically nothing new in what follows.

Though his little book appeared three or four years after
Eliot had pioneered Modernism in England with "The Love
Song of J. Alfred Prufrock," and though Stapledon always
spoke well of Eliot—even defending him, as we have seen,
against the literary commissar, Alexander Fadayev—he seems
to have learned nothing from his example. He eschews rhyme,
to be sure, and his cadences are vaguely Whitmanian; but his
diction is traditionally "poetic" and his subjects conventional.
Indeed, the collection closes with a series of panegyric set
pieces on such acceptable mythological figures as Athena,
Apollo, Artemis, Brahma, and Our Lady of Heaven. Somewhat
less expectedly (though not without precedent more than a
century after Byron), there is a sympathetic ode to Satan, whose
final lines give a fair sense, I think, of the quality of both Stapledon's thought and poetic style in 1914—particularly in
conjunction with the corresponding passage from the equally
sympathetic ode to Christ with which Stapledon (eager as always to have his cake and eat it too) balances it:

SATAN

It is thou that puttest wrath into a man among
his enemies, and into him that stands up
one against the world.
Thou art the god of heroes, and of those who
battle against fate.
Teach us thy wisdom that we may scorn the
Almighty; and thy fortitude that we may
not shrink to cast him off.
We hail thee, thou God in Man! We magnify
thee against God in Heaven.


CHRIST

Thou losest thyself in every man and woman.
Thou has forgotten thyself for ever in love.
Thou hast reached beyond man's wisdom, and
Thou hast come again into the faith of a child.
Thou understandest the wisdom of the Almighty,
and thou art gladly at one with him.
Oh thou pattern unto all men, who dwellest in
the heart of every man! Oh thou God in Man,
who knowest thyself God in Heaven!

Eventually, Stapledon seems to have lost faith in himself
as a poet. "He didn't think much of himself as a poet," Mrs.
Stapledon reported. "I think he would have liked to have been
a poet, but he was ready to accept criticism from his friends
. . . . And it was they who decided that it probably wasn't
his medium." Yet he apparently continued to write poems,
primarily for his own pleasure and that of his family; though
in his attempt to pad out *Last Men in London* he again committed some of them to print. Taken out of their fictional context, into which indeed they do not fit very well, the first four,
called "Sin," "Men," "Evanescence," and "Timber," give the
impression of having been written by an author rather different from the middle-aged thirties agnostic who created the rest
of the book: a younger man, more Christian on the one hand,
though more self-pitying on the other.

The final group of five, however, which he must have composed later, do deal with the major themes of the novel, and
are in fact among the few true "science fiction" poems in the

language. Moreover, all of them are superior to anything in
*Latter-Day Psalms*, being at once more spontaneous and more
skillfully crafted; while the last (my own favorite) is wittier as
well—though, to be sure, the Neptunian narrator objects to the
joke in its last lines, writing that, "in the final couplet there
appears the self-conscious disillusionment which is characteristic of your age."

> If man encounter
> on his proud adventure
> other intelligence?
>
> If mind more able,
> ranging among the galaxies,
> noose this colt and break him
> to be a beast of draught and burden
> for ends beyond him?
> If man's aim and his passion be ludicrous,
> and the flight of Pegasus
> but a mulish caper?
>
> Dobbin! Pull your weight!
> Better be the donkey of the Lord,
> whacked on beauty's errand,
> than the wild ass of the desert
> without destination.
>
> Vision! From star to star the human donkey
> Transports God's old street organ and his monkey.

Finally, however, Paul—like Stapledon—switches from
poetry to prose; since he sees himself as a prophet, and knows
that verse is a poor medium for preaching a "new truth" or
attracting disciples to collaborate in his mission. But he turns
out to be a not very eloquent persuader even in the other medium. To the unconverted he appears not a savior but "a crank
and a bore"; and as he grows ever shriller, even old friends
and former comrades desert him. To Catherine he seems sick,
in need of a rest; to the Communists "an incorrigible bourgeois"; and to the author of *Last and First Men* "a lunatic."
With the last diagnosis, the police finally concur, releasing
him from the prison cell where they had locked him away
"after several disorderly scenes in Hyde Park," to a madhouse
conveniently located near his suburban home.

Stapledon tells us nothing about Paul's experiences in the
asylum, except to say that he remained the "compassionately
amused spectator of his own madness"; and that "after some

months of enforced meditation he was at last released, thoroughly cured of his disease." But I find myself imagining his conversations with the skeptical psychiatrist in charge, trying to explain the nature of the extraterrestrial being who had "possessed" him; or recounting the hallucinatory and masochistic episodes he had suffered in childhood on his way to a final "illumination." Indeed, these episodes are for me the only truly memorable scenes in the book, largely, I think, because they are the "craziest." Not that they stand alone in a fiction fraught with images of insanity from beginning to end.

Toward the book's close, for instance, we are given in a garbled message from the Neptunian narrator, a description of his once utopian world as it approaches collapse: "Eat the mad, who come to grief. The many mad. Mad men with knives. Mad women with smiles, with skull faces . . . ." And we remember the doubts of the earthling Paul about his own sanity at the beginning of it all. It is as if the future half of Stapledon's split protagonist is obliged to act out, in effect to verify, the most terrible doubts of the present-day half. From the moment he had sensed the presence of that other, Paul had "feared he was going mad"; or at least that he was "possessed" by a creature not merely "alien" but "irrational, insane." A little later, he convinces himself that however "alien," that intruder into his consciousness is "sane and joyous"; and finally—after he has become its willing instrument—insists that though the new "I" he has thus become may indeed be mad, " . . . this madness is better than sanity. Better, and more sane."

He was not always so sure about that, however. Indeed, Paul's initial reactions to the visionary experience which extended his consciousness were visceral and violent—more like symptoms of a breakdown than harbingers of a breakthrough. When, for instance, he first sees and feels "beyond the normal limitations of his species," a simple green pebble, he winds up in bed for two weeks with a "bilious headache." And things get worse when he psychically enters (and is entered by) another human being; emerging from a psychic close encounter with his friend Dick in pain so intense that he lies "whimpering, with his hands over his eyes"; and when a second interpenetration is cued by a quarrel, he ends up vomiting, screaming, and running off in terror.

But the end is not yet. When his ego boundaries are

stretched far enough to include simultaneously two others, "a beastly little Jew," whom he despises, and the schoolboy bully who is tormenting him, he goes completely out of control; picking out of the fire with his naked left hand a glowing coal with which he both drives off the bully and punishes himself—then faints. But he loves the pain; and, indeed, a similar sense of masochistic pleasure persists all the way to his final liberating vision of the starry heavens.

Several times before that total "illumination," Paul has walked out on the down near his suburban home to stare at:

> . . . the immensity . . . of the galactic universe, with its intermingling streams of stars, its gulfs of darkness . . . . Then, fastening his attention once more on the stray atom earth, he would seem to see it forging through time . . . . He would conceive and sensuously experience . . . the age-long but not everlasting down-pour of human generations . . . . Along with this richness and splendor of human efflorescence I established in him the emotional certainty that the end is downfall and agony, then silence . . . . Suddenly the horror, the cruelty of existence burst upon him with a new and insupportable violence, so that he cried out, stumbled and fell . . . .

But not until he has learned to inflict pain on himself deliberately does he achieve it:

> . . . sitting up in the grass, he took out his pocket-knife, opened the big blade, and forced the point through the palm of his left hand. Looking fixedly at the Pole Star, he twisted the blade about while the warm blood spread over his hand and trickled on to the grass . . . . His forehead was wet and cold, and faintness surged over him; but he still looked at Polaris, and moved the knife . . . .
>
> Then it was that Paul experienced the illumination which was henceforth to rule his life . . . . Lest he should afterwards fail to recapture what was now so exquisitely clear he put his finding into words . . . .
>
> " . . . Formerly I was dismayed by the knowledge that pain's evil is intrinsic to pain. But now I see clearly that . . . though pain's evil to the pain-blinded creature is an absolute fact in the universe, yet the very evil itself may have a place in the music which spirit is . . . ."

Since what is revealed to Paul in terror and self-inflicted pain is so like the vision embodied in *Last and First Men*, we are left with the question: Was the actual inspiration of Stapledon's first novel the benign contemplation of seals at erotic play attributed in *Last Men in London* to the Neptunian and his mate? Or the darker, thanatic one attributed to his alter ego, Paul? Or some uneasy and ultimately irreconcilable blend of the two? Whenever asked that question, Stapledon, as we have seen, always opted for the first; and Mrs. Stapledon, when queried about whether her husband had ever, like Paul, actually sought illumination through self-mutilation, answered: "The incident of Paul mutilating his hand in order to induce in himself a sort of sublime mastery of pain and its consequent exultation was not a practice of Olaf's, but he told me of someone he knew who deliberately burned his own arm by pressing a lighted cigarette into it in order to obtain this exultation and the clarity of vision which it induced . . . ."

It is hard to know, however, how candid Stapledon was with his wife in such delicate matters; since he considered her "not very bright." Not untypically, in any case, people confess things about themselves which they want simultaneously to disclose and conceal, by speaking of them as having happened to someone they knew. But it is, alas, vain to speculate about such irrecoverable "facts"—and finally irrelevant to the fiction in which they have been either imagined for the first time or radically reimagined. Considerably more to the point is the fact that writing in 1932, Stapledon set such pain-induced "clarity of vision" in a context which calls its validity into question: telling us that the first building Paul sees as he descends from his experience on the down is a lunatic asylum; and the first sound he hears, ambiguous enough to have been the squeal of a cat or a run-over dog, he takes to be "the asylum's comment on his meditation."

This is not Stapledon's last word on Paul or the possibility of ecstatic transcendence; though we are likely to remember it when, on the last page devoted to his adventures, he ends up in this very asylum. It is only a temporary stay; and—we learn in the course of brief Dickensian epilogue—he keeps his vow never to return. Instead, he marries, has children, becomes a headmaster, "bent on reform but cautious," and finally retires, promising himself to commit suicide while still in possession of all his faculties. Clearly, this is Stapledon's notion of the optimal Happy Ending to human life; but Paul does not keep his vow, since by the time there is "no further reason for him to remain alive," he has already lost "the resolution to kill himself . . . trapped in the quagmire of senility." It is an anti-tragic, if not downright comic ending to a melancholy life; and though Stapledon tried hard to make the doom of his second Neptunian protagonist truly tragic, it seems finally only pathetic:

> "Man, a moth sucked into a furnace, vanishes; and then the furnace also, since it is but a spark islanded in the wide, the everlasting darkness. If there is a meaning, it is no human meaning. Yet one thing in all this welter stands apart, unassailable, fair, the blind recollection of past light."

# 6

# A FAILED SUPERMAN AND HIS FAITHFUL HOUND

*Odd John* had from the start the widest appeal of all Stapledon's books, not just in England but in America where it found a publisher immediately, as *Last Men in London* had not. Moreover, unlike *Last and First Men*, which got its most enthusiastic notices in fanzines and technical journals, it was reviewed in influential newspapers and literary periodicals by critics of some repute. Best of all, however, was the fact that though none of those critics was associated with the science-fiction community, by and large they liked it. Alfred Kazin, for instance, still a bright young man, wrote in the *New York Herald Tribune* book section for July 19, 1936, that despite being a little too "elaborately fantastic," it was "worth reading . . . because it happens to be, on occasion, a legitimate and moving novel . . ."; while the established journalist Elmer Davis observed in the *Saturday Review of Literature* of July 1936—a shade less enthusiastically, perhaps—that "students of this very unusual writer will be interested . . . in a fresh treatment of similar ideas in his other writings." But he was righter than he knew; since in the years between now and its original publication not merely has *Odd John* continued to interest Stapledon lovers, but it has been reprinted and translated more often than any of his "other writings," and alone among them has been optioned by moviemakers.

Why this is so is a problem not as simple as it first appears. Brian Aldiss suggests that *Odd John*'s popularity is due to the obvious fact that it "is the nearest its author ever came to 'a good read' and is therefore suitable Stapledon for beginners." He bases his conviction, however, on an assumption I do not share; that *Odd John* is a "pleasant" little story, its mood "light and cheerful." It is, to be sure, a shade jollier than the unmitigatedly gloomy *Last Men in London*—humorous in intent, or so anyway its subtitle, *A Story Between Jest and Earnest*, assures us. But if it is in any sense really a joke, the joke is on all present-day humanity, on *us*! Indeed, the only reader who could laugh over *Odd John* is one who finds funny the predicament described in what is surely its most often quoted passage: "Homo sapiens is a spider trying to crawl out of a basin. So long as he's on the bottom he can get along quite nicely, but as soon as he starts climbing he begins to slip."

It is, however, an easier book, more coherent, slimmer, tidier than its immediate predecessor; and though not entirely free of tiresome editorial asides, on the whole more faithful to its fictional *donnée*. In other respects as well, it is more like what the mass audience thinks of as a "novel"; moving its single protagonist through a single time-space continuum in something close to a conventional plot. Moreover, though it is clearly "science fiction," like Stapledon's two earlier books, unlike them it is not a quasi-allegorical cosmic history but a case study of a superman; which is to say, a genre familiar not only to science-fiction fans but to readers of mainstream literature and philosophy as well.

A similar notion of the Superman and his fate had first been propounded in fact in a long parabolic essay by the philosopher, Friedrich Nietzsche, called *Thus Spake Zarathustra* and published in installments between 1883 and 1885. It is by all odds the most widely read and influential of Nietzsche's works; so that long before 1932, the term "Superman" had passed into the public domain, along with certain key phrases from its opening sections, often garbled perhaps, but recognizable all the same: "Could it be possible! The old saint in the forest had not yet heard of it, that *God is dead!*"; "*I* teach you the Superman. Man is something that is to be surpassed. . . . Man is a rope stretched between the animal and the superman . . . not to the people is Zarathustra to speak, but to the companions. . . . Men are not equal . . . beyond good and evil."

It is scarcely surprising then, that those phrases echo and re-echo in Stapledon's fiction from the start; and that when in *Odd John* he deals head-on with the possibility of man surpassing himself, they move to the center of his consciousness.

Even if he had never read Nietzsche, or, as seems more probable, found him politically unpalatable, Stapledon would have encountered in more sympathetic writers like H. G. Wells or George Bernard Shaw, the notion that the death of God makes inevitable the emergence of the Superman. Shaw's *Man and Superman*, which appeared in 1903, and his *Back to Methusaleh*, which was published in 1921, already combine in a way which reminds us of Stapledon, Nietzschean insights with an unorthodox kind of socialism; and Wells's *Food of the Gods* (1904) does much the same. Though the least successful of his "scientific romances," Wells's study of a utopia established by superintelligent giants apparently inspired J. D. Beresford's *The Hampdenshire Wonder* (1911) to whose protagonist, "the unhappy Victor Stott," Stapledon refers (as if he were a real person) three times in the early pages of *Odd John*.

Not until the 1930s, however, did the Superman story become a major sub-genre of science fiction; perhaps because the notion of transcending human limitations had a special appeal in a time when men were confronting problems they feared insolvable though of their own making. At any rate, at a point when the Great Depression promised to go on forever and war threatened everywhere, Eric Temple Bell published (under the pseudonym of John Taine) *Seeds of Life* and Philip Wylie *Gladiator*, both intended for an adult audience; even as children, teenagers, and marginal literates of all ages were responding to similar mythologies in semi-iconic comic books. Siegel and Shuster led the way, appropriating the Nietzschean honorific for their "Man of Steel"; and scores of imitators followed, inventing invulnerable saviors sometimes scarcely distinguishable from their model. But their names and images, too, still resonate in our remembering heads, all the way from Captain Marvel, Wonder Woman, and Batman to Spider Man, the Fantastic Four, and the Incredible Hulk. Some of them, moreover, translated to television and the movie screen, promise to live on into the twenty-first century.

Most comic book superheroes, however, are upholders of

the status quo; not rebels and "immoralists" like Nietzsche's
Superman, but supercops like Siegel and Shuster's. Moreover,
like the Man of Steel, they tend to be in their personal lives
impotent losers, moving among us between heroic exploits, in
humble guise—and consequently neither honored nor feared
like Zarathustra, but ignored or despised. But the counter-
tradition has survived in certain science-fiction novels, whose
protagonists are enemies of law and order, threats to established society; and who despise ordinary humanity, yearning
for community only with their own kind. Kept alive in the
forties and fifties in works like A. E. Van Vogt's *Slan* and
Theodore Sturgeon's *More Than Human*, that tradition fully
flowered in the sixties with the emergence of a dissident youth
audience which sought in fantasy and science fiction not escape but models for alternative life-styles.

It was such young readers who made unprecedented best-
sellers of Arthur C. Clarke's *Childhood's End* and Robert Heinlein's *Stranger in a Strange Land*; the latter extraordinarily
close in plot detail, however different in tone, to *Odd John*.
Moreover, both its protagonist and the multiple superchildren
of *Childhood's End* are portrayed as "sports," the mutant offspring of normal parents like Stapledon's John; rather than
laboratory products like the force-fed giants of Wells's *Food
of the Gods* or the genetically engineered quasi-immortals of
Shaw's *Back to Methusaleh*. In his first novel, Stapledon had
imagined supermen of the latter sort: abortive failures of science like the almost bodiless Fourth Men; or triumphs of se-
lective breeding like the Fifth and Eighteenth Men—who are
also "cyborgs," i.e., hybrids created by the fusion of human
flesh with synthetic materials. They represent, in any case, not
merely the creation of something new in the evolutionary
chain, but also the replacement of nature or God by human
technology as the evolutionary force; in mythological terms,
the creature becoming the creator.

To those for whom the God of the Bible still lives, such an
assumption of his role seems diabolic; and in their renderings
of the myth, therefore, those who attempt it are depicted as
frustrated or doomed: like Faust with his Homunculus, Dr.
Frankenstein with his ill-fated Monster, or for that matter, the
academic scientists who in C. S. Lewis's *That Hideous Strength*

created a talking Head much like Stapledon's Fourth Men. Even a materialist unbeliever like H. G. Wells is so possessed still in his deep psyche by the myth of the damned Black Magician that he does not permit his Dr. Moreau to tamper unscathed with the processes of evolution. Nor, as we shall see, did Stapledon let the scientist who had created the superdog, Sirius, escape retribution. Not that Stapledon was unsympathetic to the satanic dream of men "becoming as gods," nor opposed on principle (as the hymn to Satan in *Latter-Day Psalms* makes clear) to "giving the devil his due." But he seems to have believed that only one already a superman could do so guiltlessly; and he begins therefore as early as *Last Men in London* to imagine such creatures produced by the "blind forces of nature" rather than human intent.

Stapledon devotes, in fact, most of the final chapter of his second novel to an otherwise unmotivated discussion of what he calls "submerged supermen," attributing it to the Neptunian narrator, who up to that point has concentrated on Paul. Such anomalous creatures, that omniscient narrator tells us, have appeared throughout the whole career of the First Men; but they have become more numerous during "the great ferment of the Industrial Revolution," and during its later stages have, indeed, been saved from destruction by the "growth of humanitarianism." Earlier they would have died by exposure or through neglect, being typically monstrous in appearance (bigheaded, bull-necked, and endowed with a "facial expression, which to the normal eye seemed sometimes insane, sometimes infantile, sometimes diabolic") and so slow to mature that they are apt to be confused with subnormals.

But even when permitted to survive infancy, the supernormals have remained unintegrated into the family, being physically unattractive to the opposite sex, slow to develop genitally, and after puberty given to sexual practices generally regarded with horror. Nor have they achieved in the political arena the power one might have expected them to exercise over their intellectual inferiors—refusing ever "to play the game." Not only are they likely to despise typical pleasures of the British like football or blood sports, but they tend also to reject such higher shibboleths of the tribe as patriotism, party loyalty, and churchgoing, along with the values of heroism, piety, and morality. Even science seems to them foolishness, and they are no more likely to become laboratory technicians or researchers than cabinet ministers or priests. Downwardly mobile and more comfortable among the lower classes, who though they regard them as cranks or "freaks" approach them with a certain amount of awe, they have tended to work "gigs" as postmen and truckdrivers; but even more typically they become "tramps . . . tinkering . . . poaching, stealing, breaking stones, harvesting."

This general account the man from the Far Future follows with the case history of one such supernormal, a particularly repulsive lout in his early teens, who "It so happened . . . was sent to the school where Paul was headmaster." Called "Humpty" because of his grotesquely swollen bald head, he is miserable in the classroom, and though brought out of his shell for a little while by the sympathetic approach of Paul, ends disastrously. Not, however, until he has confided to that one friendly adult his resolve to

> . . . found a small colony of supermen in some remote part of the world. This would become the germ of a new human species and a new world-order. Little by little it would gain control of the whole planet, and would either exterminate the inferior species, or more probably domesticate such members of the subhuman hordes as it required for its own uses.

Before he has begun to launch this utopian imperialist scheme, Humpty becomes convinced that he has been so hopelessly "mutilated" by his education that he is capable only of perverse and sadistic revenge against *Homo sapiens*, and so ends by willing his own death; after which the Neptunian adds a postscript forecasting the work which, when it appeared three years later, was to be called *Odd John:*

> Thus ended one of Nature's blundering attempts to improve upon her first, experimental, humanity. One other superior and much more fortunate individual was destined almost to succeed in the task that Humpty had merely imagined. Of this other, of the utopian colony which he founded, and of its destruction by a jealous world, I may tell on another occasion.

Like all Superman stories in which the author identifies with deviants from the human norm, Stapledon's brief account of Humpty, as well as the novel which was its spin-off, reflect a hatred of mankind, which is rooted—like its archetypal substrate, the myth of selling one's soul to the devil—in self-hatred. But more specifically, both "Humpty and Paul" and *Odd John* are mutant stories, beginning with an encounter between a normal adult and a mutated child. Consequently, they reembody, in inverted form, another ancient myth, preserved in the folktale of the Changeling Child. That legend projects the disturbing sense, surely felt from time to time by all parents, that the babe in one's arm, the adolescent across the table are hostile strangers, destined eventually to betray or abandon the troubled mortals who have fostered them. The original version is sympathetic to the older generation, the "normals"; but in Stapledon, the balance is tilted in favor of the later born, the "freaks," whose monstrosity he emphasizes so strongly that it seems as if he believed that to be truly admirable a new species must challenge not just ethical but esthetic norms.

In 1953, Arthur C. Clarke, most ardent and faithful of all Stapledon's disciples, made fully explicit in *Childhood's End* the mythological meanings which remained half implicit in *Odd John*. But not until the later sixties, when the "Generation Gap" became a journalistic byword for the threatened old and a revolutionary slogan for the threatening young, did that novel become a cult book. The American paperback edition, for instance, which was reprinted only four times between the date of its publication and 1960, was reissued ten times between 1967 and 1970. Only at that point had a whole generation emerged which took the myth of the Changeling Child as their very own, and therefore could read with a thrill of troubled recognition the passage toward the conclusion of *Childhood's End*, in which a bewildered parent asks of his mutated offspring, "What shall we do about our children?"; and an extraterrestrial observer answers, "Enjoy them while you may. . . . They will not be yours for long," then goes on to explain:

"All the earlier changes your race has known took countless ages. But this is a transformation of the mind, not of the body. By the standards of evolution, it will be cataclysmic—instantaneous. . . . You must face the fact that yours is the last generation of *Homo sapiens*. . . .

"In a few years, it will be over, and then the human race
will be divided in twain. . . . You have given birth to your
successors, and it is your tragedy that you will never understand them. . . ."

But to the following episode in which the mutated children, fused into a single telepathic community, prepare to leave
the earth forever at the behest of the mysterious Overmind, the
dissident youth of the sixties must have responded with unqualified joy:

> There was no sound or movement from the children. They
> stood in scattered groups along the sand, showing no more
> interest in one another than in the homes they were leaving
> forever. . . . Few were crying: some were puzzled, clutching
> nervously at their small belongings, but most seemed to be
> looking forward with eagerness to some great adventure. . . .
> Those who were leaving now were no longer children, what-
> ever they might be. And this time there would be no reunion.

It was the dream of the dissident young that Clarke had
translated into print on the page, the dream they were acting
out, however imperfectly, on the streets and campuses of half
the world during the events of 1968. If in the eighties, we see
the dreamers, untranslated into an unimaginably new world
but themselves become troubled parents in the old one, it
scarcely matters—for their fantasy, as long as it lasted, had a
reality of its own. In the mid-thirties, however, scarcely anyone was ready to dream the dream Stapledon had anticipated
without quite knowing it. Those who thought they liked *Odd
John*, therefore, were apt to be those who did not quite realize
what it was saying, taking it for a "good read"; while those
with some glimmering of what he was up to tended to respond with a hostility, verging on rage. But this was in part
understandable; since Stapledon was, after all, a man of almost fifty, betraying his own generation in behalf of mutated
youngsters not yet even born, the contemporaries of his children's children.

In any case, *Odd John*, despite its popularity, received some
of the harshest reviews ever given any of Stapledon's books.
*The Left Review*, for instance, which only the year before had
attacked *Waking World* for its refusal to accept the Soviet
Union as a model of utopian perfection, this time condemned

Stapledon for his "defeatism" and his contempt for humanity. How, their reviewer asked, was it possible for him to reject the "grossness" of ordinary men and women, while accepting, even approving a "scandalous" adolescent, who begins his career by committing murder and ends by living with certain of his fellows "in aesthetic nakedness and promiscuity"? But chiefly that reviewer seemed vexed by Stapledon's willingness to believe, like other bourgeois prophets of doom, that there is no way out for humanity, which in fact "cannot be defeated since we [i.e., the Communists] exist and work." Indeed, no matter how close Stapledon grew to the "comrades," they could never forgive him for refusing to make the final commitment.

Yet even less doctrinaire critics, to whom his politics seemed perfectly acceptable, were troubled by *Odd John.* M. D. Coles, for one, writing in *Life and Letters*, found the novel in some ways "a nice bit of propaganda," but was put off by the sheer ugliness of its protagonist ("an infant prodigy of the most objectionable sort, whose looks are even against him . . ."), as well as by "his peculiar companions . . . all certifiable and some actually certified . . . ," who "talk big of worship etc., and small of Homo sapiens, yet . . . don't seem to do much in the way of worship. . . ." She objected, moreover, to the book's nameless narrator, "a faithful, fascinated and gormless Dr. Watson," who approves all of the Superman's infractions of ordinary morality, not even caviling at murder. As late as 1976, in fact, critics were still quarreling with that narrator's (and presumably the author's) tolerance of Odd John's willingness to destroy any mere human who gets in his way.

Curtis C. Smith, for example, in a sensitive and intelligent study which appeared in *Voices for the Future: Essays on Major Science Fiction Writers* (edited by Thomas Clareson), has especial difficulty in dealing with certain of John's genetic experiments, reminiscent of Nazi "science" at its shameless worst, which the "gormless" narrator describes as follows:

> I was shown a series of thirty-eight living human embryos, each in its own incubator. These startled me considerably, but the story of their conception and capture startled me even more. Indeed, it filled me with horror, and with violent though short-

lived moral indignation. The eldest of these embryos was three months old. Its father, I was told, was Shâhin, its mother a native of the Tuamoto Archipelago. The unfortunate girl had been seduced, brought back to the island, operated upon, and killed while still under anaesthetic.

It is a difficulty which I share; for though I realize, as Mr. Smith does, that it is a fictional narrator who speaks these words rather than Stapledon himself, and that there is a hint of irony qualifying the statement "it filled me with horror, and with violent though short-lived moral indignation," the irony is directed not against the short life of the narrator's "horror," but against his philistine morality, his tender heart and the failure of "objectivity" which they imply.

But we must linger a little longer over these matters; since the problem posed by *Odd John's* narrator is a rather complicated one; and a full understanding of the book depends upon a prior understanding of him and the role he plays in it. He is, to begin with, nameless. All of the other major characters in the book are identified by their family or Christian names, though some are given nicknames, like Odd John himself, his mother called "Pax" because of her peaceful nature, and his father, known as "Doc" for obvious reasons. But the teller of the tale is never referred to as anything except "Fido," "faithful hound," "puss," "slave," "the Bean," or—somewhat condescendingly—"my dear," all names bestowed on him by the superboy he serves and adores. To be sure, that boy assures him at one point that "Fido" is from a Greek root meaning "brilliant" rather than the Latin word signifying "faithful" and long associated with canine pets.

The narrator, however, is anything but "brilliant," being both "gormless" and almost invisible, faceless at least. We are never told what he looks like, how tall he is, what color his eyes, in a novel in which John and his freakish associates are described in almost painful detail; and even his mother is sketched in a few words as "a large, sluggish blonde." True, we learn his age, approximately that of John's parents, and his profession, a free-lance journalist. Essentially, however, he is a disembodied voice, important only as he interacts with the protagonist and tells us—at some point after John is already dead—the story of John's life.

What is hard to understand is why Stapledon felt the need for a fictional narrator of that life different from his authorial self, and why he chose this particular one, not merely obtuse but abject. In part, I think, it is because he disliked telling any tale without such framing, as his two earlier novels suggest. Though *Last and First Men*, for instance, is written in the first person, the "I" of the Preface warns the reader that "throughout the following pages the speaker, the first person singular, is supposed to be, not the actual writer, but an individual living in the extremely distant future." To complicate matters further, this second "I" describes the first "I" as having a "docile but scarcely adequate brain," which is to say, as a classic obtuse narrator trying to report the perceptions of a superhuman intelligence. The same device of a double narrator is continued into *Last Men in London*, where things are made even more complex; since the omniscient Neptunian observer is this time recording through his dull-witted surrogate the experiences and perceptions of another inferior though half-awakened twentieth-century human, called Paul.

At the end of that novel, in fact, the Neptunian speaks (always, of course, through "W.O.S.") of a "hidden superman" known to Paul, of whom he says, "I may tell on another occasion." But the "I" who takes up the tale of Odd John three years later, we are made aware in the very first paragraph, is neither half-awakened nor omniscient:

> When I told John that I intended to write his biography, he laughed. "My dear *man!*" he said. "but of course it was inevitable." The word "man" on John's lips was often equivalent to "fool."
> "Well," I protested, "a cat may look at a king."
> He replied, "Yes, but can it really *see* the king? Can you, puss, really see me?"

Clearly, this time around it is the first person narrator who is "obtuse," as opposed to his subject and even to Stapledon himself, rather than vice versa; and in any case, Stapledon is no longer present in the text.

He has, that is to say, much simplified the relationship between his tale and its teller; though he has not fallen back on third person narration, in either omniscient or limited form, as he was to do in *Old Man in New World* (1944) and *Death into Life* (1946) respectively. Instead he employs a rather old-fashioned device, spurned by elite Modernist writers, but standard in popular fiction of the late nineteenth and early twentieth century, like Rider Haggard's *She* or, most notoriously, Conan Doyle's Sherlock Holmes stories; in which the adventures of a more than normally brilliant protagonist are related by a more than normally dull adulator—bonded to his subject by an abject love which verges on the pathological. Stapledon was to use similar narrators, though none so abysmally dull, in *Sirius* (1942), *The Flames* (1947), and *A Man Divided* (1950).

Unlike Haggard and Doyle, however, he does not use this device naively; finding in it a strategy for embodying in the very way he tells his tales the conviction otherwise embodied in their fables and editorial asides: that *all* men are men divided or "possessed"; and that the artist in particular is at the moment of creation the beneficiary or victim of incursions from elsewhere and elsewhen. Even when, as in *Star Maker* (1937), or *Darkness and the Light* (1942), he writes stories in a first person scarcely distinguishable from that of the author, he makes it clear that there was collaboration from other sources; actually describing in the former the telepathic hybridization of the narrator's "I" with many alien intelligences, and confessing toward the beginning of the latter that "I must, I think, have been strengthened by the felt presence of other and superhuman spectators."

But in some ways poor, faithful Fido performs a quite different function from the rest of Stapledon's narrators, human and superhuman. Like his prototype, Dr. Watson, he leaves the reader feeling superior to him, and therefore less likely to resent the arrogance of the protagonist. Moreover, our contempt for Fido's philistinism and moral obtuseness tricks us into condoning in Odd John actions which we might otherwise have considered intolerable—like deliberate incest and cold-blooded murder. Murder, indeed (as the hostile critics of the book perceived from the start), is the central theme of a novel in which the superhero becomes aware of his true nature and his fated mission only after his first killing. Nor are we kept in ignorance of this crime, as might perhaps have been expected, until sympathy has been established with its perpetrator. " . . . I know little of the amazing facts of his career," the narrator confides toward the very beginning of his biography of John Wainwright. "I know he never walked until he was six, that before he was ten he had committed several burglaries and killed a policeman . . . ."

It is not just the taking of any life that we are asked to accept in this disconcertingly matter-of-fact passage but the murder by a boy of a full-grown man, a representative of law and order who was also his friend: "my own particular pal, Smithson, who had unwittingly taught me so much!" The act, moreover, climaxes a series of challenges to older males in positions of authority. The house John had been burglarizing when Smithson caught him had, for instance, belonged to a prosperous businessman, known only as "Mr. Magnate," whom John had mercilessly baited not long before. In similar fashion, he had also mocked certain mathematicians and scientists who had come to observe him, as well as "Doc" himself, between whom and John, Fido tells us, there was "no spontaneous sympathy and little common unity of taste . . . . I have often seen on John's face while he was listening to his father a fleeting contortion of ridicule, even disgust."

It is not, of course, his father whom John actually kills, but—in what psychiatrists would identify as a typical act of "displacement"—only a fatherly cop. It is clear, however, who the real Enemy is; though Stapledon, who never missed a chance to denigrate Freudian theory, would have rejected such an interpretation out of hand. But the Oedipal configuration is completed when somewhat later John sleeps with his mother, if that indeed is what he has done. The text is reticent enough at this point to have slipped by Stapledon's wary publishers, who eight years afterward were to refuse to sponsor *Sirius*, in which the copulation of a girl and a dog is only a little less circumspectly described. But it is hard to read Fido's account any other way:

> . . . he sought delicate and intimate contact with a being whose sensibility and insight were not wholly incomparable with his own; with a being, moreover, who was beloved, who also loved him deeply . . . . Second, he needed to assert his moral independence of *Homo sapiens*, to free himself of all deep unconscious acquiescence in the conventions of the species that had nurtured him. He needed, therefore, to break what was one of the most cherished of all the taboos of that species.

It is enlightening in this context to note that Mrs. Stapledon believes Pax to have been intended as a portrait of her; and if so, it is a flattering one in its own way: "Some said she was 'just a magnificent female animal,' and so dull as to be subnormal . . . . Yet she was no fool. Her house was always in order, though she seemed to spend no thought upon it. With the same absent-minded skill she managed her rather difficult husband . . . "; and, we gather, made love to her son, who badly needed such help. Before their union, he had carried on only adolescent flirtations, some of them homosexual, all of them unconsummated. The one time he actually made it into bed, however, with a young woman who responded to his caresses, he fled from her with "revulsion and horror" (as if, he puts it, "a dog were smelling around me, or a monkey"), and he barely resists the impulse to knife her, fleeing instead to his mother's arms.

Years later, when he has founded a colony of supernormals of both sexes, John takes part in the round-robin sex which is part of their communal living. Yet even with Lo, the one girl of his mutant kind he seems to love as deeply as he does Pax, he never sleeps until just before his death. And their mating, which occurs offstage, is dismissed in a few words. Why he holds off for so long remains as mysterious as why Stapledon, although he clearly identifies with John, modeled the mother John so passionately loved not on his own mother, but on his wife. Perhaps, we are tempted to think, it is because Agnes Stapledon was in fact the daughter of his mother's brother, his mother once removed, so to speak, just distant enough to be no longer taboo. Or maybe it was only that unable when young to ask sex of his mother like John, he settled for demanding mothering of his wife after he grew old. So, at least, his last novel, A Man Divided, seems to suggest.

Yet outside his fictions Stapledon always claimed that what he had most resented in the woman who bore him was her having smothered him in affection, thus refusing to let him grow up. Odd John, however, suggests that on a deeper level, he did not find delayed maturity an unmitigated disaster; since a part at least of what fosters John's extraordinary development is the slowness of his entry into adulthood. He seems sometimes, in fact, mythologically as much Peter Pan as

Superman, a Superboy who never grew up. At eighteen we
are told, "He still looked a young boy," and even at twenty-
three, the year of his death, he was "in appearance, little altered." All the more reason then that at fourteen, when he was
still "physically comparable with a normal child of ten," he
could cuddle up to the warm flesh of his mama without guilt
feelings on either part. Yet he seems to have learned such "innocence" rather than preserved it, since four years before he
had been troubled for a while at least by the death of Smithson. Or maybe it is simply that for both him and his author
murder was a more vexing problem than the infringement of
even the most sacred sexual taboo.

What John tells Fido after the murder, however, is that he
"had not yet reached the stage of liking *whatever* had to
be done." All the same, he seems never to have doubted for a
moment that he had no other choice, and ends by accepting,
not yet in love but fatalistically, that "What must be, must
be." The "new 'I' " which has been awakened by the act of
killing feels neither remorse nor shame over the folly of the
old "I"—only a desire "to make amends as far as possible."

What he considers "amends" turns out to be the "mercy-
killing" of Smithson's bereaved widow, but circumstances
conspire to prevent this and he is left a little frustrated. More
murders lie ahead, however; since at the critical juncture of
each of the three sections into which the book is tidily divided
(it is Stapledon's most symmetrical fiction), he performs one
or more acts of ritual slaughter—in order to pass on to a higher
stage of ego development, or to confirm his already having
reached one.

The first section, which consists of ten chapters, is divided
into an account of John Wainwright's infancy and childhood
(beginning *ab ovo*, as it were, with his eleven-month-long ges-
tation); a description of his attempts to find a vocation (he
becomes in turn a burglar, a financially successful inventor
of handy household items, an even more successful speculator
in stocks, and an amateur "anthropologist," studying contemporary society); and a summary indictment of the human race.
The first of these sub-divisions seems to me the most inven-
tive and moving part of the book; treating ingeniously not just
John's unorthodox education and maturation but his first mur-

der and consequent alteration of consciousness. The Oedipal
sexual initiation which is its complement does not occur,
however, until well into the second, where it climaxes an account of his "scandalous adolescence."

It is immediately preceded by a description of John's in-
ventions which I find quite humorous; though I suspect that
Stapledon may not have realized quite how funny was the indignation of his young *Homo superior* over *Homo sapiens*
having proved too set in their ways to buy his "untearable and
detachable trousers pockets" or his "startlingly efficient dodge
for saving time and trouble in the water closet." The report on
his anthropological investigations which follows, however, is
straight-faced to the point of pomposity, and tedious besides;
since what John learns as a self-righteous gatecrasher and
snooper turns out to be very little different from what Paul
had earlier discovered about his society in *Last Men in London*. We find ourselves, therefore, enduring a rehash of Stapledon's own never very original and by now hopelessly over-
familiar notions about priests, psychiatrists, philosophers,
scientists, and an unnamed poet clearly intended to be T. S.
Eliot, as well as Bloomsbury once more—and, of course, at
greatest length, the Communists.

It is in the course of discussing the latter, who to the end
of his days attracted and repelled Stapledon like nothing else
except perhaps the God of his forefathers, that he develops a
theory about the three root causes of the world's plight: "the
almost universal need to hate something"; "economic disorder"; and "the growing sense that there's something all wrong
with modern solely-scientific culture." With the latter feeling
Odd John and, presumably, Stapledon sympathize, though they
are both aware of how the "revulsion from mechanism" can
lead to a rejection of rationality, democracy, and sanity—"a
confused craving to be mad, possessed in some way." That
"craving" Stapledon, however ambivalently, shares; but not
Odd John, who considers it only further evidence that mankind has reached a point where redemption is no longer possible.

Up to his seventeenth year, John had dreamed that with
his efforts they could be saved; and in hopes of launching such
a rescue had accumulated the wealth he had come to realize

meant power. But his study of their institutions at close range
has disillusioned him. "Homo sapiens," he declares, "is at the
end of his tether, and I'm not going to spend my life tinkering
with a doomed species." But this leaves him, despite all his
gifts, like any adolescent who has lost his childhood illusions,
stripped of his identity, lonely, and in tears. High time, then,
for him to begin again.

And so he does, though not until he has fled from everyone who has known him, including Fido; bidding farewell only
to his mother, to whom he confesses, "sobbing like a child
that cannot wake from a bad dream, Oh, Pax, I'm so *lonely.*"
Indeed, he is crying still, his face "streaming with tears" (he
who has never wept since birth and whose signature is uncanny laughter) when next we see him, through the eyes of a
couple of strangers, hikers who have come upon him in a solitary mountain cavern. But before their departure, he manages
to laugh again his characteristic laugh, a "sharp cackle," that
makes their spines tingle. Moreover, he performs for them his
first "miracle": lifting, or hypnotizing them into believing he
has lifted ("The truth of the matter," he explains later, "was
something much more subtle and tremendous than any plain
little physical miracle could ever be") the tons of snow and
rock over their heads, and sweeping away the storm clouds to
reveal the beauty of the starry heavens.

Later, too, he tells Fido how he had gotten to that point,
by confronting in aboriginal nakedness the wilderness and
the elements. He had, in fact, relived the whole history of man's
rise from barbarism: reinventing music by blowing on reeds
plucked from the riverbank, and art by scratching images on
a deer's horn. But first he had, ritually and reverently, to kill
the deer, bringing it down with a knife, of course—though
this time one chipped from stone.

> . . . With my soul I saluted him. Then I pitied him, because
> he was doomed, and in the prime. But I remembered that I too
> was doomed. I suddenly knew that I should never reach my
> prime. And laughed aloud, for him and for me, because life is
> brief and wild, and death too is in the picture.

That initial insight was confirmed and enriched for him by the
sight of the stars:

. . . when I did see the stars (riotously darting in all directions according to the caprice of their own wild natures, yet
in every movement confirming the law), the whole tangled
horror that had tormented me finally presented itself to me in
its true and beautiful shape. And I knew that the first, blind
stage of my childhood had ended.

But it was the slaughter of a beast and the eating of its
carcass which first taught John not only to laugh again in the
teeth of disaster, but to *love* all suffering and death, as an essential part of the beauty of the whole. If it seems a little anti-
climactic to discover that the illumination attained by the
Superman is the same as that of the Eighteenth Men or of poor
"possessed" Paul, or, for that matter, of William Olaf Stapledon writing his Ph.D. dissertation, we can console ourselves
by noting that at least its occasion is different. For John,
such illumination is the fruit not of passive suffering or self-
mutilation, but (however odd this may seem in a book written
by a pacifist and hater of "blood sports") of killing a fellow
creature.

Small wonder, then, that John commits murder throughout
the rest of his career whenever it seems necessary to further
what he calls, mysteriously, "advancing the spirit." Asked at
one point by the faithful narrator to define that term, he answers, "Even if I *knew* . . . I couldn't put it into English, or
any 'sapient' language. And if I could, you wouldn't understand." Nor does that "old stupid" understand the multiple
killings committed in its name, not just by Odd John himself
but by the other supernormals he gathers about him.

The ten chapters which constitute the third section of the
novel are devoted to telling how John finds those supernormals, persuades some twenty-one of them to join him, then
transports them to a South Seas island and builds with them
a society at once communistic and individualistic, orderly and
free. Before, however, its inhabitants attain the spiritual perfection to which they aspire, they are destroyed by the jeal-
ousy and incomprehension of *Homo sapiens*. Or more precisely, they blow themselves up when confronted by the
battlefleet of the six Great Pacific Powers: England, Russia,
Holland, France, America, and Japan.

I myself do not much like the novel's action-packed conclusion, which may, indeed, be what makes it seem to many a better "read" than Stapledon's slower-paced philosophical books. This is not because I distrust action, however, but rather because I do not think Stapledon is particularly good at handling it. Nor am I especially fond of his portrayal of the nature of the utopian colony, though it is impossible to deny its influence on much later science fiction, including Aldous Huxley's last novel, The Island (1962) and Heinlein's Stranger in a Strange Land (1961). Nonetheless, Stapledon's description of the ethical, esthetic, and spiritual breakthroughs presumably achieved by this new society remain disconcertingly vague. His forays into hinting at its technological advances, moreover, are often downright silly; as in John's account of how he releases from the heart of the atom the energy which provides his chief source of power:

> ". . . there's the hell of a lot of energy locked up in every atomic nucleus. . . . It's no use trying to *overcome* those terrific interlocking forces. You must *abolish* them for the time being; send them to sleep so to speak. . . . What I do, then, is to hypnotize the little devils so that they go limp for a moment and loosen their grip on one another. Then when they wake up they barge about in a hilarious freedom, and all you have to do is to see that their barging drives your machinery."

Stapledon does considerably better in describing the denizens of the island; since his powers of invention wake when he imagines the goblin-like supercreatures whom John telepathically finds and tries (sometimes in vain) to recruit. Often in his work, it is the grotesque visual images which remain in the mind long after the ideas and even the plots are forgotten. So here, the nightmare figures survive the narration which surrounds them: the six-fingered English flute player in the lunatic asylum, for instance, who breaks years of silence to cry to John, "We two, NOT MAD! But these—All mad, quite, quite mad"; the stunted African child with his "sombre red" mop of wooly hair and his mismatched eyes—one huge and black, the other tiny and blue; the Hungarian girl with a harelip and short bandy legs, whose distorted head in profile "suggested a croquet mallet"; but especially the nameless Hebridean infant, a sickly mute with "no legs, arms like a newt's," who almost kills John on their first encounter by simply opening its hitherto impenetrable mind to his telepathic scrutiny.

John manages somehow to survive that experience, whose horror he tries to explain to Fido:

> ". . . The mental oyster opened wide and tried to swllow me into itself. And itself was—just the bottomless black pit of Hell . . . . I found myself dropping plumb into the most appalling gulf of darkness, of mental and spiritual darkness, in which there was nothing whatever but eternally unsatisfied black hate; a sort of dank atmosphere of poison, in which everything I had ever cared for seemed to moulder away into nastiness. I can't explain. I can't explain."

Later, that malevolent cripple plays a mysterious part in John's destruction; though not before John has himself destroyed many others. The cold-blooded climax of his career as a killer comes, as we have already noted, when he presides over the death of the native girl from the Tuamoto Islands. Fido, however, is even more distressed by two earlier incidents, which resemble the standard practices of naval warfare and imperialist expropriation rather than the excesses of Nazi "science."

The first occurs at sea when, en route to his island, John rescues some passengers from a sinking British steamer. Two of them have actually been taken aboard his own ship before he realizes that their return home could put his whole venture in jeopardy. He, therefore, after telepathic consultation with his supernormal shipmates, shoots them down and feeds their bodies to the sharks, while his comrades finish off the rest in a lifeboat they have taken in tow. "Long afterwards, when John told me about his shocking incident," his faithful Fido writes, "I was as much perplexed as revolted. . . . If this was the way of *Homo superior*, I said, thank God I was another species . . . ." At first he is not convinced by John's explanation that "Had we been members of your species . . . what we did would have been a crime. . . . But just as you kill wolves and tigers so that the far brighter spirits of men flourish, so we killed those unfortunate creatures. . . ." But finally he yields abjectly, writing, "Such is my faith in John, that though I cannot approve, I cannot condemn. . . . John, I feel, *must* be right."

With the second example of self-justifying mass slaughter he has even more difficulty; since the victims were the inhabitants of the island on which John sought to found his colony, its owners by right of prior possession. They are, moreover, victims of a kind of unfair psychological warfare; persuaded by ritual hocus-pocus that the invaders are "gods," and that they must therefore lie down on a funeral pyre of their own making and await the flames that will destroy them. Such genocidal final solutions, Fido is uncomfortably aware, have long been the stock-in-trade of European colonizers justifying expansionist greed with talk of "taking up the White Man's Burden"; and he is hard put to it to say how John's plea of "taking up the Superman's burden" is morally less reprehensible. At least, he assures himself, these supernormal imperialists carried out their task in "the cleanest possible way," i.e., frankly and in an instant, rather than hypocritically and over the long haul with the "gifts" of baptism, booze, modest clothing, syphilis, and tuberculosis. Even this, however, does not quite satisfy him; and so he ends like a devout Christian, confronted by the inscrutable justice of God, "kissing the rod": "But who am I that I should judge beings who in daily contact with me proved themselves my superiors not only in intelligence but in moral insight?"

Fido's solution and Stapledon's apparent endorsement of it, pose it seems to me even knottier problems, esthetic as well as moral, for readers of the book. Nowhere in the whole body of Stapledon's work is the contradiction between his avowed and subliminal politics more disturbingly evident. On the conscious level, he is the heir to socialist humanism: a believer in communal decision making as well as communal goods; but on the deeper psychic levels from which his fiction comes, he is a shameless elitist—in the suspect tradition of Nietzsche—convinced that the "more fully awakened" among us (and who is to decide who they are, except themselves?) have an obligation to lead, the rest of us to follow. Moreover, to the leaders everything is permitted (after all, God is dead!) including mother incest, genocide, and cannibalism; since only by the flouting of the taboos, not just of Christianity but of liberalism, can a utopian community be created in the midst of the shambles to which Homo sapiens has reduced his world.

It is a notion that Heinlein was to elaborate fictionally and
Charles Manson, for whom *Stranger in a Strange Land* was
Scripture, was to attempt embarrassingly to translate into "real
life."

Skillfully and insidiously, Stapledon allows us to identify
both with the supercilious Superman who spurns our dearest
pieties and with the self-depreciating ordinary human who
relishes such sacrilege. But this means that *Odd John* functions much like pornography: permitting us to indulge simultaneously the sadist daydream of exercising absolute power
over an adoring victim and masochist reverie of submitting
absolutely to the power of such a beloved. Such an analysis
perhaps takes too seriously a work which Stapledon himself
indicated in his subtitle is ambiguously suspended "between
jest and earnest." I for one do not choose to believe him, however, finding the esthetic strength of *Odd John* in its appeal,
at psychic depths where the distinction between jest and earnest is meaningless, to leftover infantile fantasies of absolute
omnipotence and utter dependence.

Toward the end of the book John is portrayed as *beginning*
at last to grow up, and in doing so becomes a little less the
moral *provocateur.* He concedes, for instance, that despite their
inveterate stupidity and selfishness, ordinary humans possess
some endearing qualities. Moreover, just before his death, he
makes a declaration of love to Fido, whom he has recalled to
the island: "Yes, say in the biography that I loved you very
much." So, too, Lo, his best-beloved, declares, "We do love
you, Fido"; then adds, "If they were all like you domestic,
there'd have been no trouble"; reminding us, uncomfortably,
of Humpty's prediction in *Last Men in London* that someday
a colony of supernormals would "domesticate such members
of the subhuman hordes as it required for its own uses."

Finally, John decides *not* to destroy the human forces who
invade their island, as it is within his power to do. What mo-
tivates him, however, is not "humanitarianism," but a realization that a long war would leave him and his cohorts no
longer "fit mentally . . . for the founding of a finer species,
and for worship." "Perhaps if we were thirty years older . . ."
he ruefully muses, knowing that they are—as Stapledon never
tires of reminding us—still only kids. It is, in fact, with the

heedless zest of kids that after the decision to destroy their enemies totally, they use psychological warfare to turn against each other a horde of drunken "hooligans" sent ashore to destroy them.

It is, at any rate, with those slaughtered bodies heaped up on the beach, and with a battleship representing the Great Pacific Powers lying at anchor in the harbor that John and his remaining colonists (some have already willed their own death when threatened with arrest) blow themselves up. So powerful is the blast that it destroys not just them, but all their buildings, gardens, and works of art; indeed, the island itself, whose sinking creates a kind of *tsunami*, which washes overboard half the "sub-human" crew of the threatening vessel. We do not see the mass suicide and murder directly, however, we only learn of it through a vision vouchsafed to Pax by John and reported by her to Fido, along with the news that before their death John and Lo were "like lovers at last." It is fitting that the final words of the book be neither John's nor his faithful hound's, but those of the mother who bore him, bedded him, and, in some sense, presided over his death: "Suddenly there was blinding light and noise and pain, then nothing."

# 7

# THE MACROCOSMIC MYTH, OR GOD IS NOT LOVE

*Star Maker* did not appear until 1937, two years after the publication of *Odd John*. But it had been incubating in Stapledon's mind ever since *Last and First Men*, in which the Eighteenth Men were portrayed as intuiting before their end the whole history of the cosmos of which their own constitutes so small a part:

> In the beginning there came into existence . . . that all-pervading and unimaginably tenuous gas which was the parent of all material and spiritual existences. . . . It was in fact a very multitudinous yet precisely numbered host. From the crowding together of this great population into many swarms, arose in time the nebulae, each of which in its turn condenses as a galaxy, a universe of stars . . . and for a few moments somewhere in between their beginnings and ends a few, very few, may support mind. But in due course will come the universal End . . . .
> But the cosmic events which we call the Beginning and the End are final only in relation to our ignorance of the events which lie beyond them . . . .
> From the Beginning to the End is but the span from one spoke to the next on time's great wheel. There is a vaster span, stretching beyond the End and round to the Beginning . . . .
> The Beginning precedes the End by some hundred million million terrestrial years, and succeeds it by a period at least nine times longer . . . .

Indeed, when Stapledon manages finally to tell that longer story, all the events of *Last and First Men* are resumed in a few sentences:

> We saw Man on his little Earth blunder through many alter-
> nating phases of dullness and lucidity . . . . We watched him
> in his desperate struggle with the Martian invaders . . . we
> saw him driven, by dread of the moon's downfall, away to
> inhospitable Venus. Later still . . . he fled before the explod-
> ing sun to Neptune . . . only to be burnt up like a moth in a
> flame by irresistible catastrophe.

But in 1930, so close to the beginning of his career, Stapledon
was not ready to undertake what must have seemed to him at
that point a final as well as an all-inclusive work. He retreated,
therefore, to a microcosmic, close-up examination of the present in the main narrative of Last Men in London and in all of
Odd John.

Yet in the latter we can see the macrocosmic myth strug-
gling once more to be born, when, John tells Fido that, in their
meditations, he and some of his supernormal peers had
"glimpsed the myriads of peopled worlds, and even the minds
of stars and of nebulae." (It is the first hint of minded life on
so vast a scale.) Moreover, in their last encounter, John gives
to his biographer-to-be "an amazing document, written by John
himself, and purporting to give an account of the whole story
of the Cosmos": a work which it is tempting to identify with
Star Maker, particularly in light of Fido's comment, "Whether
it should be taken as a plain statement of fact or a poetic fantasy I do not know." More probably, however, the "whole story
of the Cosmos" to which Stapledon refers—typically making
a future fiction part of an earlier one, before launching it in
the real world—is the first version of Star Maker, left unfinished but preserved in manuscript and published in 1976 as
"Nebula maker" (the quotation marks indicating, I take it, that
the title was chosen not by Stapledon but by the editor, Harvey
Satty).

Nonetheless, as in the case of Odd John, the attribution of
authorship shifted, as the book that would eventually become
Star Maker was delivered from the novel in which it was originally conceived. Even in "Nebula maker," though it is nar-
rated in the first person singular, the narrator's "I" is clearly
not John or Fido, but someone rather like Stapledon himself.
He is portrayed, that is to say, as living in a part of the world
resembling West Kirby and involved in just such a warm but

troubled relationship with his wife as Stapledon seems to have had with his own. At the moment the book opens, in fact, he has been driven out of his "mean little villa" by a marital crisis; but as he stands in anguish on "the heathery top of the hill which overlooks our suburb and the sea," he is overwhelmed by a vision of "God creating the cosmos, watching its growth, and finally destroying it."

He is so awestruck and embarrassed by the anthropomorphic literalness of what he sees, that he spends most of the opening pages of "Nebula maker" apologizing for it:

> Anxiety for my sanity forced me to take firm hold on myself. Derisively I reflected that this was too crude, too banal an illusion for a scientifically minded person like me. Maidservants or savages might be haunted by such a phantom; but I, with my sceptical intelligence, could surely dismiss it by merely ridiculing it . . . .

Apparently the author, was afflicted by a similar sort of insecurity and snobbism; since in the final recension of Star Maker, the embarrassing hallucination is not merely moved to the end of the book, but it is reduced to a single vague and rather abstract paragraph:

> Confronted with this infinity . . . I, the cosmical mind . . . was appalled, as any savage is appalled by the lightning and the thunder. And as I fell abject before the Star Maker, my mind was flooded with a spate of images. The fictitious deities of all races in all worlds once more crowded themselves upon me, symbols of majesty and tenderness, of ruthless power, of blind creativity, and of all seeing wisdom . . . .

I do not doubt, however, that the occasion which cued Stapledon's long-deferred "last word" on the universe, was not such general reflections on power, creativity, and wisdom (which are, after all, only the Christian trinity in disguise), but precisely the "banal" hallucinatory experience that he spells out in the first section of "Nebula maker":

> . . . I recognized that an immense and dimly lucent face was regarding me from behind the stars . . . .
> The fearsome thing was spread over half the sky. And it was upside down. . . . Down toward the northern horizon loomed titanic shoulders, and far below them a confusion of many arms . . . .

The celestial face was like no other face, or like all faces.
. . . I was subtly reminded of the grotesque gods of Egypt and
India, and also of the mild enigmatical expression of certain
African carvings . . . .

Presently the apparition was transformed. I discovered that
it was no single constant face but a succession of face forms
imperceptibly changing into one another . . . . I saw it now
as a mythical beast, now a fair young man with battle in his
nostrils, now as a sphinx, now as a mother bowed over her
child, now as the child crucified, now as a jesting fiend, now
as a huge inhuman insect face with many-faceted eyes and
pincer mandibles, now for a fleeting moment as the white-
bearded Jehovah . . . .

The transformations became more rapid, more bewildering
. . . . Instead of a face there were a thousand eyes intermingled with a thousand searching or constructing hands. I seemed
to detect also, in the obscure depths of the vision, a thousand
phallic shapes, flaccid, rampant . . . .

It is a fascinating enough peek into the author's well-
stocked unconscious to make us wish for a moment that he
had not (at the urging, he tells us in the preface to *Star Maker*,
of Professor L. C. Martin, Mr. L. H. Myers, and Mr. E. V. Rieu)
revised the passage almost out of existence. Yet in the end
they were right; since the writing is flat, forced, and dull—
uninspired, as all attempts at rendering actually "inspired,"
and therefore ineffable, experiences tend to be. The inertness
of language throughout must have been, in fact, one of Stapledon's major reasons for beginning again; but there were other
good and sufficient reasons as well. He did not, for instance,
seem to know what to do with the "I" of that earlier version,
whose insufficiently explained omniscience taxes our credulity; and whom the author, in any case, keeps forgetting. In
many passages, chiefly toward the end of the fragment, in fact,
that "I" drops out of sight, or reemerges in a generalized cho-
ral "we."

It is a problem which Stapledon solves in *Star Maker* by
integrating the "I" into the myth itself; fusing him, after a
long journey through time and space, into a quite different
sort of "we," in which is focused all truly awakened consciousness in the universe: the Cosmical Mind, in short, which
for one beautiful, deluded moment sees itself as the intended
"bride of God." But to make this possible the original order of

events had to be reversed—the Vision displaced to the end,
where it could be confronted by a narrator-protagonist at a
maximum psychical remove from the simple-minded, embit-
tered husband on the suburban hilltop.

In any event, first time around, Stapledon found himself
obliged to begin with the minded Nebulae. And though his
fantasy successfully met the challenge of representing their
alien physical and psychological mode of existence (chiefly by
drawing on metaphors of the Dance), when he tried to invent
for them a politics and history, he ended up writing pop sociology. This he must have realized in retrospect, since he reduced to four pages in *Star Maker*, an account to which he
had devoted a hundred in the earlier version, de-politicalizing
it completely in the process. He was able to do so largely, I
think, because in the later version he exorcized his immediate
social concerns in a description of life on a planet which he
calls the "Other Earth," whose humanoid inhabitants we find
it easier to imagine living through crises like our own. But in
"*Nebula maker*," there was no one else except the inappropriate Nebulae on whom Stapledon could project his awareness of the menace of fascism and the imminence of war.

Small wonder, then, that as he wrote, the alien Nebulae
turned into allegorical representations of all-too-familiar human dilemmas. He could not even abide by his original resolve to imagine for them modes of existence compatible with
creatures different from us in their scale, tempo, and "ignorance of other minds." Quite like our own troubled kind, they
build empires, fight mass wars, and create a technology which
becomes their master rather than their slave. Moreover, their
cosmos is finally rent by a conflict, strangely reminiscent of
human history between "Bright Heart" and "Fire Bolt," foun-
ders of two parties: one dedicated to the creation of world
community through mutual love and the rejection of technology, the other to the use of technology in a world revolution
aimed at overthrowing the oppressors.

At this point, however, the book begins to fall apart; since
try as the half-forgotten narrator will, he cannot convince us
that either of these solutions bears on the larger questions
raised by his initial Vision; nor committed to sterile allegory,
can Stapledon do justice to the cosmic myth which had for so

long possessed him. Indeed, matters get worse as what began on a fairly high level of abstraction grows ever more specific and parochial. Postulated as the Saint and the Revolutionary, Bright Heart and Fire Bolt became particularized as the Christ of the New Testament and the Lenin of thirties pamphlets (the latter is even portrayed as being bald!). Finally, we are given in the guise of fantasy a barely camouflaged journalistic account, the real names typically suppressed, of course, of Lenin's death, the struggle for succession, the triumph of Stalin, the plotting of Trotsky, "prince of all cynics," and the Moscow Trials.

Clearly, this is a dead end; and consequently I do not believe, as Harvey Satty apparently does, that there may once have been more of the *"Nebula maker"* than has survived. Though the last section of the manuscript is labeled tantalizingly "Interlude," it marks not a transition but a final stuttering out. When he begins again *da capo*, therefore, Stapledon not only cuts out the whole tedious allegory of Bright Heart and Fire Bolt, but eliminates the improbable discussions of Nebular psychology and scoiology as well. Even the dance patterns of the Nebulae, over which he lingered so lovingly, are reassigned to the Stars; while the Nebulae themselves are poetically reimagined as great, sluggish "megatheria," "amoeboid titans," impelled by two "blind, passionate urges" to unite with one another and "to be gathered up once more in the source whence they had come."

To be sure, Stapledon preserves, as we have noted, a collapsed account of the original anthropomorphic Vision; and at somewhat greater length a creation scene in which the "Big Bang" theory of modern physics and the myth of Genesis are oddly conflated: "Then the Star Maker said, 'Let there be light.' . . . From all the coincident and punctual centers of power, light leapt and blazed. The cosmos exploded . . . ." The only scene from *"Nebula maker"* which he actually expands, however, is the description of the "torturing personal contact" which had sent the narrator out on to the hill. Dismissed in a few lines in the original version, this falling out with "the person, in whom . . . all sweetness and bitterness were together embodied," becomes in *Star Maker* a fleshed-out story, which opens and closes the book.

The cause of their quarrel remains vague, though its "bitterness" is emphasized by the repetition of the word three
times on the first page. But the suburban setting is described
this time in more detail ("Beyond our estuary, a red growth of
fire sprang from a foundry"), as if to make even clearer that it
is Stapledon's own home town where the action begins; and
the other "person" involved, whose gender was not even
specified in the original, is identified as the narrator's wife
("We were just a married couple, making shift to live together
without undue strain"), whom, like Stapledon's own, he had
"first met when she was a child" and with whom, again like
his author, he has children of his own. They have, moreover,
like the Stapledons at the time of the book's composition, been
cohabiting for so long that, despite their awareness of their
need for each other, on the husband's side at least, there is a
tendency to take their union for granted: "Coldly I now assessed her as merely a useful, but often infuriating adjunct to
my personal life . . . . We left one another a certain freedom,
and so we were able to endure our proximity."

Though finally their lifelong symbiosis becomes in the
symbolic pattern of the whole—or at least so the narrator insists in editorial asides—"a little glowing atom of community," "evidence that all men and women . . . were at heart
capable of a world wide love-knit community," the narrator's
attitude as well as the author's remain ambivalent to the end.
And the dark side of that ambivalence is confessed in a fable
that begins with the narrator's running away from home to the
ultimate Wilderness of Deep Space, in which domestic memories (rendered in terms of a lonely woman sitting beside the
fire and sewing, her brow furrowed with worry that her absent
mate may be dead) are portrayed as a sweet temptation to
abandon the quest whose rewards are incommensurably greater
than those of the hearthside. Moreover, in the course of his
centrifugal flight from home, the Time and Space Traveller
who tells the tale finds companions who prove invariably to
be males. There is not a single encounter with a female on any
of the alien worlds he reaches, and therefore as far as he is
concerned nothing even faintly resembling heterosexual love.

At least once, however, he is bonded to a fellow male in a
symbolic union much like marriage ("In time each of us came

to feel that to taste the flavour of life in isolation from the other was to miss half its richness and subtlety"), yet "spiritually" superior to it, because incorporeal, disembodied. That psychic mate, however, an inhabitant of the "Other Earth" called Bvalltu, turns out to be more alter ego than "other half": an "aging but still vigorous" philosopher, "whose eccentric and unpalatable views had prevented him from attaining eminence"; one so like the narrator, in short, that their union seems finally more narcissistic than homoerotic. Nonetheless, an American reader cannot help thinking of our own classic runaways from Rip Van Winkle to Huckleberry Finn; though, to be sure, Stapledon's refugee from home and women does not, like the latter, keep seeking forever "the territory ahead," nor like the former, return only after his wife is safely dead. Perhaps, then, he is more like certain British prototypes who make the Journey There and Back, Jonathan Swift's Gulliver, for instance, or even Enoch Arden.

Yet even these versions of the myth of Returning Home have dark or equivocal denouements; while Stapledon's novel concludes with the closest thing to a Happy Ending he ever imagined. True enough, his narrator is alone when we leave him, as he was when we first encountered him—but flooded with feelings of "peace" and "wild joy" simply at seeing the lighted windows of his house. If as readers we feel cheated because we are not permitted to enter that house and witness his reunion with his wife, we recall that we have never seen them together, never seen her at all; since *Star Maker* is essentially a male fantasy, in which women exist as faces in a crowd or images remembered in solitude. Yet marriage, though it remains abstract and offstage, as it were, is portrayed as representing the only viable alternative to a cold acceptance of horror: a last, best way of creating some small beauty in the brief instant of consciousness between the vast darkness out of which we come and not to which we return when our minuscule comings and goings on earth are over.

"Small," "brief," and "minuscule" are the operative words; since it is, Stapledon seems to be suggesting, only by knowing the pettiness of the lives we live that we can appreciate the awesome magnitude of the universe in which we live them. A further function, then, of the marriage frame story in *Star*

*Maker* is to establish a scale by which the immensity of the cosmic history it frames can be measured. "Things are of course only large and small," Stapledon writes in "A Note on Magnitude," a kind of last word appended to his novel, "in relation to one another." Originally, that appendix had been one among many entries in a glossary (preserved still in manuscript), in which he defined all the key words used in his novel; and the fact that the definition of "size" was printed should alert us to its thematic importance. Indeed, from the moment his narrator leaves the hill outside his home to begin a disembodied flight through space and time, we are made aware of the immensity of the universe through which our dwarf planet moves, the multiplicity of its inhabitants, and the complexity of their societies.

Though the lives and deaths of single individuals, be they minuscule insects or minded galaxies almost too huge for imagining, are left unspecified as in *Last and First Men*, it is not the acceleration of the narrator's passage through time which blurs them to indistinction. It is rather the ever-widening scope of his vision, as he himself without ceasing to be an individual becomes a federated community of spirits, whose compound vision is adequate to the perception of the whole. From that point of view, time is fused into eternity. Yet the "I/we" who tells the tale never ceases to be, like all of Stapledon's narrators, an historian: recounting the rise and fall of cultures, nations, empires, in a single macrohistory, at once utopian and tragic. When all the minded worlds have been delivered from war, selfishness, and mortality, when even the final conflict is resolved between the Stars and the multiform "vermin" on their satellites, it is too late to stay the entropic drift toward stasis and the extinction of mind. Moreover, though the Cosmic Spirit which Stapledon's narrator has become perceives beyond this catastrophe other universes, past and future, he intuits that they, too, will at the inscrutable Star Maker's behest flicker briefly and be snuffed out.

Later writers of science fiction, though inspired by Stapledon's example have tended to neglect his Vision of the End of Everything in favor of his macrohistory: sometimes borrowing quite out of context aeon-long episodes; sometimes trying to open up infinite vistas of their own. More often than not, however, they end by creating space-time horse operas, intergalactic feudal romances, or pseudo-epics, in which petty earthside heroism is projected upon the empty stretches between stars. Nonetheless, no matter how ineptly, they are responding to the challenge which Stapledon made clear constituted a chief *raison d'être* for the genre: to replace traditional mythologies of a universe tailored to the human scale with one which—without falsifying the findings of modern science or denying the terror they have stirred in all our hearts—can redeem them for the imagination. No one has succeeded in doing this as successfully as Stapledon; which explains, perhaps, the uniquely baleful charm of *Star Maker*, its all but intolerable appeal.

In any case, it is not size for its own sake, Stapledon explains, in his view of magnitude; "A living Socrates or Lenin has more importance than a lifeless galaxy . . . . But the spatial and temporal immensity of a cosmos favors richness of mentality. . . . The cosmos in which we live seems to have the potentiality for mental development incomparably greater than our own." To understand what he means by this, however, we must turn back to the glossary, in which the long entry under "Size" is sandwiched—for reasons, I am convinced, more than merely alphabetical—between "Religious" and "Spirit." There is no entry at all under the former heading, which Stapledon seems to have introduced as an afterthought; perhaps because he discovered that he had said all he wanted to say on the subject under "Spirit," "Star Maker," "Waking," and "Worship." Among these key terms, only "Star Maker" is new, a nonce word invented to spare the author the embarrassment of having to use (as he did earlier and would again) the shopworn name "God" for the Creator of the Universe. "Waking" had not only appeared in the title of his first attempt at popular philosophy, but along with the form "awakened" had been an essential part of his vocabulary from the start. These terms come to him not from Christian sources, however, but from an "occult" tradition, which includes the writings of Madame Blavatsky and Rudolf Steiner, and with which he carried on a lifelong flirtation.

"Worship" and "Spirit," on the other hand, are almost as closely associated with Christian doctrine as the word "God"

itself; and though Stapledon had employed them earlier, he
had never made them as central as they became in *Star Maker*.
Earlier, indeed, he had used instead of "Worship" the less
compromised terms "ecstasy" and "admiration," which do not
even appear in the glossary. Quite aware of the risks he is
running in turning to so conventional a vocabulary, he pre-
fixes both entries with an apology; beginning the one for
"Spirit," "I have dared to make use of this emotive and danger-
ously ambiguous noun . . . though now debased, it was once
a good word . . . ," and that for "Worship," "At the risk of
rousing thunder on the Left, I have used this word. . . ." In
the preface to *Star Maker*, however, in which he salvaged some
of the material from the glossary, he amended this to read: "At
the risk of raising thunder both on the Left and the Right, I
have occasionally used certain ideas and words derived from
religion . . . "; and his afterthought was more on target, since
it was from the Right that the most rabid response came: from
certain practicing Christians, to be specific, who seemed more
troubled than the Communists by the fact that *Star Maker* was
essentially a theological book—and, from their point of view,
a heretical one.

C. S. Lewis was their most articulate spokesman, actually
travestying in his second attempt at anti-science fiction, *Perelandra*, the religious notions expressed in the text of *Star
Maker*. It is, as a matter of fact, hard to distinguish the opinions Lewis attributed to his diabolically possessed scientist,
Weston, from Stapledon's beliefs at the moment of writing his
most ambitious, moving, and deeply religious novel. In *Perelandra*, Weston develops his ideas in an interchange, portrayed as having occurred on the planet Venus, between that
scientist and a surrogate for Lewis himself, a philologian called
Ransom. Just such a debate, I cannot help believing, Lewis
liked to imagine might have happened between him and Stapledon—who, alas, as far as the record shows, never responded at all to Lewis's sniping. Here, at any rate, is Stapledon as reimagined by Lewis:

" . . . I saw almost at once that I could admit no breaks, no
discontinuity in the unfolding of the cosmic process, I became
a convinced believer in emergent evolution . . . . The stuff of

mind, the unconsciously purposive dynamism, is present from the very beginning.

"... the majestic spectacle of this blind, inarticulate purposiveness thrusting its way upward and ever upward in an endless unity of differentiated achievements ... towards spontaneity and spirituality, swept away all my old conceptions .... The forward movement of Life—the growing spirituality—is everything .... The spread of spirituality ... is henceforth my mission .... I worked first for myself; then for science; then for humanity; but now at last for Spirit itself ..."

And here is Stapledon himself, summarizing in the unpublished glossary what he believed his whole text to have been saying on the subject:

The word "spirit" is also used in a more abstract sense, as in the phrase "the advancement of the spirit." Here "the spirit" is simply spirit in general, whether in the individual, or successive generations of individuals, or in minded worlds, or a minded cosmos. In this sense the word implies more than mere consciousness, since the advance consists of progress in or toward "spirituality." ...

It is, perhaps, a little hard to see exactly why Lewis finds this point of view so reprehensible, especially when his surrogate, Ransom, readily agrees with Weston/Stapledon that "God is a spirit": but their differences begin to become clear when Weston takes the argument a little further, and for the first time Ransom registers puzzled dissent:

"...Why, spirit—mind—freedom—spontaneity ... That is the goal towards which the whole cosmic process is moving .... The goal, Ransom, the goal: think of it! *Pure* spirit: the final vortex of self-thinking, self-originating activity."

"Final?" said Ransom. "You mean it doesn't yet exist?"

"Ah," said Weston, "I see what's bothering you. Of course I know. Religion pictures it as being there from the beginning. But surely that is not a real difference? ... When it has once been attained, you might then say it had been at the beginning just as well as at the end. Time is one of the things it will transcend."

But this, of course, is already a familiar notion to any reader of Stapledon—borrowed from J. W. Dunne, already at the heart of *Last and First Men*, and repeated with special emphasis at the climax of *Star Maker*:

For though in eternity all times are present, and the infinite
spirit, being perfect, must comprise in itself the full achievement of all possible creations, yet this could not be unless in
its finite, its temporal and creative mode, the infinite and absolute spirit conceived and executed the whole vast sequence
of creatings . . . .
. . . the Star Maker in his finite and creative mode was actually a developing, an awakening spirit . . . .

What finally horrifies Ransom/Lewis, however, is the notion, somehow connected with the theory of the Creator as
Spirit awakening in time, that He is double also in the sense
of compromising in his paradoxical unity everything traditional religion associates with an all-good God and what it has
projected as a quite separate force of absolute evil called the
Devil. Asked by Weston if he worships God because He is
"pure spirit," Ransom answers, " 'Good heavens, no! We worship Him because He is wise and good. There's nothing especially fine about simply being a spirit. The Devil is a spirit' ";
to which Weston responds:

"Now your mentioning the Devil is very interesting . . . . It
is a most interesting thing in popular religion, this tendency
to fissipirate, to breed pairs of opposites: heaven and hell, God
and Devil. I need hardly say that in my view no real dualism
in the universe is admissible . . . .
"Your Devil and your God . . . are both pictures of the same
Force . . . ."

Though it is, of course, more subtly phrased and qualified, a
not dissimilar view of the twi-natured Creator does indeed appear in Star Maker:

. . . the Immature Star Maker had seemed to regard the tragic
failure of his first biological experiment with a kind of diabol-
ical glee. In many subsequent creations also he appeared to be
twi-minded . . . . I was at first moved with horror and incre-
dulity . . . . How could such a vindictive deity command
worship? . . .
To excuse my worship, I told myself that this dread mystery lay far beyond my comprehension . . . . Did barbarity
perhaps belong to the Star Maker only in his immaturity . . . .
No! I already knew that this ruthlessness, was to be manifested
even in the ultimate cosmos . . . .
Was it, then, only the "good" aspect of the Star Maker that
I worshipped? No! Irrationally, yet with conviction, I gave my

adoration to the Star Maker as comprising both aspects of his dual nature, both the "good" and the "evil" . . . . Like an infatuated lover . . . I strove to palliate the inhumanity of the Star Maker, nay positively I gloried in it. Was there then something cruel in my own nature? Or did my heart recognize that love, the supreme virtue in creatures, must not in the creator be absolute?

For Lewis, this incredibly bleak perception of the nature of the Creator, and even more perhaps, Stapledon's willingness to accept and praise it, seem clear evidence that he has become first the mouthpiece for, then the helpless victim of the Dark Principle he purports to worship. In any case, *Perelandra* portrays the scientist who speaks words so much like Stapledon's as a man possessed by the Devil:

> Then horrible things began happening. A spasm like that preceding a deadly vomit twisted Weston's face out of recognition . . . and instantly his whole body spun round as if he had been hit by a revolver-bullet and he fell to the earth, and was there rolling at Ransom's feet, slavering and chattering and tearing up the moss by the handfuls . . . .

It is a judgment with which anyone not committed to the indurated pieties of high Anglicanism would find it hard to concur; but even for the most secular reader, there is something close to pathological in the relish with which the narrator of *Star Maker* celebrates the inhumanity of the Creator he perceives. It seems, indeed, only a final expected development of the abject masochism of Stapledon's earlier narrator, Fido, before the murderous coldness and contempt of his Superman. But whatever the suspect psycho-genesis of such "worship," it is proffered in *Star Maker* as part of a coherent theology or countertheology: an attempt to fill the vacuum, the hole left in man's mythological universe by the Death-of-God philosophers from the French Encyclopedists of the eighteenth century to Friedrich Nietzsche.

It has, indeed, been one of the chief functions of the post-Death-of-God literary genre called science fiction to create such a new mytho-cosmology in place of the defunct Judeo-Christian one. Sometimes science-fiction writers have done this unconsciously, inadvertently, sometimes in full consciousness; but scarcely any one has made that attempt more deliberately than Stapledon, and certainly no one has come closer to succeeding—on the level of theory, at least. Yet in some ways he came to the task ill-prepared.

He appears, for instance, to have had little religious instruction as a child; his father having been a communicant of no Christian sect and his mother a Unitarian, which is to say, a member of a church with minimal doctrine. In adult life, he seems to have joined no congregation, though he served under Quaker auspices in France and was married by Quakers after his return. His academic training, moreover, was in "modern" secular philosophy; and his dearest allegiances, to Science, on one hand, and Marxism, on the other, pulled him in the direction of anti-mythological materialism. Typically, indeed, though perhaps a little disingenuously, he presents himself in his earlier work as an agnostic, dedicated to perfecting an attitude toward man in relationship to the perceived indifference and vastness of the universe, which would be viable *whether or not a minded Creator existed.*

Nonetheless, "myth" was for Stapledon a lifelong concern; so that in the preface to *Last and First Men*, for instance, he describes the book as being "not mere fiction, but myth"; then goes on to define a "true myth" as "one which, within the universe of a certain culture (living or dead), expresses richly, and perhaps tragically, the highest admirations possible within that culture." Though he does not make a similar claim in the foreword to *Star Maker*, he uses the term through-out, and in the suppressed glossary, attempted another, fuller definition: "*Myth.* A story having some far-reaching intellectual and emotional significance. To have such significance it must express symbolically ideas and emotions that have deep importance for the people and the period to which the myth applies, and it must do this by means of concepts which are themselves alive in the minds of its public. The story must not be fully credible, but the more credible it is, the better." He then adds an expected apology and, somewhat more helpfully, an explanation of the novel's structure: "This whole book is a myth, though in many ways an unsatisfactory one. Chapters XIV and XV constitute a myth within a myth."

But the myth of those penultimate chapters postulates a Creator who can be if not known, intuited at least, or, perhaps better, directly apprehended—and who must, therefore, be "worshipped." It leads, that is to say, to a religious conversion and a commitment to bear witness by describing as clearly as human language is able the visionary experience of that ultimate reality. But this implies writing a mythic fiction which is also a theology and theodicy: a discussion of the nature of God (or, to use Stapledon's euphemism, the Star Maker) and a consideration of how that nature is consistent with the presence of evil and suffering in a world He has created. Stapledon decides, not unlike the author of Book of Job, that the Creator of the Universe is neither "just" nor "good," as men have defined these terms, but closer to what they would call "perverse" or "cruel." Nor is He motivated by the "Love" which the New Testament teaches transcends the "Justice" of the Old; His behavior (insofar as it is humanly comprehensible at all) seems esthetic or even ludic rather than ethical. From such perception of the Divine, at any rate, there emerges a cosmological myth which imagines the Star Maker creating and destroying universe after universe—for no other end than indulging a whim, like a spoiled child or a pampered artist. In this case, however, the Star Maker is also the fond parent and the indulgent audience.

Yet He is not entirely without an Other in the manifold worlds of his creating. In our own cosmos at least (which Stapledon postulates as occurring early in the series—a work, as it were, of the Star Maker's early maturity), not just matter exists, but mind; and mind aspires to become spirit, spirit to become Spirit: a single universal intelligence created by the communion of all "awakened" minds, and much resembling the imminent "God" of the pantheists. But though Stapledon's Cosmic Spirit is "like unto a god," It, or as he prefers to say, "She" is quite different from the transcendent power called "He." Indeed, from the moment when She becomes aware of her full and separate identity, She longs to be united with a divinity beyond her: her, so to speak, "Better Half."

> It seemed to me that the Star, my Maker, must surely stoop to meet me and enfold me in his radiance. For it seemed to me that I, the spirit of so many worlds, the flower of so many ages, was the Church Cosmical, fit at last to be the bride of God
> . . . .

It is odd, yet fitting perhaps, that the sole image of heterosexual passion in the main body of the *Star Maker* occurs at
so lofty a height of sublimation—evoking the allegorical eros
of the *Song of Songs* as interpreted by the Christian commen-
tators: "By night on my bed I sought him whom my soul lov-
eth: I sought him but I found him not . . . . Make haste, my
beloved . . . . " For a moment, indeed, Stapledon's myth
seems to tremble on the verge of a Happy Ending: a marriage
of fit mates, which on one level figures forth the union of Christ
and his Church, but on another reminds us of the suburban
connubial situation with which the novel begins. It all turns,
however, bitter, or at best bittersweet. The Spirit discovers that
Her hoped-for bridegroom "neither loved nor had need of
love," and is "felled like some swooning maiden left at the
altar. Yet finally She manages to assure herself—true now to
the spirit of *La Traviata* at her stoical best—that "It is infinitely more than enough to have been used . . ."; and ends
suffused with "a strange peace and a strange joy."

Nonetheless, though in the myth which Stapledon dreams,
the Star Maker exists independently of the questing Spirit; in
the explicit theology derived from it, we are told that He does
not fully and truly come into being until that Spirit "sees"
Him fully. He has, to be sure, created Her, but outside of time
(here logical inconsistency is proffered as ultimate paradox)
and, in some sense, as eternal as Himself. Yet He will continue to exist when She has been dissolved to the nothingness
which is both His absence and the absolute ground of His
being. But even this is not quite the end; since in a final turn
of the screw, Stapledon withdraws from paradox to agnosticism:

> . . . In some unintelligible manner all finite things, though
> they were in a sense figments of the absolute spirit, were also
> essential to the very existence of the absolute spirit. Apart from
> them it had no being. But whether this obscure relationship
> represented some important truth or was merely a trivial dream-
> fiction, I cannot say.

It is perhaps his refusal quite to believe his own myth—
and especially his compulsive need to tell us so—that undercuts it for the reader as well. Certainly we do not find it incredible in the sense in which the biblical account of the Creation in the Garden is incredible, i.e., outside the ordinary

parameters of belief and disbelief. Besides, it is too abstruse
and theoretical, not finally a story at all, but a kind of exegisis
in quest of a story, a Talmud without the Five Books of Moses.
It lacks, to begin with, particular names with mythological
resonance, like Eve, Adam, Lilith, Satan; and specific images
as well, icons more multivalent than the sum total of their
verbal interpretations. Such images, rich with allusions to leg-
ends and fables already in our consciousness, were present in
the shamelessly "anthropomorphic" Vision of "Nebula maker."
But even there, they seemed already mythology once removed, archetypal stories evoked rather than invented, as in
Eliot's The Waste Land or James Joyce's Ulysses. Here, even
such secondary myth has been rejected in favor of theological
explication. It is as if Stapledon had forgotten his own conviction, expressed in the glossary, that to be fully acceptable to
the ordinary readers myth must be based on "concepts . . .
alive in the minds of its public . . . the more credible . . . the
better." Or maybe he was simply too sophisticated to be able
to apply it.

    Certainly it seems an advantage in our own time to be na-
ive about these matters; since too much self-consciousness
tends to inhibit the mythopoeic power inherent in, say, the
characters and fables of Bram Stoker's Dracula, Edgar Rice
Burrough's Tarzan of the Apes, or Robert Heinlein's Stranger
in a Strange Land. Yet even the most sophisticated of artists
can, on occasion, create truly mythic fictions, primary mythological personae; as, for instance, Vladimir Nabokov did in
Lolita, and James Joyce in the latter part of Ulysses, where the
archetypal Leopold Bloom takes over from the autobiographical Stephen Daedalus. In Star Maker, Stapledon comes closer
to doing so in Chapters IV to XIII than in the two self-
consciously mythological chapters which follow them; or for
that matter, in the very long chapter which precedes them.
Called "The Other Earth," the latter seems to me an unfortunate digression from myth to politics, allegorical, satirical, and
unfortunately simple-minded: a betrayal not just of the novel's
essential fable, but of its unity as well.

Once Stapledon gets past Chapter III, he achieves what seems
to me the most coherent of all his longer fictions; but he was
apparently not sure how to begin. Or perhaps, he still had to

get out of his system certain notions about the "crisis" of his own era ("The struggle to emerge from an unco-ordinated, individualistic world-order to one that is consciously planned for true world community"), which the first time around he had tried to express in the obvious allegory of Bright Heart and Fire Bolt. Nor are such notions redeemed for the imagination merely by portraying the "other earthlings' as green and earless, or by moving their nostrils up between their eyes. Not even the simple-minded device of making taste rather than sight their primary sense is of much help. To be sure, for the first time in Stapledon's fiction, on this mirror planet the terran narrator is the invader of extraterrestrial minds rather than vice versa, and is therefore considered a ghost, a demon, or a symptom of madness. But the inversion delivers us only to a banal dystopia, barely distinguishable from the society we read about in our morning papers, rather than a through-the-looking-glass world answerable to no logic but its own.

It is with relief that the reader (and, I suspect, Stapledon himself) crosses in Chapter IV the border which separates the Here and Now from Neverland; and begins to move among life forms no longer obliged to function as glosses on our own, but free to work out the destinies implicit in their invention, like an extended metaphor or a conceit. I am not suggesting that Stapledon completely escaped his own conscious pieties, or his sense of needing to please the "comrades." Indeed, some of his silliest political asides come in the midst of this section of his novel; as when, for instance, he describes in orthodox pacifist terms the resolution of a particularly insane war between nations of insect-like swarms, one aggressive and the other pledged to non-resistance:

> The pacific races had the courage to disarm. In the most spectacular and unmistakeable manner they destroyed their weapons and their munition factories. . . . In reply the enemy invaded the nearest of the disarmed countries. . . . But in spite of mass executions and mass torture, the upshot was not what was expected. . . . Repression only strengthened the will for passive resistance. Little by little the tyranny began to waver. The invaders withdrew, taking with them the infection of pacifism. . . .

Perhaps the most absurd instance of such editorializing occurs when the narrator launches into what can only be read as an apology for Stalinist tyranny in Eastern Europe of 1937; though presented as a defense of societies immensely distant in space and time:

> . . . in the loosest possible sense, all were communistic; for in all the means of production were communally owned. . . . Again, in a sense all . . . were democratic. . . . But in many cases there was no democratic machinery. . . . Instead . . . a world-dictator might carry out the business of organizing the world's activity with legally absolute power, but under constant supervision by popular will expressed through the radio. We were amazed to find that in a truly awakened world even a dictatorship could be in essence democratic. . . .

In general, however, Stapledon has surrendered at this point to mythic imperatives functioning at levels far beneath such conscious pieties. He seems especially possessed by the archetype of the Quest or the Journey There and Back, classically formulated in Homer's *Odyssey*, which takes its protagonist to lands where all the polarities of consensus reality are magically fused; so that the distinction blurs between life and death, here and there, then and now, cause and effect, even yes and no. It is a world familiar enough to all of us, since we enter it each night in sleep; but only in myths can we live in it awake. On that age-old trip to Wonderland, at any rate, Stapledon takes us in *Star Maker*, but this time with a difference.

Though some storytellers have continued to imagine Wonderland up to the verge of our own time beneath the earth or on some undiscovered island, ever since the early Renaissance explorers have been expropriating one by one its customary haunts, even as the telescope has been opening up new territories to receive it. Stapledon's truly modern traveler, therefore, unlike his predecessors from Odysseus to Rip Van Winkle, finds that retreating Other Place not in some lost hollow of the hills or uncharted corner of an inland sea, but in outer space. When he reaches it, however, he finds it inhabited by creatures rather like the denizens of Faerie Land or Circe's magic isle—omnipotent, immortal, able to read the minds of ordinary men. Yet they are not reembodied remnants from the half-forgotten past, but incarnate extrapolations from a half-perceived future.

To be sure, Stapledon's cosmic voyager reaches their world

not by means as in hard-core science fiction of a machine, but of "levitation" or "astral projection," as envisaged by the occultists of bygone days. Nonetheless, Stapledon is anticipating, metaphorically, as it were, the exploration of space, which before the lapse of fifty years would have become everyday technological fact. He is responding not to an archaic need to believe in "magic," but to our quite modern need (most recently made manifest in the widespread UFO delusion) to believe that man is not alone in that vastness of space and time revealed to him by modern science; that there is something, someone out there more closely akin to us than stars and nebulae, quasars, pulsars, and black holes.

We accumulate day by day more detailed knowledge about aspects of heavenly bodies once utterly outside our ken: the lunar landscape, the atmosphere of Mars, the temperature of Venus, the nature of Saturn's Rings. But we also learn disconcertingly that everywhere we have reached with telescopes and radar, space vehicles manned and unmanned, telescopic cameras, and echoing electromagnetic impulses, there is *no life*, much less intelligence. No life on Mars or Venus or the Moon, or the satellites of more distant planets in our own solar system once populated in our imaginations. Neither do answers come to the messages we transmit beyond these parochial limits; nor, despite our watchfulness, alien spacecraft moving faster than the speed of light.

But we find this unendurable; since even those among us who have returned to the "Old Time Religion" are no longer capable of thrilling to the thought that one time only a God made in our image created life in His, confining it to this small, dying planet. Once we took the fixed or moving lights that spangle our nighttime sky as mere adornments, or centers of power which in their configurations determine our little fates. Now, however, we know them as myriad worlds with more beyond our range of sight—and cannot help asking what, then, they are *for*? Some, it is true, have imagined them our future homes, refuges provided to receive us when our sun begins to fail; and inhabited, if at all, by lesser breeds destined to give way before our technology, as the beasts of the field have retreated before our spears and guns. Even Stapledon at the time of *Last and First Men* seems to have shared this native imperialist belief, though it scarcely satisfies the deep need which nurtured it; since its scenario ends with a human population scattered through the solar system—but still *alone*.

There is, however, a rival dream, which if it has not moved more men has moved them more deeply: the dream of some day confronting on their homegrounds or ours alien life forms, benign, malign, or incomprehensible, but equal or superior to ourselves. Sometimes in the books and films bred by this fantasy those sentients turned out to be disconcertingly like the Powers and Dominions, the incubi, succubi, elves, goblins, bogeys, and demons, the centaurs and satyrs, the many-headed, many-limbed, single-eyed, sexless, or androgynous divinities of pantheons which we thought the Enlightenment had banished to our nightmares—or demoted at least to the status of hallucinations. But as the Vision which overwhelms Stapledon's narrator at the beginning of *"Nebula maker"* attests, no true god, which is to say, no enduring archetype, ever really dies.

Sometimes it seems, indeed, as if the whole post-Enlightenment project of introjecting such archetypes, pretending that what was once enthroned on Olympus or cast down into Hell, is "just in our heads," was a mistake; and the attempt to "cure" them with psycho-chemistry, depth analysis, or the primal scream an even worse error. Better by far to project them again, even in their traditional forms, as writers or archaizing fantasies, from neo-Satanists like H. P. Lovecraft to latter-day Christians like J.R.R. Tolkien, have done. But best of all, perhaps, would be to resurrect the gods and demons not by reviving old myths, but as in mainline science fiction, creating new ones, compatible with the scientific world view and, therefore, not likely to be perceived as mythology at all.

In any case, science fiction by postulating the existence of alien intelligences simultaneously satisfies two psychic needs of the post-Newtonian world: on the one hand, the need to be assured that the universe is not empty of all sentient life but us; and on the other, the need to be persuaded that the Others who seem to "possess" us are not merely fragments of our own psyches. It scarcely matters in light of this whether we imagine the aliens we have projected into outer space befriending us or invading us, delivering us from our own folly

or enslaving us to their whim, so long as they are there to
allay the child's fear of being abandoned and the adolescent's
dread of going mad. These none of us ever quite outgrows,
and indeed, modern science—in its assault on the traditional
boundaries of the cosmos and the ego—has greatly exacerbated them, as Stapledon by virtue of his own more than normal alienation and insecurity perceives more clearly than most.
His *Star Maker* is, therefore, a paradigm of all that science
fiction does best in this regard, though only where he remains
faithful to the terror that alienation and insecurity beget.

It is true enough, as Gregory Benford, a physicist and
science-fiction writer, has recently contended, that when Stapledon tries to imagine the sociology of alien worlds, "There
are no alternate realities . . . no genuinely different ways of
looking at the universe, but instead . . . a clockwork Marxism
that drives them inevitably into tired confrontations of labor
with capital, and so on." It is equally true, moreover, that his
attempts at portraying alternate technologies for such worlds
prove quite as unsuccessful. He understood little of the potentialities of technology even in his own time and place; so that
he failed, for instance, to realize that the development of "ar-
tificial intelligence" and the perfection of automated servo-
mechanisms might well imply the emergence of a new breed
of sentients in our very midst. From the time of Karel Čapek's
*R.U.R.* or Fritz Lang's *Metropolis*, the robot and the android
have haunted science fiction; but they are oddly absent from
Stapledon's work. Perhaps, though, it is not so much his invincible ignorance as his profound distaste for "the Machine"
which explains the lacuna.

In any case, he neither imagines machines as living intelligences, nor intelligent life as responding to the laws of me-
chanics. Nonetheless, for him, we must remember, everything
*not made by man* in the Heavens and on earth is living and
"minded": from the great sluggish Megatheria of the Nebulae
to the miniature flame-creatures which flicker in the coronas
of sentient Stars. Moreover, wherever mind exists, it longs for
self-fulfillment, as well as union with other mind and the
Maker of All; so that for Stapledon, impulse, desire, and esthetic whim determine even the waxing and waning of suns
and the journey through space of the galaxies. The cosmos of

*Star Maker* represents, in short, a true alternative to the dead
world envisaged by Newtonian physics, in which only the
lonely terran observer is self-moved, while everything else
continues at rest or in motion in a straight line until acted on
by some outside force. Clearly, Newton's universe is the invention of reason and expressible, therefore, in the rational
language of mathematics. But Stapledon's seems the creation
of impulses released in us in REM sleep, and describable only
in the irrational metalanguage of Edward Lear, Lewis Carroll,
or certain writers of science fiction.

When he writes in that metalanguage, rather than in the
jargon of the sciences, hard or soft; or better still, when his
words become so translucent they scarcely obscure the icons
behind them, Stapledon creates images of alienation, rich and
varied enough to represent all the nuances of our lonely plight.
Once more, therefore, we need to remind ourselves to trust the
myth and not the message, the Vision and not the exegesis.
But even before we do so, we discover that only the former
remain: the Plant Men, for example, "gigantic mobile herbs
. . . at once animal and vegetable . . . their skin was green
or streaked with green. . . . Vegetable eyes and ears . . . appeared on their stems and foliage. . . . Some spread their foliage and drifted in the wind . . ."; the Echinoderms, "a sort
of five-pronged marine animal rather like a star-fish. This creature would in time specialize one prong for perceiving, four
for locomotion. . . . Their bodies . . . were usually covered
with . . . soft spines or fat hairs. . . . The tall head often bore
a coronet of five eyes. Large single nostrils, used for breathing
and smelling and also speaking formed another circlet below
the eyes": the Nautiloids, whose "hull was a rigid, streamlined vessel. . . . The simple membranes . . . had become a
system of parchment like sails and bony masts and spars. . . .
Similarity to a ship was increased by the downward looking
eyes, one on each side of the prow. The mainmast also bore
eyes, for searching the horizon . . ."; and especially, perhaps,
the symbiotic Ichthyoids and Arachnoids, destined to play so
important a role in the history of the cosmos: "The one came
of a fish-like stock. The other was a sort of paddle-footed crab
or marine spider . . . it was covered not with a brittle cara-
pace, but with a tough pachydermatous hide. . . . The little

arachnoid, no bigger than a chimpanzee, rode in a snug hollow behind the great 'fish's' skull. . . ."

If such grotesques seem much like the bug-eyed monsters of the science-fiction pulps and comic books whom we find it so easy to scorn, this should make us rethink not our esteem for *Star Maker*, but our contempt for the bug-eyed monsters. Identifying, as we do, our essential humanity with the "normal" body image, we can scarcely conceive aliens who are not monstrously deviant, or for that matter, physiological deviants who are not alien (think, for instance, of our attitudes toward congenital malformations or "freaks"). Imagining the emergence, on the other hand, in some remote, radically different world, of an unrelated species which looks exactly like us fills us with the terror we feel in nightmares encountering *doppelgängers*, identical replicas of ourselves. There is something, I am suggesting, reassuring about the very deviance of alien life forms in science fiction, whether they are conceived of as "cute" as cuddly toys or household pets, like the extraterrestrial drinkers in the famous barroom scene of *Star Wars*; or portrayed as resembling other animal species, which though they have never submitted to domesticity, have at least long shared earth's ecosphere with us.

It is hard, indeed, to make images of sentients which do not fall into one or another of these categories, except for those based on the iconography of the old religions, which also provide a comfortable sense of *déjà vu*. Stapledon, in any case, peoples his richly swarming worlds with creatures of all three kinds. The most vividly imagined among them, however, are based on models likely to be observed by one who (like Stapledon and his wife on the rocky cliffs where he was first moved to fantasize about man's future) looks from shore to sea to sky: starfish and hermit crabs on the beach itself; kelp and sea anemones below the surface of the water, and schools of porpoises breaking it; in the air, the flycatchers and diving gulls; toward the far horizon, schooners under full sail; and above it—as light fails—planets, suns, and nebulae become magically visible. Visible and comprehensible, not only to the watcher, but (in Stapledon's deep imagination at least) to each other.

At times this telepathic, symbiotic universe seems *too*

comprehensible, too bland and euphemized to be believed. Where, we ask ourselves, has the *alienness* of the alien gone, the incommensurability of so huge an All, and the panic we feel confronting it? But the answer becomes evident before the novel's close. Stapledon has denied none of it, merely moved it from the created universe to the Creator, whose incomprehensible essence baffles language itself. Even the wildest metaphor or image of Him, would be, insofar as it was comprehensible at all, a lie. And so Stapledon attempts to suggest his essential mystery by depicting the reactions of a beholder rather than trying to describe what he beholds: "Confronted with this infinity . . . I . . . was appalled as any savage is appalled by the lightning and the thunder. And I fell abject. . . . I immediately spread the poor wings of my spirit to soar up to him, only to be blinded and seared and struck down. . . . I was blinded and seared and struck down by terrible light. . . . In my agony I cried out. . . . But no sooner had I, in my blended misery, cried out, than I was struck dumb. . . ."

Struck down, struck blind, struck dumb—through all its variations, the meaning of the metaphor remains the same: the absolute experience of the Absolute Other, who neither loves nor needs love, is an offense, an assault, a blow, too monstrous to be borne yet somehow an occasion for worship and praise. At the heart of that "worship," however, is the acceptance not just of the fact that though we are not alone in the universe we are not loved, but also that we will surely die: a bleak antifaith based on the denial of two major tenets of Christianity, that God loves us and that believing in him we shall live forever. In the structure of the novel, in any event, the encounter with the Star Maker is followed immediately by a vision of cosmic death, rather like the elegiac conclusion of *The Time Machine*, though on an immensely greater scale:

> Still probing the future . . . I saw my death, the final breaking of those telepathic contacts on which my being depended. . . . Presently nothing was left in the whole cosmos but darkness and the dark whiffs of dust that once were galaxies. Aeons incalculable passed. Little by little each whiff of dust-grains contracted upon itself though the gravitational influence of its parts. . . . But little by little the last resources of the cosmos were radiated away from the cooling lumps, and nothing was left but rock and the inconceivably faint ripples of radiation

that crept in all directions . . . far too slowly to bridge the
increasing gulfs between the islanded grains of rock. . . . And
since all change had ceased, the proper time of each barren
universe had also ceased . . . this apparently was to be the
static and eternal end. . . .

Yet Stapledon does not leave us on quite so nihilistic a
note; circling back once more (in a book finally as cyclical in
structure as the universe it envisages) to the Creator and De-
stroyer of all possible worlds, in one last attempt to define
both his nature and that of the "worship" He compels:

> It was with anguish and horror, and yet with acquiescence,
> even with praise, that I felt or seemed to feel something of the
> eternal spirit's temper. . . . Here was no pity, no proffer of
> salvation, no kindly aid. Or here were all pity and all love, but
> mastered in a frosty ecstasy. . . . Love was not absolute; con-
> templation was. And though there was love, there was also
> hate compromised within the spirit's temper . . . cruel delight
> in the contemplation of every horror, and glee in the downfall
> of the virtuous. . . . All passions . . . but mastered, icily
> gripped within the cold, clear, crystal ecstasy of contempla-
> tion. . . . And yet I worshipped.

This is not quite nihilism, perhaps, but its "positive" message offers what, in the very next paragraph, Stapledon himself calls "cold comfort" to those seeking reassurance that they
are not alone in the universe. The adjective, moreover, picks
up "icily gripped," "cold, clear, crystal ecstasy," and is reinforced by the chill clarity of the prose. It is a metaphor of
freezing which we are likely to find inappropriate to "God";
associating it with the last circle of Dante's Hell, in which the
betrayers of benefactors are forever imprisoned in a frozen
waste. But Stapledon seems to take a perverse pleasure, rather
like the Star Makers's "cruel delight" in man's defeat, in thus
cheating our expectations by similarly encasing in ice the supreme visionary moment of his book. Nor does he abandon
the imagery of eternal winter with this scene; picking it up
again when his narrator wakes upon the hill outside his home.
Even as he prepares to warm himself at its familiar fire, he remembers for one final time "the cold light of the stars . . .
with its crystal ecstasy . . . in which the dearest love is frostily
assessed. . . ."

# 8
# IN THE VALLEY
# OF THE SHADOW OF DEATH

In the five years between the appearance of *Star Maker* (1937) and *Darkness and the Light* (1942), Stapledon published no fiction, largely, it would seem, because he felt he had exhausted the mythological vein he had first tapped into with *Last and First Men*, and had worked ever since. "It will probably be my last fantastic book," he told the editor of the British fanzine *Scientifiction*, just before the publication of *Star Maker*. Certainly there is a sense at the end of *Star Maker* not only of Stapledon's having extended the limits of macrohistory as far as they would go (no more universes to conquer!), but of having used up the fictional possibilities of his two major themes: the apocalyptic End of Everything, which he had first discovered in Wells's *The Time Machine*; and the ecstatic acceptance of All, which he had first stumbled on in writing his Ph.D. dissertation. He did not abandon these themes completely, however, but tried again—as he had in both *A Modern Theory of Ethics* (1929) and *Waking World* (1934)—to present them without the trappings of fantasy in straight didactic prose.

It is quite clear that he considered his fiction and non-fiction alternative modes of presentation for what he liked to call "scientific philosophy" (he never used the term "science fiction"). Indeed, there is some evidence that he *preferred* the non-fictional mode, which permitted him to shuck the role of entertainer and assume that of teacher. The reputation he had won with his novels, however, made it possible for him to write non-fiction not on "spec" but on assignment, and for other houses beside Methuen, with whom he had hitherto published exclusively. He may even have begun to hope once more (though by this time both his parents had died, leaving him financially secure) that he could make it on his own as a free-lance writer. Between 1937 and 1942, at any rate, he completed four book-length essays, New Hope for Britain (1939), Saints and Revolutionaries (1939), Philosophy and Living (1939), and Beyond the "Isms" (1942), the first of which appeared under the imprint of his old publisher, the third under that of Penguin Books, and the last for Secker and Warburg.

Three of them were issued in a single year, the year of the outbreak of World War II, whose imminence already cast a shadow over Star Maker from the very first sentence of the preface. "At a moment when Europe is in danger of a catastrophe worse than that of 1914 a book like this may be condemned as a distraction from the desperately urgent defence of civilization against modern barbarism." The eruption of hostilities in Central Europe and the involvement of England in the conflict between the Fascist Powers and the "democracies" (the apologetic quotation marks are Stapledon's) meant for Stapledon a crisis of conscience, testing his lifelong pacifism and anti-nationalism; so that he became finally, without ever working out the theory very clearly, a supporter of his country's cause. His participation in the war effort was vicarious and peripheral, but nonetheless real. It was, for instance, his son not he who served under fire and nearly died as his ship went down; while he only served as an air-raid warden and lectured on history and philosophy to enlisted men.

But how much Stapledon understood the history of his own time, particularly the rise of Nazism, remains unclear. To be sure, he sheltered briefly in the suburban peace of his home Wolfgang Brueck, an Austrian Jewish student from Liverpool University, threatened with deportation back into the heart of Hitler's terror. And Sam Moskowitz, in an attempt to mitigate the anti-Semitism apparent in Stapledon's early fiction, describes at length Brueck's positive reaction to life with the Stapledons. But though in his later work there are no such overtly slanderous references to the Jews as appeared in Last

*Men in London*, there is also no evidence that Stapledon ever really understood the enormity of the Holocaust or was possessed by images of persecuted Jewry. What does possess him in the ambiguous image of Hitler as a kind of embodiment of the Dark Principle intrinsic to the Star Maker himself. He becomes, in fact, a major mythic persona in *Death into Life*, Stapledon's next-to-last novel, which also reveals his obsession with his own mortality, his growing sense of alienation from the present: an old man in a new world, trying to adapt outmoded values to unforeseen occasions.

Stapledon was, after all, well into his fifties when this worldwide battle fought by the young began, and he was getting ready to turn sixty by the time it had come to an end. By and large, however, the non-fiction which Stapledon published in the first few years of that war recapitulates ideas he had been exploring since the very beginning of his career. Both *Saints and Revolutionaries* and *Beyond the "Isms,"* for instance, are restatements of the dialectical interplay between ideal Christianity and pure communism, while all four of the books draw on the basic vocabulary defined in the glossary to *Star Maker*. There is scarcely a new idea anywhere; only insistent repetition, less aimed, it would seem, at converting others, than convincing himself that he had all along been right, right, *right!*

Only one of these books, I believe, was ever published in America, and none is now in print anywhere; nor would I wish it otherwise. Yet it is hard to pass over *Philosophy and Living* without a word; since it is in some ways the most ambitious project Stapledon ever undertook. In two volumes totalling 461 pages, he explicates for a lay audience in quest of enlightenment rather than diversion his double vision of the universe, in time and *sub specie aeternitatis*; concluding with an attempted reconciliation of their perhaps contradictory implications for "the wise conduct of practical life":

> . . . We may regard the human mind as having two aspects. In the one aspect a man is a finite individual; and his concern, his whole duty, is to champion the cause of personality-in-community in the human world . . . .
>
> Let us suppose, however, that he has also another aspect, in which he finds precarious contact with the eternal and per-

fected spirit of the cosmos, and in which his will tends to
conform to that spirit, in the sense that he is no longer en-
slaved to the cravings of the separate self, or even to the service of the ideal of personality-in-community . . . . He real-
ises that it is foolish and impious to demand that the universe
shall be moral . . . or that "God" shall be good . . . .

In some such manner we may try to cope with the seeming
logical conflict between the two fundamental religious experiences: between the moral protest, which seeks to alter the
universe, and the ecstatic acceptance of the universe, with all
its glory and its shame, its joy and its distress, its beauty, and
all its squalor . . . .

Much more important, however, to one interested in Stapledon as successful novelist rather than failed sage are a series of brief essays also published at this time, in which he
came as close as was possible for him to writing genuine literary criticism. In the last of the lot, for instance, a piece called
"Literature and the Unity of Man," originally delivered at a
Congress of the P.E.N. Club [an international organization of
writers] held in London in September 1941, he begins by reflecting rather defensively on his limitations as a reader. Two
"topical and idiomatic great works" in particular, he confesses, have always remained for him problematical: Dante's
*Divine Comedy* and James Joyce's *Ulysses*, which though he
respects and even admires, he has never really understood—
since he is, he notes apologetically, not merely a bad linguist
but hopelessly "obtuse." So, too, he has been baffled by other
laureates of high Modernism, including "the French imag-
ists," particularly Laforgue, "our contemporary English poets,"
and the Surrealists.

Clearly, however, these other artists disturb him less than
Joyce, who was after all his near contemporary. He was, moreover, already the darling of a critical establishment that would,
as Stapledon could doubtless foresee, always prefer *Ulysses*
and *Finnegans Wake* to *Last and First Men* and *Star Maker*.
Stapledon tries hard to be tolerant of his more difficult rivals,
adding, "God forbid that, just because stupid people cannot
follow them, they should cease to write their pregnant cross-
word puzzles." Yet from that observation, he moves on to a
position rather like the orthodox "Stalinist" condemnation of

the bourgeois avant-garde, which at the start he seemed anx-
ious to avoid:

> But excellent as this kind of literature is in itself, valuable
> as it is for those who have the gifts and the opportunity to
> appreciate it, its direct contribution to human unity must at
> present be slight. If I, a middle-class intellectual, who speak
> the same language as our modern English poets, cannot prop-
> erly understand them without help, what hope has a French
> peasant, a German engineer, a Chinese soldier?

Moreover, he goes on to ask "is there no more direct and effective way in which writers can work for human unity?"; and
in his peroration, answers, "Let us, in fact, even we moderns,
proclaim the spirit"—as presumably Joyce and Laforgue, Auden and Spender do *not*.

It is tempting to measure Stapledon's own achievement
against this theoretical model, though finally rather dis-
heartening. Though doctrinally his work abides by his own
prescription, thereby alienating the guardians of elite Modernist standards, it has never reached the wide popular audience
whose "unity" it preaches in the name of the "spirit." Its chief
hope of doing so lay not in its homilies but in the conventional narrative mode of science fiction and the futurist deep-
space mythology which Stapledon had used without ever being
quite aware of what he was doing. It is possible, indeed, that
his temporary abandonment of the novel form was in part the
result of his realization, after Eric Frank Russell had introduced him to the science-fiction pulps, that his novels were
in fact more like such escapist fiction than he had ever sus-
pected. But to understand why that revelation so profoundly
disturbed him, we must turn to his essay "Escapism in Literature," which appeared in *Scrutiny* for December 1939.

One of the most distinguished literary journals of the first
half of the twentieth century, dedicated to critical rigor and
the maintenance of "standards" according to which few practicing writers of the time passed muster, *Scrutiny* is a strange
forum for Olaf Stapledon; though its editors D. W. Harding,
F. R. Leavis, Q. D. Leavis, and L. C. Knights shared his distrust
of Bloomsbury and the academic establishment, as well as of
Joyce and the poets of the thirties. Like him, moreover, they

clung to certain bourgeois pieties, while rejecting organized
religion; and radically criticized the status quo without submitting to Marxist orthodoxy. Above all, like him, they considered both literature and literary criticism moral acts. Unfortunately however, Leavis's "standards," which have since
triumphed in English academia, leave no room in the "Great
Tradition" for Stapledon, or indeed any writer of science fiction. Certainly no book of his was ever reviewed in Scrutiny's
exclusivist pages; and though a notice of Aldous Huxley's
Brave New World did appear, that was because of his earlier
claim to be an art novelist.

Nonetheless, between September 1939, when he contributed a piece called "Writers and Politics" to a symposium on
"The Claims of Politics," and June 1940, when an essay titled
"Tradition and Innovation To-day" appeared, Stapledon was
published three times in that immensely influential magazine.
In neither his first piece nor his last, however, does he deal
with the specifics of literature. In the latter, he confines himself to high-level abstractions about socialism and conserva-
tism, science and Christianity; and in the former, hardly descends from even loftier platitudes about civilization versus
barbarism. The third, however, "Escapism in Literature," dated
December 1939, begins by talking about particular books and
his relationship to them; not, however, before he has made the
sort of self-deprecatory apology which is characteristic of him:

> . . . I must say briefly what in my view literature is, and what
> its relation is to the rest of human life. One who is not a lit-
> erary critic ought perhaps to refrain from discussing this sub-
> ject, particularly in a literary journal. The expert may be able
> to show either that my categories are false or that my whole
> view has been stated long ago, and much more aptly. How-
> ever, when fools rush in, they may with their mangled re-
> mains pave the way for angels.

He then goes on to make clear his belief that literature must
not merely express but "clarify and develop experience"; and
that, therefore, it cannot be judged solely on the basis of "ef-
ficiency of expression." Such formalist criticism is secondary.
What is primary is "the significance of the subject in relation
to the demand for the intensifying, clarifying, broadening,
deepening and unifying of experience . . . . " Moreover, such

"significance" cannot be determined intrinsically, but must be assessed in reference to "a sound social philosophy." In light of this, he contends, all imaginative writing can be categorized as "creative literature," "propaganda literature," "release literature," or "escape literature."

Though elements of "release" and "propaganda" play a subsidiary role in works of the first kind, "they are made to serve the essential literary function of clarifying and developing consciousness, of world or self." In the second, on the other hand, the writer uses clichés and slogans "simply to popularize facts, ideas and emotions with which he is already familiar"; while in the third, his goal is "the assuagement of starved needs, the release of pent-up forces"—a therapeutic use of fiction which Stapledon does not wholly spurn, any more than he does "propaganda." The latter, he contends, when used in behalf of a "good cause," may "produce a development of experience in the public, and is therefore in a sense creative," though "for the writer himself it is not an expression of developing experience . . . ."

His qualified defense of "release" is even more interesting, since among the genres included in this category, which he describes as being sometimes written "with such originality of perception and expression that they have a really quickening effect," are not only detective stories and thrillers but "romances," like, we must suppose, H. G. Wells's and his own. He is prepared, moreover, to grant that such popular forms "may benefit a wider public than that which is capable of appreciating literature of a more far-reachingly creative type." He condemns out of hand, however, "escape literature," which has an even broader appeal and which is frequently confused with "release literature"; though unlike the latter, the former has "ulterior motives" which are, he insists, "wholly bad."

There is little doubt in my own mind that when C. S. Lewis, in an essay on "Fairy Tales," defends "escape," suggesting that it is a bad word only to jailers, he is responding to Stapledon's contention that:

> The escape motive is generally an unrecognized fear, which causes an unwitting incapacity to face up to reality. A morbid blindness, a self-protective and perversely creative blindness, not only blots out the obnoxious aspect of reality but also re-

constructs the remaining characters into a coherent and lying image. This is the essence of escapism. From the purely literary point of view "escape literature" is a debased kind of literature, since it involves a gross limitation of sensibility and an insincere use of creative power . . . from the moral point of view "escape literature" is bad because it tends to prevent men from facing up to urgent moral problems.

These categories were still very much on Stapledon's mind when he returned to fantastic fiction with *Darkness and the Light*: a "caricature," he calls it in a preface dated October 1941, giving "symbolic expression two dispositions now in conflict in the world . . . the will for darkness and the will for light." These "dispositions" lead to two possible futures, one dystopian, one utopian; though both finally "somehow close knit into the dread and lovely pattern universe . . . . For light is more brilliant when the dark offsets it." In the Future of Triumphant Light, writers though tolerated and even meagerly supported are essentially impotent, their prophetic function having passed into the hands of secular mystics called "forwards."

In the Reign of Darkness, however, the authors of "propaganda" and "escape literature" (into which "release literature" has apparently been subsumed) flourish, sustained by the totalitarian regime they have helped to create:

> One of the main factors in the waning of the will for light in this period was the attitude of the intellectuals . . . above all, the writers flagrantly betrayed their trust . . . . Many were paid servants of the government, engaged in propaganda . . . . These were concerned chiefly to put a good complexion on the regime, and to praise . . . the virtues of acquiescence and obedience, and the ecstasy of cruelty. Still more numerous were the independent but futile intellectual ostriches who shut their eyes to the horror of their time and won adulation and power by spinning fantasies of self-aggrandizement and sexual delight, distracting men's attention from contemporary evils with seductive romances of other ages and other worlds . . . .

If this seems a comment cued by self-hatred, even more so does his description of a third kind of writer, clearly representing what exponents of "progressive" politics and "creative" literature have become in situations like Stapledon's own.

These saw clearly enough that contemporary society was mortally sick, and in a dream-like unearnest way they expounded their tenuous Utopias, in which there was often much common sense and even wisdom; but they preached without that fury of conviction which alone can rouse men to desperate action. And they themselves lived comfortably upon the existing system, in their flats and suburban houses . . . .

Beyond this he can imagine no really heroic artists, but only "the very few sincere and impotent rebels, who flung away their lives in vain and crazy attempts to be great prophets."

No book of Stapledon's was ever undertaken with less faith in its own *raison d'être*. "A reviewer of an earlier book of mine," he tells us in the preface, "said that it was difficult to see why such a book should ever have been written . . ."; then goes on to observe that "the fact that the great majority of books ought never to have been written must give the writer pause," especially in light of "the paper shortage and the urgency of war work." But publish it he did, leaving the question of "Whether this book has enough significance to justify its appearance . . . to the judgment of reader and reviewers."

Those readers and reviewers have by and large decided that it was *not*. It was apparently the least reviewed of all Stapledon's novels; and when it finally appeared in the United States in 1974, it had long been out of print in England, a fate, in my opinion, richly deserved. It is on all counts the most undistinguished of Stapledon's books. Nowhere are his ethnic stereotypes more blatantly obtrusive. Americans, for instance, are described as given to "extravagance in ideas, either in the direction of hard-boiled materialism or toward sentimental newfangled religion"; the Chinese as "so fastidious and so friendly" but "liable both to cold cruelty and passionate vindictiveness"; and the Japanese are "far more successful in imitating the worst features of European commercialism, than in absorbing the best spirit of European civilization." His prose style, moreover, often sinks to the level of the pulps at their weariest:

There is no need to give details of the fighting. At one time it seemed that resistance had broken, yet the Tibetan leaders and fighters maintained their irrational confidence. "Hang on, hang on," it was said. "The tide will turn." And sure enough it did.

There is a sense throughout of Stapledon's whipping himself on to perform a task he neither quite understands nor much likes—as autotherapy perhaps or out of a desire to reenter realms of his own unconscious which he had not explored since turning his back on fantasy; or maybe to reestablish himself in the minds of the reviewers. In any case, nothing really worked, though he returns as a kind of charm to the format and theme of *Last and First Men.* But the structure seems somehow arbitrary, the narrator remains scarcely realized, and the psychic intervention which extends his vision is only sketchily specified. The historical scope of the whole has, moreover, shrunk to the time span of a single human species on earth rather than of eighteen on three planets.

What *Darkness and the Light* recapitulates is merely the foreground of the first novel, a Near Future, in describing which Stapledon once more betrays his political naiveté and historical blindness. He is aware of the latter to be sure, confessing in the preface that "Certainly I, who entirely failed to foresee the advent of Fascism cannot lay claim to describe the next phase of European change." Yet much of what follows is dedicated to short-term prophecies, which range from not quite right to absurdly wrong. It is perhaps not entirely misleading to suggest that World War II "ended in a British victory of sorts." But it is an oddly parochial way of putting it, taking into account neither the massive American intervention nor the key role played by the Soviet Union; much less the falling apart of the United States and Russia after the victory, and the beginning of the Cold War.

The present-day reader cannot help being uncomfortably aware, as well, that Islam is left entirely out of Stapledon's vision, though his own childhood had been spent on or near the Suez Canal, nor does he foresee the establishment of Israel. He failed also to perceive how the early victories of Japan over imperial Britain (and later the United States) would kindle dreams of independence in the non-white peoples of South East Asia, eventuating in some of the bloodiest conflicts of our time. His two most egregious errors, however, were his failure to realize that nationalism would prove the most dynamic political force of the immediate future, and his old-fashioned notion that a chief threat to mankind in the years ahead would be the falling birthrate among the fittest and best, which is to say, white Europeans. In both his futures, at any rate, he foresees the triumph of internationalism, whether in the form of a free federation of humanity or a world empire imposed by force; and a decline in population, soluble only by an enlightened eugenics, which sterilizes the unfit, on the one hand, and breeds, on the other, a race of long-lived and fertile superhumans.

Though he predicts that America and Russia, along with China, will play key roles in creating that world state, he does not foresee either as finally determining whether that world will be benign or malign. In *Darkness and the Light*, he is somewhat kinder to America and considerably harder on Russia than he had been earlier and would be later. Yet though he foresees how by the time history had reached its crossroads "Adversity had purged Americans of their romantic commercialism" and "their cherished formulation of the Rights of Man was now supplemented by an emphatic statement of man's duties," the pseudo-utopia they create proves too "comfortable and amiable . . . stagnant and mediocre" to fulfill the spiritual possibilities of mankind. They are, therefore, overwhelmed by "the second Russian Empire, the evil offspring of man's first great though ill-starred attempt to organize society for the many rather than for the power of the few."

In the alternative world of Light, Americans are imagined as triumphing temporarily over the "not very efficient tyranny of Russia," with the revival of "a more or less benevolent and restrained capitalism"; but they eventually capitulate to the even more benevolent values of a Worldwide Communist Federation. It is, however, Tibet, which he portrays as not very different from the spiritual oasis invented in the Sunday Supplements and mythicized in James Hilton's *Lost Horizon*, that Stapledon foresees as playing the decisive role in the struggle between the Darkness and the Light. Fascinatingly, despite his insistence that the true strength of that tiny nation lay in its devotion to the "spirit," Stapledon conceives it as having, along one time track, turned back the forces of Darkness by military means, including germ warfare. To be sure, the decisive factor is, he insists, its air force, which he describes as not only "trained to the highest technical proficiency," but "one and all, conscious servants of the light." When, however, on the other track, "the pure pacifists became strong enough to blunt the edge of resolution," Tibet goes down to defeat, and the world heads toward inevitable disaster.

It is a strange, unsatisfied moment of Stapledon's life out of which this strange, unsatisfactory book emerges. A crisis of fifty-five, I am tempted to call it, borrowing the noun he used to describe the world's political climacteric and applying it to a psychological one of his own. It was, also a time of political soul-searching for him, as confronted by a war in which he did not quite believe but could not quite disavow, threatening the existence of an England whose social system he despised but which nonetheless he loved, he was forced to rethink his simple-minded earlier attitudes toward organized violence and patriotism. Besides, there was the problem of the Soviet Union (or Russia, as he preferred to call it), which had passed from the alliance with Hitler that had unleashed the attack on Poland to one with America, symbol of all Stapledon most feared in capitalism, without ever ceasing to repress all dissent in the name of military necessity and national security. Only a world revolution at the war's end, he believed, could redeem everything. But that revolution, he feared, might never come—not surely if it depended on the efforts of men like him, who seeing the Light, refused to sacrifice personal comfort in the struggle to attain it.

Yet none of this quite explains the miasma of total depression which hangs over *Darkness and the Light*, or the self-hatred which permeates it. It can scarcely be the identity crisis, typical of "male menopause," which is troubling Stapledon. For him, his own identity had always seemed problematical; providing, in fact, a recurrent subtheme for his most successful fictions, in which an uncertainty about ego boundaries is typically built into the very structure. Telepathy, mental symbiosis, and the preempting of one consciousness by another are his favorite metaphors for a range of psychic phenomena called in the language of psychiatry "schizophrenia," "split personality," and "acute manic depression." Such metaphors are, however, played down in *Darkness and the Light*, whose narrator talks vaguely about "possession" by extraterrestrials from the Far Future ("I must,

I think, have been strengthened by the felt presence of other and superhuman spectators"), but then pretty much forgets it.

What replaces them is the new conceit of the narrator's posthumous vision. "As I write this book," he tells us, "my own death must lie somewhere in the near future . . . . Seemingly it is at the time of my death, that the strange experience begins . . . ." He is aware here, that is to say, as never before of the imminence of his own death and of *having grown old.* "No young man," Hazlitt somewhere remarks, "believes that he shall ever die"; which does not mean, of course, that many young men are not obsessed with a *general* awareness of human mortality. Certainly it obsessed Stapledon throughout his prolonged adolescence, but for a while he was able to project his fear of death onto the cosmos, simultaneously magnifying the horror and protecting himself against it. In the early forties, however, he could no longer pretend—his parents ten years dead, his children grown, he himself a long-established writer—that he was at the beginning of anything. And as he became more and more aware of his impending end, he began to look back over his whole career as if he were already dead.

Small wonder, then, that his novel is shot through with evocations of mutilation and death, rendered with sadomasochistic relish. Such thematic scenes are at least plausibly motivated in the first section of the book, which deals with the victory of Darkness. Here we are prepared to accept accounts of gratuitously brutal brainwashing, not unlike those Orwell was to portray in 1984; or descriptions of public torture sessions, in which before an audience of "fascinated and nauseated spectators," leading bureaucrats of the dystopian state would "perform the office of tearing out the eyes or bowels or genitals of the sacrificial victim . . . without a qualm." Nor do we cavil at this section's ending with the portrayal of a shrunken and degenerate population eaten by rats:

> At last there came a crisis. Some climactic change covering the whole planet seems to have made life . . . more difficult for man and therefore for his parasite. Driven by starvation . . . they attacked men themselves. They began by devouring the babies whenever they were left for a while unguarded. Sleeping adults were also attacked. Sometimes a host of hungry rodents would waylay a lonely hunter, seize his legs,

clamber up his body, drag him to the ground and devour him
alive . . . .

The prose remains somehow inert. Yet a genuine nightmare struggles toward expression behind it; a vision of horror
which ends with great armies of rodents driving the diminishing tribes of sub-men into the woods, where, feeding on roots
and worms, they manage still to gather "at the full moon in
solemn conclave to chant their spells against the rodent enemy, and assert with stupid pride their superiority over all
beasts." For a moment, Stapledon's concept for humanity's self-
betrayal almost brings the words to life. But the fervor fades,
and the passage ends, oddly flat once more: "At some time or
other, unmourned and unnoticed, the last human being was
destroyed"; as if the End of Man, which had for so long
haunted him, has come to seem an anti-climax.

Similar horrific scenes are by no means absent, however,
from the second part of the book, dedicated to the description
of utopia; though here, where they enter unbidden as it were,
such nightmares achieve a prose style adequate to their horror. Only the Happy Ending we have been led to expect is
rendered perfunctorily, without resonance or conviction, as if
Stapledon's imagination is incapable at this point of sustain-
ing anything but visions of disaster:

> . . . I emerged from my vision in weariness but also in peace
> and joy, for it seemed that those new men, though I could not
> keep pace with the movement of their minds, were loyal to
> the light and well equipped to serve it, loyal to that same light
> which my own generation so vaguely sees and falteringly
> serves.

It is "new men," the so-called "secondary" ones, whom
Stapledon portrays as attaining such unspecified bliss: meaning a species of *Homo superior*, which has rendered *Homo
sapiens* redundant. We find, in short, that the triumph of Light
entails as as surely as the victory of Darkness the end of men
like us. Yet for a little while, as cosmic time goes, mankind
seems to be faring very well indeed. Out of a Communist world
state, which has conquered war and poverty forever, there
gradually emerges a decentralized "village culture," in which
handicrafts and folkways exist side by side with a limited

technology. In that ideal commonwealth, the only issues which divide men are debates over the exploration of space and the remolding of *Homo sapiens* through eugenics. Moreover, whatever way they are decided, Stapledon suggests, humanity will continue to flourish.

At that point, however, the "forwards" attain through meditation an intolerable vision of "occult" reality which calls into question the values and achievements of the world around them. In all of Stapledon's books, the ecstatic apprehension of the deepest truth about the cosmos is fraught with terror. But nowhere is it perceived as more horrendous than here:

> They had discovered, they said, that the universe of familiar space and time . . . though fully actual and no mere figment of man's mind, was but spindrift caught up by occult winds and driven along the surface of an occult ocean of existence . . . . It was . . . in order to have access to the occult reality, that the forwards had been working during the preceding centuries.
>
> At last, they said, they had momentarily penetrated to the deeper truth . . . .
>
> But the experience, far from being beatific, had been terrible. They had recoiled in horror from the unspeakable facts. Servants of the light . . . they had discovered that the light itself in their own eyes was but a subjective figment . . . . For a moment they had succeeded in opening their eyes, but only to discover a deeper and more formidable darkness. Or was it something worse than darkness?

To give some sense of that nameless something "worse than darkness" to their less-awakened fellows, the "forwards" invent a myth which though fantastic and petty, did, they affirmed, convey "the essence of that strange and desolate truth." But unlike the abstract monist myth of *Star Maker*, the Manichaean myth of the "forwards" evokes images out of popular demonology; reinforcing that childhood paranoia, which none of us ever completely outgrows—and which, I cannot help believing, must have possessed Stapledon at the moment he was writing *Darkness and the Light*.

> . . . This universe, they said, of galaxies and atoms, of loves and hates and strifes, is no more than a melting snowflake which at any moment may be trampled into slush by brawling and indifferent titans . . . . Myriad upon myriad of the snow-

flakes, each one a great physical cosmos, faltered downwards
and rested on the field of snow. The footmarks of the "titans"
. . . were areas where thousands of these universes had been
crushed together into a muddy chaos . . . . At any moment
the fundamental physical structure and substance of our own
many-galaxied cosmos might be reduced to chaos, so that in a
flash all its frail intelligent worlds would vanish . . . .

Nonetheless, the "forwards" did not preach supine acceptance of calamity; offering instead the slim hope that "brilli-
ance of spirit" might yet overcome the "titans," though only
if "a whole race . . . a whole conscious world . . . united in
most intimate spiritual communion." To do this, they taught,
all men must give up completely ordinary pursuits, art and
science, procreation, "the gentle bondage of personal love,"
finally, eating itself. Ironically, however, the immediate result
of the supreme communal effort is the deteriorating of community, along with the growth of sadistic crime, perversion,
and diabolism. Then, even as this trend is being temporarily
reversed, a "hideous epidemic" breaks out, the result, the narrator hints, not of natural causes, but of the intrusion into the
cosmos of "some obscure powers of darkness."

The initial symptoms of the disease are physical. But they
are described with an uncanny vividness which suggests that
they may be based on hallucinations which had apparently
possessed Stapledon in this darkest hour of his life; and which
he therefore felt compelled to exorcise—however improbably—at the intendedly utopian climax of his story.

The first symptom of the disease was violent vomiting and
diarrhoea. So formidable were the spasms that the gullet and
rectum might be torn and even forced outwards. . . . Another
effect was the extravagant growth of the skeleton, such that
the overstrained flesh and skin would split on every limb, revealing the bare bone. But a softening of the bony structure
was also a frequent symptom, causing the limbs to bend in
unnatural places and the head to turn as soft as an over-ripe
orange. Or the skin might grow till it became a voluminous
garment. Sufferers were often in danger of tripping on the folds
of skin trailing from their own legs. Another frequent result
was rapid confusion of sex. . . . Most distressing of all, perhaps, was the frequent and fantastic exaggeration of sexuality.
The organs became grossly distended. The secondary sexual
characters, such as the female breasts were repulsively en-
larged.

With the mention of sex, the symptomology moves from the physiological to the psychological:

> The mind became so enslaved to the pressure of the body's superabundant sexuality that . . . even the most self-disciplined found themselves swept away in a continuous orgy of fornication and all kinds of perversion. . . . Sometimes a sudden access of hate would force the patient to kill or torture whoever was at hand. . . . One common effect was a crazy dread of isolation. Another was such panic fear in the presence of other human beings that, when the patient was surprised by a visitor, he might leap out of an upper window or dash himself against the wall like a terrified bird. Yet another effect was a reduction of sensibility. Blind and deaf, without taste and smell, almost without touch, the wretched creature would snatch a morbid pleasure from the only sense that remained to rouse him to some faint interest, namely pain. With fumbling eagerness, he would tear back his finger-nails, crush his eyes, bite his tongue to bloody pulp.

The inexorable drift of the disease is toward atony, loss of affect, lethargy, catatonia—the classic indications of an acute depression, from which the whole sick litany represents perhaps a desperate effort to escape:

> . . . But in every case the final emotional state was identical and permanent. The patient emerged into profound apathy. In extreme cases he cared for nothing but the satisfaction of bodily needs of nutrition and excretion . . . so that, if left to himself, he might lie inert from morning till night. . . . Most people recovered so far as to behave in a normal manner in respect to all simple animal impulses, but they no longer found any satisfaction whatever in the activities which are distinctively human. . . . Abstract thought, even when their intelligence was capable of it, they found unutterably boring. . . . Art no longer had any meaning for them . . . . The life of the spirit was wholly fatuous to them. The great common discipline and adventure, which they formerly accepted with enthusiasm, now stimulated them only to yawn and shrug their shoulders . . . .

But Stapledon's catalogue of the horrors consequent on the presumed Triumph of the Light does not end on a yawn. Though most of the survivors of the plague were left indifferent, apathetic, or alcoholic—addicted to what had proved the sole effective antidote—a saving remnant survived in Tibet and New Zealand. In these two remote oases we learn, "every woman of child-bearing age was devotedly producing a child every year," indeed, after a while with the aid of science, triplets; while elsewhere "Fornication of a lazy, unenterprising sort, was general, but procreation was prevented by birth-control." Despite the fact that missionaries from those two fertile lands eventually reversed the decline of population and intelligence, the promised renaissance of man failed to materialize. Even as a reborn scientific culture seemed on the verge of creating "a superior human type," the demonic intelligences attacked the very earth on which men lived and worked:

> . . . the surface of the planet began to suffer from immense upheavals and subsidences, buckling and cracking like the skin of a roasting apple. Prodigious volcanic eruption calcined whole countries. The seas poured torrentially into new depressions . . . or was sucked down in gigantic maelstrom . . . to issue again . . . as spouts of superheated water and steam, tearing apart the solid crust of the earth, boiling the cities, and soaring to the stratosphere . . . .

It is as if, try as he will, Stapledon cannot keep his most hopeful reveries from turning into bad dreams. Yet he makes one final attempt, imagining a new Atlantis rising from the depths of the new Deluge; and, populated by refugees from Europe and America, producing "the new human type" for which humanity had for so long yearned. Even such "secondaries," however, can live "happily ever after" in the world of Stapledon's fantasy only by utterly destroying the "primaries," which is to say, us: "In these conditions," the narrator informs us, "the primary population inevitably dwindled into extinction. The secondaries possessed the earth and proceeded in a way that seemed good to them." Or maybe it is more accurate to say that for Stapledon the one true Happy Ending is the end of Homo sapiens.

At any rate, before the next nightmare overwhelms him, Stapledon moves quickly, quickly to be done. Perhaps he had become aware at this point, that the occult "titanic" forces which have over and over again undermined his utopia come from within his own troubled psyche, and are as much the embodiment of his deepest wishes as of his profoundest fears. It is not simply a matter of a covert desire to be punished for some primal sin, perhaps that of having been born; though this plays a part. Nor are we simply confronting the familiar syndrome of the prophet of doom coming to *desire* what he has darkly surmised, in order to prove himself right in the face of his mockers. It is all of this, but something more; something which C. S. Lewis would have called "satanic," but which Stapledon's narrator has already tried more ambiguously to define: "Though pity implores that all horror should turn out to have been a dream, yet for the light's own sake some sterner passion demands that evil may have its triumph . . . Nay more! My heart demands them both."

# 9
# DEATH BY FIRE

*Darkness and the Light* was not the only futurist fantasy in which Stapledon responded to the personal crisis of finding himself an old man confronting death. In their titles, his two other World War II novels, *Old Man in New World* (1944) and *Death into Life* (1946) confess the troubled awareness of age and mortality which underlie the rather blithe sociology of the first and the fundamentally reassuring metaphysics of the second. *Old Man in New World*, moreover, ends with its venerable hero reduced to tears by the words of a privileged Jester, who at ceremonies honoring the thirtieth anniversary of a utopian New World order, reminds the celebrants "But death dogs you. . . . We are mere sparks that flash and die. . . ."

Yet is is finally the most optimistic of all Stapledon's books, as well as the briefest (some thirty-three pages of text, it seems scarcely more than a short story) and the most colloquial. It projects the triumph of worldwide revolution by 1968, and the development before the end of the twentieth century of a world state in which "psychosynthesis" and telepathy are well advanced, "sub-atomic" energy so developed that spaceflight seems to lie just ahead, and the air of the largest cities sparkling clean. Moreover, monogamy (with, of course, extramarital privileges) had been "rehabilitated," and even the dread "decline in population" has been reversed—at least in Britain, whose contingent in the Anniversary Procession is headed by "a rank of young mothers carrying babies." It is all a little too

166

pat and propagandistic, perhaps; less a freely invented fiction than a fictionalized version of the pamphlet *The Seven Pillars of Peace*, which Stapledon also published in 1944. But this seems fair enough in light of the fact that *Old Man in New World* was produced on request for the P.E.N., an organization left of center and dedicated to "freedom of artistic expression, and international goodwill."

Stapledon's "international goodwill" did not, however, at this point, extend as far as the United States. America emerges as the villain of the postwar years, which, in his imaginary future, endured a catastrophic super-Depression:

> . . . Everywhere there were ruined factories, deserted mines, streets of dilapidated houses, whole cities neglected and in ruins. Those that still functioned at all were inhabited by a few ragged and unhealthy, and mostly middle-aged, people who had lost all hope. The few boys and girls, moreover, seemed prematurely old and grim. . . .

To the Old Man of the story's title is entrusted the task of explaining that America bears the burden of guilt for helping this disaster come to pass:

> How I remember the wild hope when peace came! Never again should gangsters rule! Never again should money power mess up everything. . . . People really believed that the incubus of the old system could be shifted as easily as that! Unfortunately they forgot that everything depended on the Americans, and that those former pioneers were still stuck in the nineteenth century. The American money-bosses were able to bolster up our own tottering capitalist rulers and prevent our revolution.

To these charges, a young pilot, entrusted with flying the aged revolutionary to his place of honor in the reviewing stands, protests that "the Americans did well at first pouring food and goods into Europe without expectation of payment." But this, of course, does not satisfy the still resentful revolutionary:

> "Yes," replied the old man, "but think how the American rulers, the men of big business, when they had recaptured the state after the decline of the New Deal, used the power of the larder and the store-cupboard to establish swarms of their own people in charge of relief throughout Europe. These 'relieving' Americans settled down as a kind of aristocracy. . . . In the name of freedom and mercy they set up a despotism almost as strict as Hitler's."

Clearly the Old Man is not identical with Stapledon; since he is described as having been born during World War I to a working-class family, and having dedicated almost all of his eighty years to political activism. In many of his basic opinions, moreover, he differs radically from his author; distrusting, for instance, the institution of matrimony (a lifelong bachelor, he had experienced only a "late, desperate, childless marriage," which ended in a "stormy separation"). And he is stubbornly hostile not just to organized religion but to anything which smacks of "spirituality." He serves, nonetheless, as the author's mouthpiece on the subject of the United States. Without a clearly defined public enemy, some historical, secular embodiment of the Powers of Darkness, Stapledon was driven, as in *Darkness and the Light*, to self-hatred and the paranoic fear of occult, "titanic" forces. For his own mental health, then, Stapledon *needed* to return to the wholehearted hostility toward capitalist America with which he had begun in *Last and First Men*, and which was to sustain him in his public life right up to the 1949 Communist-inspired world conference of intellectuals at the New York Waldorf. In *Old Man in New World*, therefore, he imagines the American "bosses" not just as utterly hateful once more, but for the first time as totally defeated; and in some way the sanguine tone of the whole depends on his maintaining this Good Dream.

Yet the Old Man is in a sense the victim as well as the beneficiary of that dream; justifying in its name the rigid imposition of repressive discipline. Without such controls, he argues, the "precious old-dead-as-mutton liberal democracy" will be revived, with its hypocritical slogans: "Individual initiative, private enterprise, freedom of thought" and its long-compromised cant about "spirit," "that ancient opium." But the young man who pilots him remembers what the older one has forgotten: that the Revolution they both applaud triumphed not merely over the embattled capitalists of the United States, but over the corrupted bureaucrats of the Soviet Union as well, being led by "airmen, skilled workers and—the agnostic mystics . . . those modern saints. . . ," with their "purged and clarified *will for the light.*"

At this point, the younger man becomes the spokesman for Stapledon; "remembering forward," and therefore aware that

"individual initiative" and "freedom of thought" must become the goals of society, once regimentation has become the
chief threat. The new regime has, therefore, built into itself
safeguards against rigidity and solemnity; institutionalizing,
as it were, the anti-institutional principle. In the grand 30th
Anniversary Procession, that principle is represented by "un-
attached individuals whose task it was to clown hither and
thither beside the marchers. . . ."

> Each of these comedians was dressed in a stylized and ex-
> travagant version of some costume prominent in his own na-
> tional contingent. All were clearly meant to represent the un-
> disciplined individuality of the common man. . . . Sometimes
> they merely blundered along enthusiastically beside the col-
> umn, vainly trying to conform to the regimented conduct of
> their fellows. . . . Occasionally one of them would attach
> himself to a leader of the column, mimicking his pompous
> bearing and military gait . . .

One of them finally speaks:

> ". . . The stars give no answer. But within ourselves . . . the
> answer lies . . . And from the depth of each one of us, and
> from our community together, a will arises. . . . 'Live, oh fully
> live!' it bids us. To be aware, to love, to make—this is the
> music that I command of all my instruments. . . . And we,
> little human instruments, though death will surely hunt us
> down, and though our species is ephemeral, we shall obey.
> Weak we are, and blind, but the Unseen makes music with
> us."

His is not the last word, however. Nor does it belong to the
World's President, who takes the microphone from him to echo
the conclusion of Stapledon's first novel: "I say no more but
that your leaders, who are also your comrades, will go forward
with you to make the living music that is man."

The last words are reserved for the Old Man, speaking for
what in a tired and aging Stapledon still resists waking to a
wisdom that transcends social utility. "Oh yes, it was a great
feat of stage-craft," he says of the interchange between Jester
and President. "One could not but be moved. But it was dangerous, and subtly false to the spirit of the Revolution. . . . It
was all a cunning bid for popularity. Worse, it was a reversion
to religion. . . . Where would this thing end?" Yet even this
response is not quite final; since the author, who is both the

Old Man and the young, adds, in a muted prose, scarcely distinguishable from that of the Old Man's interior monologue,
"But tears were in his eyes."

Clearly, Stapledon after his return to fiction found it hard to
achieve a proper fictional voice, as well as to rediscover a viable fictional subject. The latter, however, seemed to him an
easier problem. He would simply revive the formula which
had brought him success: mingling macrohistory with a tragic
vision that transcended time. It had worked well in *Last and
First Men* and, following the failures of *Last Men in London*
and the radio play, *Far Future Calling*, spectacularly in *Star
Maker*. So why not once more? or twice? or three times, if he
lived so long? But it did not work in either *Darkness and the
Light* or *Old Man in New World*, the former turning out unen-
durably incoherent, and the latter unredeemably slight. In both,
moreover, Stapledon was unable to recapture the temporal and
spatial magnitude which his readers had come to think of as
the hallmark of his fiction. In *Darkness and the Light*, the time
span had shrunk, as we have already observed, to the lifetime
of a single human species, and the arena of action to our tiny
earth; while the main plot in *Old Man in New World* occurs
in one day. Even in retrospect (there is *no* prospect), it covers
only half a century, and its events are confined almost entirely
to the city of London.

Besides, in neither of these books does Stapledon manage
to evoke the secular-mystic encounter with the ineffable Creator. In the former, he reaches no further than an apprehension of "ultimate horror" in the form of the "titanic" destroyers (there is a hint that beyond their seemingly final darkness,
there may be "the true light," but it comes to nothing); and in
the latter, ends with a couple of cryptic references to the "Unseen," who remains just that. He failed in both instances,
moreover, to imagine a "possessed" or telepathically reinforced narrator capable of seeing any further or deeper. Finally, in neither case did he attain a level of language capable
of evoking the old grandeurs. It seems, indeed, as if he had
lost faith not only in the Far Future and the icy ecstasy, but
in the old-fashioned high rhetoric which he had sustained in

a time when its overstuffed Victorian virtues were being challenged, on one side by Ernest Hemingway and on the other by James Joyce.

Though the outbreak of World War II had inspired Stapledon's return to storytelling, while it still continued the uncertainty of its outcome seems to have made successful fiction impossible for him. When the war was over, he assured himself, and its meanings could be assimilated into the cosmic myth he had been creating from the start, the spell might be broken. At any rate, he tried again as the bells were tolling for victory with *Death into Life*, his last macroscopic and metaphysical futurist novel. By 1946, when it appeared, he had already published *Sirius* (1944), in which he had employed a new fictional strategy, microscopic, erotic, and rooted in the present. But he seems to have felt it somehow irrelevant to his main concerns; returning to unfinished business—to which I feel obliged at this point to return with him, leaving for later discussion that less pretentious and infinitely more successful book. Considerably longer than *Old Man in New World*, *Death into Life* is still only half the size of *Last and First Men* or *Star Maker*, though it is padded out with seven "Interludes" and an "End Piece," some seventeen or eighteen pages of autobiographical meditations on marriage, parenthood, old age, and death, a version of one of which had been published earlier as "The Core," in a journal called *The Windmill*.

Unlike his other fantasies with bipolar titles, the last of Stapledon's mytho-histories has no explanatory or apologetic preface; only a one sentence "Author's Note," insisting, "This fantasy is not a novel." What else it might be called, however, is difficult to say. It begins as a mimetic account of a British bombing raid during the last days of the war on a target referred to as "The City," but clearly intended to be Berlin. Moreover, in its early sections, quite like a proper novel, it stays largely inside the consciousness of one of the seven members of the bomber's crew: a gunner, portrayed as a repressed petty bourgeois virgin with a limited vocabulary and a tendency to blame the world's troubles on the Jews, and whose sole redeeming virtue is his loyalty to his mates. It is a loyalty shared by the only other crew member whose point of

view Stapledon lets us enter, a working-class Communist who
has learned in enforced proximity with politically alien others
to transcend his parochial bitterness and paranoia.

However imperfectly, Stapledon would have us believe, that
confraternity of airborne warriors represents a paradigm of
personality-in-community—like the few to whom so many
owed so much (the words of Churchill on the Battle of Britain
continue to ring in Stapledon's head, despite himself), to
whom he had also alluded in certain passages of *Darkness and
the Light* and *Old Man in New World*. An impassioned bird-
watcher in fact, Stapledon had, in fiction, used images of flight
everywhere (most notably, perhaps in the description of the
winged Seventh Men in *Last and First Men*) to symbolize freedom, innocence, and a kind of ludic transport. In this para-
novel, however, in which for a while "realism" triumphs over
fantasy, the flyers are neither artists like the Seventh Men, de-
fenders of humanity's Last Best Hope, like the Tibetan squad-
rons in *Darkness and the Light*, nor an enlightened revolutionary vanguard, like the pilots of *Old Man in New World*. They
are instead dealers of death, destroyers of women and children; flattening in a brutal assault, churches, schools, and the
fragile homes of the powerless poor—all out of grim necessity,
but not without guilt.

Yet as the plane is caught in enemy fire, the guilt of the
tail-gunner is extinguished at the same moment as his frail
ego; and his spirit is gathered along with those of his dead
mates into a greater "I," the Spirit of the Crew. This in turn is
metamorphosed, in an ever-widening upward spiral of deaths
and rebirths; first, into the Spirit of all this war's victims on
either side, next, of those killed in any war, then, of the whole
congregation of the dead. And finally, it fuses the spirit of
every human, dead, living, or yet to be born, into the single
Spirit of Man. At each stage, it more easily transcends the fear
of mortality and welcomes its own dissolution. Never, however, does it cease to raise the question, "But I, I, what is it
that I really am?"—in which the identity crisis and the dread
of personal annihilation that haunt our little lives are translated to the loftiest metaphysical level without loss of their
familiar pathos.

With the emergence of the perfected Spirit of Man, the book

reaches its first plateau; and abandoning mimetic fiction Stapledon turns to myth. But myth of the Primal Adam with which he begins ("Out of that darkness he had sprung to life . . . a male child, the first true human being, off-spring of subhuman parents . . .") lacks archetypal resonance; and soon degenerates into a brief chronological account of mankind's successes and failures: the dreariest portion of the book, more like another Outline of History according to H. G. Wells than the New Scriptures it obviously aspires to be. Yet it evokes Stapledon's familiar pantheon of prophets, unnamed but recognizable: Buddha, Socrates, and Jesus, Spinoza, Marx, and Lenin, then adds another—also anonymous in the test, but clearly Adolf Hitler.

"A false prophet," Stapledon calls him, insisting that "In him the true fire of the spirit was subtly blended with the heats of personal resentment against a society that had scorned him." It is fascinating, I think, that of all the political leaders granted quasi-mythological status by the horrors of World War II, only Hitler possessed Stapledon's imagination. Nor does Stapledon ever forget his "false prophet"; bringing him back for a reprise toward the book's end, as the Spirit of Man reflects on all the dead souls which have been fused into his living own. He evokes first the petty bourgeois gunner; then the revolutionary engineer; then a "saint" of the City, a committed and selfless Christian destroyed by the British bombardment; and last of all, Hitler once more—this time allowed to speak for himself:

> . . . "I did great evil," he mused, "epoch-making evil. Of my own will I wickedly did it. . . . And now I see my little hateful self no longer hateful, but transfigured. . . . Now looking back, I would not change that life. I would not have it otherwise. My evil, though in me utterly evil, was a needed feature of the whole's form. Someone had to play that part. And so I, even I, who was so wicked, find salvation. . . ."

Only then can the Spirit of Man pray his last prayer. "Strange peace possesses him. He whispers in his own being's depth, 'Oh, Thou, Thou! So be it!' "

That prayer has been wrung from him once before—as he contemplated the Spirit destined to supersede him: the Cosmic Spirit, which Stapledon tells us is hermaphroditic, but ends up calling "she." First, however, the Spirit of Man perceives a future considerably less equivocal than either of those evoked in *Darkness and the Light*, since in the millennia just ahead he foresees mankind achieving a kind of limited utopia. War and poverty will be eliminated, and technology made the slave rather than the master of men, who will learn to breed descendants viable on six planets of the solar system. Telepathy, however, will remain always just outside their grasp, nor will they ever achieve interstellar flight. As their "perfect" social order becomes first stereotyped, then comatose and the sun threatens to "nova," therefore, they will believe their doomed species alone in the universe. Indeed, by that time, they will have lost all faith in the Spirit and the dread Other they had once surmised beyond it, devoting their last hours to hedonistic orgies. Moreover, the Spirit which has survived their disbelief will not be able to outlive their demise but even as their six worlds go up in flame will be "annihilated," like the gunner, the engineer, the "saint," and the "false prophet."

Yet also like the human characters he "remembers pastly," the Spirit of Man is transfigured, metamorphosed into "an alien self that was not his familiar self yet had always been rooted in him." Though he begins by resenting his assimilation into that larger self, he finally identifies with her, embracing her "I"; and perceiving through it the life and death of worlds to come in which powers of telepathy and clairvoyance have made possible the emergence of that loftier Spirit. Because of those powers, moreover, the myriad beings of those other worlds can foresee their own inevitable death and the annihilation of the Cosmic Spirit; and they join in a concerted effort to make possible a union between her and the dread Other, "her unseen lover." But, we are told, before that yearned-for consummation, she is subsumed into "the single and essential and universal Spirit . . . the very Spirit, identical in all the innumerable spheres of created being of which our cosmos is but one."

Even then, or at least so the Spirit of Man seems to recall— brought back from his vision of the Far Future by the insistent clanging of the victory bells—the synthesis of all possible universes still aspires "for Communion with that Dark Other, her creator." But we are vouchsafed no glimpse of that final encounter, no assurance that it did, does or will ever occur. Unlike *Star Maker, Death into Life* climaxes not with a series of metaphors suggesting a vision of ineffable reality, but with a confession of invincible agnosticism:

> But the lowly spirit of Man, peering from eternity's foothills, sees only the universal Spirit, fulfilled with the beauty of all the spheres of created being, dies. And whether in that ultimate death she, like all lesser spirits may strike free; or whether, dying, she swoons into blissful union with her creator; or whether, even for her, the dark Other remains utterly inscrutable and inaccessible, the lowly spirit of Man cannot know.

Stapledon is no longer, it would seem, in that "Dark Night of the Soul" into which he was plunged after the loss of the Vision he first recorded in "*Nebula maker.*" He ends his final cosmic fantasy, therefore, not in despair and terror, but with a provisional faith that makes possible the prayer in which the Unseen becomes (surely Stapledon must have been reading Martin Buber) an intimately addressed "Thou."

> But now the spirit of Man finds his new peace still precarious . . . . And once more doubting, he fears once more for the salvation of his fellow spirits; so uncaring seems the Other, so unresponsive, so heartless. Yet, fearing, the spirit of man still adores . . . .
> The spirit of Man's mood changes . . . . The strange intoxication leaves him. And at last he complains, "The Other? What Other is there but the blind idiot, Fate, or the quite unworshipful outer darkness, the thoughtless void?" . . .
> But once more his mood changes. "At least," he cries, "if the Other is a mere projection of my own desire and fear, there is the Spirit . . . . And to the Spirit I shall be loyal without reserve." The spirit of Man prays to the Spirit, "Possess me wholly! . . . Give me the heart, the wit, the imagination, to serve effectively in your cosmical war against the darkness, and the void, and idiot Fate!"
> But no sooner has he prayed, than . . . he is seized again by the irresistible presence of the Other; so that he can only whisper, "Thou! Oh, Thou!"

*Death into Life*, whatever its merits, seems oddly out of place among the fictions produced during the last years of Stapledon's life. More characteristic of that period are *A Man Divided* (1950), *Sirius* (1944), and *The Flames* (1947); all three centrally concerned with parapsychology, human love, or some

combination of both and told by an obtuse time-bound narrator. They are, therefore, limited to our present-day earth, with
no full-scale incursions into the Far Future, and no ventures
into a past outside the memory of still living men and women.
Cosmic breadth, temporal and spatial, has given way to psychological depth. Yet the interpretations of psychological phenomena tend to be "occultist" rather than "scientific."

The two personalities of the main character in *A Man Divided*, for instance, are not explained away in medical text-
book terms like "split personality" or "manic depressive," but
are left a "spiritual" mystery. Similarly, in *The Flames*, though
we are offered the tantalizing possibility that the vision of the
parapsychologist who is its protagonist may be only "madness," the weight of the evidence seems to go against that hypothesis. In any case, his nickname, "Cass" for Cassandra,
suggests that he is indeed a true prophet destined not to be
believed. Though no other character in all of Stapledon's books
is portayed as engaged in a study of the paranormal, telepathy
and "psycho-synthesis" were on his mind from the very beginning. Indeed, the narrative method of both *Last and First
Men* and *Last Men in London* demands at least a suspension
of disbelief in those occult powers on the part of the reader.

Yet is is hard to be sure of how seriously Stapledon himself takes them, in light of the fact that those early novels pur-
port to be "myth" rather than a direct representation of reality.
Nor do his rather cryptic remarks in the preface to *Last and
First Men* help very much; since after insisting that the "fiction" of psychic communication and control from the Far Future is "not wholly excluded by our thought," he hastens to
add, that "only by some such radical and bewildering device
could I embody the possibility that there may be more in
time's nature than is revealed to us."

More helpful, perhaps, is an entry in the unpublished glossary to *Star Maker*, which reads:

*Telepathy*. Immediate, extra-sensory, contact between minds.
A mind's direct access to another mind without physical meditation. Whether such an activity can occur I do not know.
There is some striking evidence for it, but it is not yet generally accepted among psychologists. I have made great use of
this concept, partly for the very reason that it suggests the in-
completeness of our established scientific outlook. . . .

This is, however, by no means his final word on the subject, since in 1948 and 1949 he contributed three articles to a journal called *Enquiry*, whose "Editorial Advisory Panel" included not only Carl Jung, of all the onetime disciples of Freud the one most interested in the occult, and Dr. J. B. Rhine, whose experiments with the blind reading of playing cards had made ESP a household word, but also a certain D. J. West, described on the masthead as "Research Officer, Society for Psychical Research."

How deeply involved with occultist circles Stapledon had been earlier is hard to determine; though it is safe to assume that he must in his Victorian childhood have been exposed to the then reigning fad of "spiritualism." It seems doubtful though that he could have had any connections with the theosophists or the anthroposophists, or even the Order of the Golden Dawn, to which writers as different from each other as William Butler Yeats and Charles Williams, friend and spiritual cicerone to C. S. Lewis, had been attracted. But this is a matter for future biographical investigation.

What we do know is that between the middle of the thirties and the end of the forties, Stapledon had moved from the study of J. W. Dunne to the reading of such explorers of the "paranormal" as S. G. Soal, F.W.H. Myers, G.N.M. Tyrrell, Edmund Gurney, Henry Sedgwick, and A. W. Verall. As a result, his earlier doubts seem to have been pretty much resolved; so that he writes in an article called "Data for a World View," published in *Enquiry*: "It seems clear by now that overwhelmingly strong evidence for some kind of paranormal experience has in fact been established"; including, he goes on to specify, telepathic contact between minds in the same time frame, precognitive and postcognitive telepathy, clairvoyance, telekinesis, psychometry. Also, he suggests, though he seems less certain on this score, there is evidence for "communication with the dead"; the special concern, it is worth noting, of F.W.H. Myers.

Stapledon then argues that even what slim knowledge we have in these areas "makes crude materialism untenable," and "strongly suggests that the whole universe of ordinary experience . . . is but a superficies behind which are unimaginable depths of existence." These are, however, by no means new notions for Stapledon, who had conceived them in fantasy before he discovered the serious investigators who attempted to "prove" them. Nor are readers of his fiction unprepared for his most far-fetched extrapolation that "It is not inconceivable that all physical action (say of electrons and other units) is inwardly a combination of telekinesis and telepathy"; since they had encountered it earlier in Odd John's old explanation of his colony's power source.

There is, however, something new—not just in emphasis and vocabulary—in another essay called "Conflict of Wisdoms," which appeared in Enquiry for August 1949. In it, he contends that evidence for paranormal phenomena makes it clear that "When the ancient wisdom was in full flower," not only was a "good deal of sheer quackery" tolerated under the rubric of witchcraft, second sight, and magic, but "there was also prevalent a whole range of experiences that have since been almost lost," as the modern wisdom of science has prevailed. To the recovery of that "ancient wisdom," at any rate, Stapledon pledges himself in such non-fictional manifestos as this; and in A Man Divided, which appeared close to the same time, dramatizes for the first time the inextricable link between "witchcraft" and human love.

In his somewhat earlier Sirius, however, whose subtitle is A Fantasy of Love and Discord, eros itself is the only magic; while in The Flames, the paranormal pushes love's rival mystery to the periphery of the action. The major issue raised is the question of whether the telepathic communications which Cass believes himself to be receiving from a sentient flame are genuine or more figments of insanity. What society has decided on this score we know from the start, since Cass's epistle is penned in a madhouse. But for Cass himself they are real. And the eighty-four pages of this novella consequently revolve around the secondary problem of the motives of certain solar flame-creatures, trapped ever since the creation of the planets in the cooling core of the earth.

They claim that they want nothing more than to coexist with man; and plead with Cass to persuade the rulers of his world to create for them, by atomic means, a reservation of radiant heat. But Cass comes to suspect that they dream really of a total atomic holocaust (the memory of burned-out Berlin

and bombed-out Hiroshima, along with the prospect of an
apocalyptic World War III, haunts Stapledon in this little book
as in no other), which will leave them the sole possessors of
a radioactive earth; from which they hope eventually to flee
and rejoin their fellows in the sun.

The nature of such creatures had teased Stapledon's imagination from the time of *Last and First Men*, in which he writes:
" . . . we have evidence that in a few of the younger stars
there is life, and even intelligence . . . we know not . . .
whether it is perhaps the life of the star as a whole . . . or the
life of many flame-like inhabitants"; to that of *Star Maker*, in
which he tells us:

> In the outer layers of young stars life nearly always appears
> . . . in the form of parasites, minute independent organisms
> of fire, often no bigger than a cloud in the terrestrial air, but
> sometimes as large as the Earth itself. These "salamanders"
> either feed upon the welling energies of the star in the same
> manner as the star's own organic tissues feed, or simply prey
> upon those tissues themselves. Here as elsewhere the laws of
> biological evolution come into force, and in time there may
> appear races of intelligent flame-like beings . . . .

When, however, one of these solar parasites is introduced
in *The Flames*, he is considerably reduced in scale, though
rendered with hallucinatory vividness:

> Suddenly a minute white flame appeared to issue from the
> stone itself. It grew, until it was nearly an inch tall; and stood
> for a moment, in the draught of the fire. It was the most re-
> markable flamelet that I had ever seen, a little incandescent
> leaf or seedling, or upstanding worm, leaning in the breeze.
> Its core seemed to be more brilliant than its surface, for the
> dazzling interior was edged with a vague, yellowish aura. Near
> the flame's tip, surprisingly, was a ring or bulging collar of
> darkness, but the tip itself was a point of brilliant peacock
> blue . . . .

Once he has postulated the parasites in this guise, Stapledon
works out the implications of his hypothesis, with a fidelity
to its inner logic and an extrapolative ingenuity found only in
certain great metaphysical poets of the seventeenth century
and gifted science-fiction writers of the twentieth. From that
central conceit comes most of what I find genuinely moving
and memorable in the book.

But *The Flames*, though it devotes only three or four pages to the subject, deals interestingly also with love between men and women, a truly new theme, central to Stapledon's last two major novels, *Sirius* and *A Man Divided*. In this novella, however, which appeared between the two of them, such love is not only presented as tragic and doomed, but is kept, as it were, offstage. It enters first in an "Introductory Note" signed "Thos." (short, we are told, for the "Doubting Thomas" of the New Testament), who informs us that he owes "a debt of deep gratitude" to Cass, author of "The Letter" which follows and contains the main narrative. Cass, Thos. goes on to explain, "saw me heading for a most disastrous love affair, and by magic (no other word seems adequate) he opened my eyes to the folly of it." Cass's "magic," however, seems to have failed him in his own love life; which though it had begun promisingly enough with a marriage rather like Stapledon's own, as the telepathic flame-creature explains, ends in misunderstanding and death.

> . . . For many years the two of you grew ever more intimately and sweetly dependent on one another. Your tendrils entwined inextricably with hers. You knew well that deep, quiet passion or mutual cherishing and mutual kindling, the piquant delight in your endless diversity and deep identity. And you found in this experience of personal loving a significance which seemed to point beyond your two ephemeral selves . . . .

But it is Cass's obsession with the paranormal, "a vast new ocean of experience," into which his wife first timidly ventures, then draws back, which destroys their relationship. Yet precisely this disaster, the sentient flame goes on to explain, has made possible between Cass and him the "special sympathy" which makes their telepathic communication possible.

He, too, has been a lover whose love ended in grief, when after "many millions of terrestrial years" he and the androgynous "dear companion," with whom he had created "an exquisitely harmonious 'we,' " are sundered by an interstellar catastrophe:

> For a while we kept in touch telepathically . . . . But . . . communication between the terrestrial exiles and the solar population became increasingly difficult, and at last impossi-

ble. Little by little our intertwined tendrils were torn apart. We agonizingly adapted ourselves, stage by stage, to self-sufficiency. And now only memory unites us.

On the basis of their common bereavement, he argues, and the loftier love for each other created by their several griefs, Cass is obliged to help him and his fellow exiles to regain their ancient powers. But this means—Cass begins to suspect—the enslavement or destruction of the human race. Perhaps, he tells himself, the flamelet has already manipulated him, even caused the break-up of his marriage, by kindling in him the "obsession" which alienated him from his wife and in turn bred the "phobia" that led her to throw herself under a bus. Calling, therefore, on the last remants of "free will" left him, Cass douses the fire in which he has hitherto nurtured the telepathic flame, and is of course overcome by guilt:

> . . . When the air had cleared, I saw that the centre of the fire was black, and the flame had vanished. I listened inwardly for some communication, but there was silence.
> Christ! There is no silence like the silence when one has murdered a friend.

Yet what else was there for him to do, caught in an unnatural triangle, torn between the conflicting claims of human marriage and an androgynous passion which transcends sex. Not even the deliberate murder of the alien being to whom he is symbiotically bonded can quite make up for the half-inadvertent killing of his own wife. So he goes through the world destroying other manifestations of his beloved enemy (who has assured him that, in some sense, he and all his fellows are one) in hearthfires and blast furnaces, until at last he is caught and locked away with the mad. In the madhouse, however, he becomes convinced that the flames have all along been benign; or that at least the only threat to him among them are members of a sect which believes in the existence of a living God, a hypercosmological Lover, with whom they are striving to attain union. Another rival sect (to which Cass himself belongs, like the flamelet he has murdered and, for that matter, Olaf Stapledon), insists that such matters are unknowable and to pursue them vain.

The fact that Stapledon at this stage of his life entrusts the case for cosmic agnosticism to a classic paranoia, persuaded

that the believers in a God of Love are "trying to undermine
my sanity, and if I resist this threat, they will probably kill
me," dissolves it in multiple ironies. And those ironies are
even more confusingly confounded when Cass dies in a fire
which Thos. suspects he may have set himself "by focussing
the sun's rays through a large reading glass which was found
in his room."

# 10
# LOVE AGAINST DEATH, OR BEAUTY AND THE BEAST

Sirius appeared in 1944, the same year which saw the publication of *Old Man in New World* and *The Seven Pillars of Peace*; and it was followed in 1946 by *Death into Life* and *Youth and Tomorrow*, the last of Stapledon's sociological tracts for the times. Not until a year later was *The Flames* published, while *A Man Divided* did not come out until 1950. Yet I have chosen to discuss *Sirius* along with the latter, to which alone among his works it has any real affinities. Both stand apart not only because they are love stories, but because, even more exceptionally, they have as main characters nubile and sexually attractive women. This is worth insisting upon, I am convinced, because other scholars of Stapledon have somehow failed to notice it.

Curtis C. Smith, for instance, in an immensely useful bibliography which appeared in *Science Fiction Studies* for Fall 1974, describes *Sirius* as: "The Frankenstein theme in an exploration of the complex relationship between animal and human nature: the tragically isolated Sirius, a dog with an artificially heightened intelligence that makes him in some ways more but in others less advanced than *Homo sapiens*, both rebels against and longs to join mankind." And he summarizes *A Man Divided* as: "The story of Victor Smith, who alternates between long periods in the merely human or unawakened state and shorter periods in the fully human or awakened state. . . ." While in some ways this is fair enough,

*183*

particularly if one is more interested in establishing the connections of these two works with Stapledon's total oeuvre than
in indicating their uniqueness, it pays also to remember that
the former without Plaxy, the girl who loves a dog, and the
latter without Maggie, the waitress who loves a dolt, are *Ham-
let* without the Prince twice over.

Despite its similarities to *A Man Divided*, however, *Sirius*
is in certain respects *sui generis*, a sport among Stapledon's
novels. To begin with, it turns out to be—ironically enough,
since one of its major characters is an animal—the most *human* of all his fictions. Only *Odd John*, which like it descends
from the icy empyrean to the warm hearthside, is as available
to the general reader. Both are books, as Mrs. Stapledon re-
marked to Harvey Satty, "anybody could pick up and find interesting," in large part because of their erotic interest. In *Odd
John*, however, the erotic element is peripheral, muted, and
the only sexual consummation fully described is between a
mother and her son; so that it evokes in us the guilt-ridden
fantasies of childhood rather than the pleasurable experiences
of adult love.

The eros of *Sirius* is also "unnatural" and even more disturbing. It verges, indeed, on the pornographic, insofar as it
infringes on an even deeper taboo and forces us to imagine,
in graphic physical detail, the coupling of a human female
and a male animal. In this sense, Stapledon's editors at Methuen were, however cowardly, right, when they refused to
publish the novel on the grounds that many readers might find
it "offensive." It might seem as if a similar case could have
been made against *Odd John*. In it, however, the tabooed erotic
is not merely cryptically rendered and kept well offstage, but
it is incidental: a mere prelude to more important events, rather
than the very heart of an ambiguous, doomed idyll. In any
event, Stapledon managed to find a braver publisher for *Sirius*, Secker and Warburg, who also issued *The Flames*, though
why this time Methuen again demurred is considerably harder
to say.

I find it inconceivable that *Sirius* could have remained unpublished. It is not only the most salable of all Stapledon's
works (it would make, it seems to me, an eminently successful
film), but by all odds the best of his fictions—with the possible

exception of *Star Maker*. More coherent and elegantly struc-
tured than anything which preceded it or was to follow, it is
also more archetypally resonant, more genuinely pathetic, more
truly a product of deep psychic impulses for once blessedly
out of the author's control. It begins, indeed, as a reworking
of the Frankenstein myth: itself an adaptation of the more ancient legend of Faust to a moral crisis created by the rise of
modern science. Stapledon's version, however, dispenses with
the Gothic trimmings of Mary Shelley's tale, in which the quite
unspecified act of "creation" seems more like black magic than
laboratory science. Though his scientist, like hers, is insensitive to the possible consequences of his experiment and is
eventually charged by the ignorant with having "sold his soul
to the Devil," he never himself views his activity as satanic.
Moreover, what he produces, with prenatal injections of hor-
mones into an already living fetus, is not a metahuman like
Mrs. Shelley's Monster, created by revivifying scraps of mold-
ering corpses, but a dog superior in intelligence to others of
his kind. He may, it is true, have dreamed of someday applying the process to make a superman, but that scheme never
comes to fruition.

It was, in any case, specifically the notion of breeding a
superdog which had been in Stapledon's mind ever since *Last
and First Men*; in which the Third Men are described as having developed a "plastic vital art" that enabled them to produce, among other controlled mutations, an "exceptionally intelligent or sturdy variety of herdsman's dog." As practiced
by a species whose basic flaw was a tendency toward sadism,
however, that "very remarkable new art" turned out to be eth-
ically ambiguous. Though in one of its modes, it "sought to
evoke the full potentiality of each natural type as a harmonious and perfected nature," in another, it "prided itself on producing monsters." Moreover, we learn, despite the fact that
"This *motif* of the monstrous and the self-discrepant was less
prominent than the other, the *motif* of harmonious perfection
. . . at all times it was apt to exercise at least a sub-conscious
influence." Often, indeed, the Third Men ended by pitting such
hyperdeveloped beasts against each other or against humans
in "sacred" gladitorial combats. But they were also bonded to
them by a love which rose "sometimes in the case of domes-

ticated animals, to an exquisite, almost painful adoration"—
an interspecific passion reminiscent of the "strange love"
which developed between Sirius and the "fay and cat-like"
but fully human Plaxy.

The phrase "plastic vital art" suggests, however, that Stapledon may have come on the idea which he was to develop
fully in *Sirius* not in Mary Shelley's *Frankenstein* but in H. G.
Wells's *The Island of Dr. Moreau*, in which wild animals are
metamorphosed by a sadistic scientist into higher life forms
by vivisection and behavioral conditioning. In Wells's fantasy,
moreover, Dr. Moreau's unstable hybrids eventually devolve,
and casting off the human law by which their creator, in a last
brutal turn of the screw, has forced them to abide, attack and
destroy him. So, too, Sirius reverts to his "wolf nature," killing and eating a member of the species which had burdened
and blessed him with "spiritual" values in conflict with his
animal inheritance. It is not his actual "begetter," Dr. Treloney, whom he murders. But—as if in response to mythic imperatives of which Stapledon was never fully conscious—that
good doctor does die in agony, quite like Wells's bad doctor
before him. And his wife dies shortly thereafter, like the
doomed spouse of Dr. Frankenstein. Yet in Treloney's case,
though he is struck down, as it were, from the heavens, the
blow is delivered by a Nazi bomber rather than the God in
whom neither he nor Sirius, nor, for that matter, Olaf Stapledon, believes; while his wife perishes not at the hands of the
"Monster" he has created, but in simple grief.

Treloney is not portrayed, therefore, as subject to remorse
or terror over what he has done. Yet he is plagued by occasional doubts about the plight of the singular creature he has
brought into being: as when, for instance, Sirius asks, "Why
did you make *me* without a world for me to live in. It's as
though God had made Adam and not bothered to make Eden,
nor Eve . . . ," and he answers, "It's my fault that you are
more than a dog . . . . I'll do my best for you I promise . . . ."
Moreover, after his "best" turns out not to be good enough, he
confesses to his wife, "What a fool I was . . . not to foresee
this psychological trouble. I don't think I ever *really* realized
that if things went wrong with *this* experiment I couldn't just
wash my hand of it all, and start again . . . . I feel as God

ought to have felt towards Adam when Adam went wrong—
morally responsible. But "God" to that skeptical scientist is
just a metaphor; and, in any event, he has thought of himself
in relation to Sirius as an earthly father rather than a surrogate
Heavenly one. Furthermore, he acted that way, neither locking
his creature into a cage and demanding his worship, like Dr.
Moreau, nor casting him out of the Earthly Paradise and
dooming him to rebellion, like Dr. Frankenstein. Instead, he
took him into what was presumably all the paradise anyone
needed, his own home, where he loved him and raised him as
if he were just another child.

It is in some ways a quite ordinary suburban household in
which Sirius finds himself, presided over by "enlightened"
modern parents, wary about the ill effects of sexual repression
and determined to raise their young free of bigotry. Somewhat
more disturbingly, they seem equally determined to protect
them from the vulgar culture which sustains the values of that
unredeemed world. Consequently, though there are sensible
toys about, as well as good books and musical instruments
suitable for family concerts, there seems to be no radio; and
no one goes to the movies, or for that matter the popular thea-
ter. Nor does anyone attend football, rugger, or cricket matches,
much less play in them—and they all stay safely out of church.
Though the festivals of the Christian year are marked by school
vacations, there is no hint that they are celebrated at home.
No Christmas tree, no sprig of ivy, no hanging mistletoe is
ever mentioned; and the wassail bowl seems inconceivable in
an environment where no one ever overeats or overdrinks,
either ritually or just for the hell of it. Indeed the only mention of alcohol comes in *The Lamp-post, A Study of the Social
Life of the Domestic Dog*, a book we are asked to believe Sirius
tries to write, which begins: "In man, social intercourse has
centered mainly on the process of absorbing fluid into the or-
ganism, but in the domestic dog . . . the act charged with the
most social significance is the excretion of fluid."

If this is, indeed, England, we find ourselves thinking, it is
an alternative England in which Dickens either did not exist
or has been disavowed, along with the Victorian values against
which he made his sentimental, Dionysiac protest. But entering it in *Sirius* and meeting the family which inhabits it, we

know, if we are faithful readers of Stapledon, that we have been here, encountered them before. An almost identical cast has appeared in a nearly identical setting in Stapledon's earlier experiment in what Northrop Frye would call the "low mimetic mode," *Odd John*. Here once more is the doctor father with his skepticism and commitment to scientific method; the warm, not very articulate mother with her sensitivity and allegiance to domesticity; the protected children, male and female, one of them "odd"; plus the servants necessary for their comfort, and a pet dog to romp with or take for walks in the countryside. This time, however, the pet and the "odd" son have been fused into the single figure of the superdog, Sirius, who must compete for the attention of his beloved foster mother against his foster sister, Plaxy, and for Plaxy's attention against the other household pet, a cat.

It seems as if Stapledon could imagine when he turned to realistic fiction only one family; or more precisely as if he preferred to use his own as a model rather than to invent at all. Yet it was not the family into which he had been born which he re-created, but the one he had himself begotten. As we have noted, he remembered his own mother without much tenderness, and he apparently considered his actual status as an only child too lacking in conflict to be fictionally interesting. Oedipal tensions were not enough for him, and he therefore augmented them with sibling rivalry—multiplying his own two children by doubling his one son in *Odd John* and *Sirius*, and splitting his single daughter in the latter. Two kids at a time turned out, however, to be all he could handle on scene, and the supernumary others therefore tend to fade into the background in both books. When he does remember them, he bestows on them adventures which had befallen one or another of his own offspring: in *Sirius*, for instance, portraying Plaxy's hitherto almost invisible brother Maurice as having, like Stapledon's son John, gone down on a British cruiser, and being for a while thought dead.

Plaxy herself, in her progress, from childhood to attractive full womanhood, is clearly a portrait of a daughter (Stapledon's Mary was twenty-four when *Sirius* appeared) drawn from life by a loving father; and Elizabeth, her mother, is, like Pax in *Odd John*, modeled on his wife. Interestingly enough, however, the father in both these novels is not based on Stapledon himself but on *his* father. He chose, even as he approached his own sixtieth birthday and that father had been long dead, to identify with the "odd" sons, the more or less than human offspring of successful but all-too-human sires. It is as if certain old scores had not yet been, maybe could never be, settled between him and the man who begot him. He seems, therefore, to be reenacting yet one more time in Sirius's refusal to become a worker in Dr. Treloney's Cambridge laboratory his own refusal to stay in the family business. But it is not quite as simple as all that; since vis-à-vis his daughter, Treloney is Stapledon's surrogate, affording him an opportunity to exorcise both his own vestigial incestuous impulses and his lingering suspicion of (or wish for?) corresponding feelings in her.

In any event, at the point when Thomas Treloney is reluctant to send his daughter off to school, the narrator of *Sirius* tells us:

> I am inclined to think that there was another reason why Thomas was reluctant to send Plaxy away from home, a reason which, I suspect, Thomas himself did not recognize . . . . I felt that behind his detached and ostentatiously "scientific" interest in her lay a very strong feeling for his youngest child . . . . Plaxy, on her side, was always rather aloof from her father . . . . She sometimes teased him about his mannerisms . . . . She was never infected by his passion for science, but when he was criticized she sometimes defended him with surprising ardour. For this reason, and in the light of subsequent events, it may be inferred that Thomas' submerged passion for her was reciprocated. Yet many years later . . . she ridiculed my suggestion that there was any strong feeling between her and her father, arguing that, like so many amateur psychologists, I was "always looking for a parent complex."

He insists throughout, moreover, that the union after her father's death between Plaxy and Sirius represents not merely the resolution of their not-quite-sibling rivalry in not-quite-brother-sister incest, but also a kind of father-daughter incest once removed, writing, for instance: "I should not mention the problem of Plaxy's relation with Thomas did I not feel that it may throw some light on her extraordinary deep, though conflicting feeling about Sirius, who was Thomas' crowning work, and the apple of his eye."

Of the man who makes these judgments we learn little except that he is called Robert, has been a civil servant, a novelist, and at the moment the action of the book begins, has joined the Royal Air Force. Meanwhile Plaxy, after her father is killed by a Nazi bombing raid, has slipped off to keep house for Sirius in a remote Welsh cottage. But by the novel's close—though the war continues—Sirius is dead and Plaxy has married Robert, to whom she has revealed that her relationship with the dog is fully sexual and declared that "in spirit I can never be yours." ("How," he confesses, "I hated that brute Sirius. . . .") Yet, even before the superdog's death, Robert had begun to share her with him; trying hard not to imagine her mounted by a beast fresh from an encounter with some bitch in heat. Later, to be sure, he boasts that "my love for Plaxy had been from the start unpossessive; owing to the fact that I myself, like Sirius in his canine style, had sometimes loved elsewhere."

It is hard, however, to know whether or not to believe this, since his involvement in the "strange triangle" makes him a very unreliable narrator indeed. His matter-of-fact unsentimental tone, moreover, seems oddly out of keeping with a tale eventuating in a romantic *Liebestod*; though perhaps for this very reason Stapledon has chosen him to tell it. From the very start, in any case, Robert misleads us, insisting that "this book is about Sirius not Plaxy." Yet the very first word of the first chapter is "Plaxy," and for the whole of the last chapter we remain inside her consciousness, see through her eyes. The final word of the book, moreover, is "Sirius"; and most of what comes before belongs to him, too, as dog, as human or more than human, as allegory and as myth.

It is the rendering of Sirius's quintessential dogginess which seems to me the supreme achievement of the novel as science fiction. We are given first a portrait of the formidable canine body inside of which Sirius's frail, uncanine spirit will struggle to awake.

. . . In the main he was an Alsatian, perhaps with a dash of Great Dane or Mastiff, for he was a huge beast. His general build was wolf-like, but he was slimmer than a wolf, because of his height. His coat, though the hair was short, was superbly thick and silky, particularly rough around the neck, where it was a close turbulent ruff. Its silkiness missed effeminacy by a hint of stubborn harshness . . . on back and crown it was black, but on flanks and legs and the undersurface of his body it paled to an austere greyish fawn. There were also two large patches of fawn above the eyes, giving his face . . . the appearance of a Greek statue with blank-eyed helmet pushed back from the face. What distinguished Sirius from all other dogs was his huge cranium . . . The dome reached almost to the tops of his large Alsatian ears. To hold up this weight of head, the muscles of his neck and shoulders were strongly developed . . . .

Stapledon seldom lets us forget the cruel parameters which that beautiful brute's body impose on Sirius's questing super-intelligence. We see the familiar world through eyes to which it remains blurred and without color; hear it through ears to which what seems to us soothing melody is aching torment, but which can hear music beyond our range; sniff it through nostrils that can discriminate by smell person from person and mood from mood—and to which, consequently, eros depends largely on aroma. And especially, we touch it, awkwardly, ineffectively, with paws that have never become hands. It is his lack of handiness which most torments Sirius, as he attempts to realize potentialities for power and control which he can perceive though they remain forever just beyond his "grasp."

He learns, indeed, with teeth and prosthetic aids to perform certain tasks at home and in the field, besides sheepherding for which nature has so splendidly equipped him. He teaches himself, moreover, against all odds, to write; beginning, though never finishing, two books. And most improbably, he manages, despite the limitations of his speech organs, to talk—producing a series of modulated whimpers, grunts, and growls comprehensible to those who know and love him. But all of these "unnatural" efforts involve a mounting frustration, which compounded by his contempt for the benightedness of the handier but less "advanced" humans he encounters, eventuate in a wolf-like rage: a ravening desire to rend and kill. This his "awakened" spirit knows is wrong; since the taboo which forbids murder, unlike those which keep the "tyrant species" from pissing anywhere or copulating at will, is based not on repressive convention, but on ethical insight attainable only by man.

Yet men, too, kill from time to time not just "lower" animals like him, but each other, as the continuing war keeps reminding Sirius. Indeed, he learns from his maker that humans *must*, despite the eternal wrongness of murder, sometimes *choose* to kill, as a lesser evil.

> Sirius, no less than Thomas, now realized that the war had to be won, otherwise all that was best in the tyrant species would be destroyed. But he lived in the depth of the country, and he was wholly absorbed in his new work . . . Moreover, though one side of his nature was wholly identified with this glorious human species, another side was secretly and irrationally gratified by the tyrant's plight. Intellectually he knew that his future depended on the future of Britain, but emotionally he was as detached from the struggle as, at a later stage, the threatened millions of India were to be emotionally aloof from the menace of Japan . . . .

But this is no longer the dog Sirius talking; which is to say, no longer the voice of Stapledon's profoundest feeling of alienation from kith and kin, and the child's sense of being a changeling from another universe, another species. This conviction of being a stranger in a strange land, an exile in a world we never made does not die in our deep psyche, no matter how "adult" we become. But when it speaks, it fantasizes not editorializes, as Stapledon does here; rationalizing, justifying his personal plight as a long-time internationalist and pacifist, forced by unforeseen circumstances to support the war effort of a country and a class he hates, even as he secretly hates his own father and what of his father persists in himself. Nor do these casuistical asides on the war represent the only occasion on which Stapledon turns his protagonist from an alien observer of mankind into an all-too-human mouthpiece in dog's clothing.

At points in the book, when, for instance, Sirius is described as "cowardly" or "lazy," or it is explained why he prefers Browning and the early Eliot to more recent Modernist poets, he seems more like Paul in *Last Men in London*, John in *Odd John*, or Victor in *A Man Divided* than his own doggy self. But he is most out of character when, again like the young men of those quasi-autobiographical *Bildungsromane*, he makes a pilgrimage into the great world beyond his home. Here he learns (and we are once more reminded) of the suffering of the poor, the vacuity of the rich, and the inability to help either of the scientists, the intellectuals, the new poets, the old labor leaders—and especially the Christian clergy. There are problems of probability involved in giving a dog the full Cook's Tour of Contemporary Culture. But after all, as Dr. Treloney tells us, explaining why he has chosen to raise the intelligence of dogs rather than apes or even cats, "They were capable of much greater movement in our society."

Yet even their social mobility is limited; so that Stapledon does not ask us to believe that Sirius has carried on that flirtation with communism so central to the *éducation sentimentale* of other provincial young men. This he consigns to Plaxy, using the occasion to rehearse once more all his ambivalences about the Bolshevik Revolution:

> . . . For a short spell she had been a member of the Communist Party, but she had resigned, "because, though they are energetic and devoted, they're also intolerably cocksure and unfair." Nevertheless she remained very much under the influence of Marxism, though she was hard put to it to find room in Marxism for her faith in "the spirit" . . . And she insisted that if Communism was not, after all, the whole truth, then nothing short of a great *new* idea, based on Communism, could win the war and found a tolerable social order . . . .

Stapledon has no difficulty, however, getting Sirius into church, where he ends up signing an anthem from behind a screen, scandalizing the congregation, and winning the affection of a saintly priest, whom he then defeats in a theological argument about whether God is really Love. If God does indeed exist, he argues, using the metaphors appropriate to his canine senses, he is not that ultimate sweetness we at first seem to perceive, but something utterly and terrifyingly *Other*.

> "But presently, as I paced up and down the little room, a queer thing happened. It was as though my wandering imagination came upon a new quality, different from all I had ever

known; yet one which was also more familiar and intimate than the smell of Plaxy in the mood of love, more piercing sweet than bitches, more hunt-worthy than the trail of a fox.

". . . If it was a fragrance at all, it was the fragrance of love and wisdom and creating, of these for their own sake, whether crowned with success and happiness or not. . . . It was this fragrance, trailed across the universe . . . that had so often enticed me; but now in my excited state it presented itself to me so vividly that I had to dramatize it to myself as a new quality, neither odour nor sound nor visible form, but most like an odour to be pursued.

"And I did pursue it . . . and as I pursued, lessening the distance between myself and the quarry, the scent grew clear and more compelling . . .

"At last a terrible thing happened. As I drew nearer, the quality of the heavenly quarry seemed to change. Though its exquisite sweetness remained . . . a new, pungent tang, a stinging, choking, bitter, exquisite and terrifying perfume was mixed with it. There was something in it . . . fierce, like the mighty smells of tiger and lion, but with a grimness that no earthly smell ever had . . . . The thing I was hunting must surely be the source of all fragrance in the universe, and all the horror also . . . in the end surely not *I* should devour *it*, but *it* would devour *me*. Surely, the thing I was crazily hunting must be the very thing that men called God, the dear and beautiful and dread . . . ."

Nor is this quite the end; since after the first intensity of the vision had departed, Sirius tells us, the whole universe remained imbued "with a new quality, as though my monochrome vision had suddenly gained the glory of colour . . . . And even now . . . I still see everything coloured by the light of the spirit." It is a little churlish, perhaps, to resent, after so gallant an attempt, the fact that the insight attained through a dog's alien senses turns out to be so little different from that suggested in the concluding chapters of *A Modern Theory of Ethics;* and that the language and imagery are finally a bit too literary, reminiscent, in fact of Francis Thompson's much anthologized Victorian poem, "The Hound of Heaven." At least, in all of this Stapledon does not flagrantly betray his conceit and break the illusion, as he seems to me to do later, when his invention begins to flag or is overwhelmed by his desire to make it clear that Sirius represents not just the unique plight of a man-made monster, but the condition of all creatures, including ourselves, who are both "spirit" and matter.

He is already moving in this direction when he has Sirius reveal that, like all Stapledon's surrogates, he remains an agnostic even after his visionary experience. ". . . But what God actually *is*," the dog-man tells the Christian minister, "whether the maker of all things, or just a dream in our own hearts, I have not the art to know. Neither have you, I believe; nor any man, nor any spirit of our humble stature." And he threatens to dissolve Sirius completely as a particularized character into a "hideous and intolerable allegory," when in the final pages of the novel, he tells us through Plaxy that ". . . Sirius, in spite of his uniqueness, epitomized in his whole life and in his death something universal, something that is common to all awakening spirits on earth, and in the farthest galaxies"; that he is, in short, as Curtis C. Smith suggests in his bibliographical note on the book, a fictional embodiment of certain abstract ideas expressed in the non-fictional *Waking World*. While it is hard to deny the unfortunate allegorical element in Sirius, he stubbornly refuses translation one to one into some preexistent meaning; but remains to the end as evasively polysemous as a myth.

Though Stapledon does not insist on the mythic nature of his tale in the text itself, the archetypal nature of the "man-dog" is unequivocally established by his names. Called "Sirius" by his maker, Thomas Treloney, he is rebaptized "Bran" by Pugh, the Welsh shepherd to whom he is apprenticed: both appellations with mythological resonances of which Stapledon must have been aware, although he never made them explicit. Only in the very last sentence of the book does he remind us obliquely that Sirius is the name of the morning star, the Dog Star which, in the constellation of Orion, follows at the heels of that hunter, close behind the eternally fleeing Pleiades.

Much less does he inform us that the ancient Egyptians had oriented the entries to the Pyramids to make possible the observation of Sirius through his whole trajectory; or that they identified that brightest of all the fixed stars, which they called Sothis, with the god Thoth, the goddess Nut, and especially the Great Mother, Isis. Indeed, as Stapledon might well have learned reading James Frazer's *The Golden Bough*, the Egyptians began their sacred year on July 23—the start of what we

still refer to as the "dog days"—since, three or four thousand
years before Christ, that was the date at which the star Sirius
"appeared at dawn in the east just before sunrise about the
time of the summer solstice, when the Nile begins to rise." In
Frazer, too, Stapledon could have discovered the connection
of Sothis with the mystery of the slain and resurrected god
Osiris. And from similar sources, he might have found out
that for the Magi of the Persians, the Dog Star was the guardian
of Ormazd, the Divine Principle of Good, preserving mankind
by preventing the sun from breaking out of his proper bounds.

It is less likely that he knew of the crucial importance of
Sirius for such "occultists" as Gurdjieff and the sinister Aleis-
ter Crowley; though they were both his contemporaries, and
he may have been introduced to their work by his friend L. H.
Myers, who moved in such circles. From him, too, Stapledon
could have heard of the arcane speculations which identified
Sirius with the Star of the Tarot pack, and that which had
shone above Bethlehem when Christ was born. What he could
not possibly have been aware of, though it would have tickled
him immensely in light of his own commitment to both the
paranormal and the notion of interstellar communication, was
the fact that certain African tribes had long been aware of the
existence of Sirius's dark twin, only recently confirmed by
telescopic observation. On the basis of this, it has been argued
by Robert K. G. Temple in *The Sirius Mystery* and less soberly
by Robert Anton Wilson in *Cosmic Trigger* that the first contacts with humans from outer space (which may, according to
him be continuing still) originated from a planet orbiting Sirius. What is clear, in any case, is that the name "Sirius" possessed for Stapledon, and should possess for us, mythic con-
notations; and the same is true for "Bran," which he also leaves
tantalizingly unglossed.

A little research, however, reveals that its legendary roots
are in a native British tradition, surviving chiefly in folklore
and fairy tales. In Celtic lore, there are, in fact, three Brans,
one of whom is the legendary discoverer of America. But Stapledon is obviously thinking of Bran and Sceolan, the favorite
hounds of the heroic Finn MacCumhal, father of Ossian. In the
Highland version of their tale, they are monstrous beasts, won
by Finn from an ogre who ate babies, and controllable only by

a magical golden chain. But according to the Welsh, they are beautiful and so wise that they seem almost human. This is fair enough in light of the fact that they were born of a human woman, Tuiren, the sister of Finn's mother, while she was temporarily transformed, by a jealous queen of the Shi, into the guise of a bitch. Bran seems, in many ways a more fitting name for a creature, the crucial moments of whose life occur in the magic-laden back country of Wales: a talking dog, who cohabits in a lonely cottage with a human girl. It is a situation, after all, which, however strange in the everyday world of adults, is not uncommon in the Realm of Faerie, where communication between men and animals occasions no more surprise than in children's waking fantasies or the deep-sleep dreams of us all.

The archetypal fairy story, however, which possesses Stapledon's imagination at a level inaccessible perhaps to his own consciousness, is not that of Bran but of "Beauty and the Beast"; or as the folklorists prefer to call it, "The Animal Groom." It is a tale which appears in various forms in many cultures. Best known in the modern West are "Snow White and Rose Red" and "The Frog King" or "The Frog Prince," both published in France in the eighteenth century, and "Cupid and Psyche," retold from ancient sources in Apuleius' second-century Latin romance, The Golden Ass. In all of them, an extraordinarily beautiful maiden is married to a monstrous non-human creature, whom at first she finds utterly repulsive, though from the start he loves her. The threat of death, moreover, whether to the girl or those she holds dear, is present throughout (in "Cupid and Psyche," Psyche actually dies and is reborn), and she experiences their first union as a rape. But coming eventually to love the Beast, she transforms him into, or comes to realize he has been all along, a spouse not only faithful and good, but beautiful, i.e., fully human or even divine. And "they live happily ever after."

In his justly renowned study of the tale as told by Apuleius, the Jungian analyst, Erich Neumann, makes it clear that the myth which underlies it represents developing feminine consciousness as it moves from a matriarchal horror of phallic domination to a conjugal awareness of the full selfhood of both the male and the female in love. That it was a male who not merely transmitted but gave its classic formulation to this archetype, seems to Neumann more than a little puzzling. He attempts to explain it as due in part to Apuleius' having been inducted into the maternal mysteries of Isis (whose star, we remember, was Sirius/Sothis)—though even more, he suggests, to the fact that the author of "Cupid and Psyche" was "one of those creative men who, like the feminine, must give birth, one of those 'whom Psyche guides.' " So, too, we must believe, was Stapledon. But only, in the writing of *Sirius*, at the point where that book ceases to be the life story of the dog-man and becomes the love story of Plaxy (what is the mythic origin, if any, of that odd name I have been unable to discover)—or rather, of that of the androgynous beast-human, Sirius-Plaxy, which their love begets.

Though the novel actually opens with a visit of Robert to the cottage where Sirius and Plaxy have already established their strange ménage, we do not fully understand what is happening until Robert, beginning again with the creation of the superdog, has brought us step by step back to that moment. Sirius, we learn, has retreated to rural Wales from the world of "intellectuals" after his disillusionment with Cambridge and London and his growing awareness of the "wolf-side" of his nature. The latter has not only more and more tinged with sadism his coupling with bitches and his affection for Plaxy, but has led him finally to kill a ram, a pony, and a man. There are many ostensible "good reasons" for his eventual exile to the countryside where he ends up managing Pugh's farm: his need to lie low lest the law catch up with him for his crimes; the aging of Pugh; the coming of World War II and the consequent shortage of labor. But he had come there chiefly to meditate on his plight and to discover whether there was not some way to mediate in himself the conflicting claims of the Beast and the "spirit." If he is impelled also by a desire to escape for a while from the consequences of his ever-burgeoning desire for Plaxy, he is not quite as aware of it.

In any case, even as the bestial elements in him threaten to dominate the spiritual, she joins him in his retreat. For her move, too, there are "good reasons": her father has been killed, leaving her desolate; she is growing bored with the students she has been teaching; she cannot bring herself either to marry

Robert or to give him up completely; and finally, her mother
dies of grief over her husband and her son, whom she falsely
believes has also been killed in the war. But this provides Plaxy
with a final excuse; since her mother had at the end of her life
been helping Sirius and Pugh on the sheep farm, and they
need, she persuades herself, a substitute.

Eventually, the war is to part them again, as Plaxy is recalled to a job more suitable to her talents and more immediately useful to a beleaguered England. But they do not separate until she and Sirius have set up housekeeping in an
isolated cottage called Tan-y-Voel, remote even from the farm-
house of the Pughs. "I congratulate you, Mr. Sirius, on your
bride," Old Pugh says when Plaxy first arrives, and he thinks
he is joking. But the neighboring farmers, the local kids
scrawling obscene pictures on their walls, and a lubricious
clergyman who weekly sermonizes against "unnatural sin" are
closer to being right in their suspicion that the dog and the
girl have indeed become one flesh as well as one spirit. However "unnatural," theirs is initially a happy union, though
never without an undertone of sadness, a disturbing awareness that it is destined to end soon and tragically:

> . . . Sirius said, "This is not real. It is a very lovely dream.
> Presently I shall wake up." And she, "Perhaps it will not last
> long, but it is real while it lasts. And there is a rightness in it.
> It had to be, to make us one in spirit for ever, whatever else
> may come. We shall be happy, never fear."

But as the hostility and suspicion around them mount, and
they are accused of not just bestiality but witchcraft and even
espionage, their relationship becomes ever "more passionate
and less happy." Yet they do not begin to fall apart, not even
when Robert reenters, turning their lonely idyll into a ménage
à trois. Indeed, even after Plaxy and her former lover have
made love human-style, and Robert, seized with "A revulsion
little short of horror . . . at the thought of leaving her with
the non-human being who she strangely loved," pleads with
her to come away with him, Plaxy answers:

> "No, dear Robert, you don't understand. Humanly, I do love
> you very much, but—how can I say it—super-humanly, in the
> spirit, but therefore in the flesh also, I love my other dear, my
> strange darling. And for him there can never possibly be any-

one but me . . . he can't give me what as a girl I need most.
But I am not just a girl. I am different from all other girls. I am
Plaxy. And Plaxy is half of Sirius-Plaxy, needing the other half.
And the other half needs me."

But Plaxy is at last conscripted, and Sirius begins to distrust all humanity, regarding even his old friend Pugh through
eyes ever more alien and remote. Then he disappears completely, and dreadful reports begin to come back: a dog with
whom he has earlier fought is found dead with his throat torn;
a stray sheep discovered killed and partly eaten. Then, inevitably the half-consumed corpse of a man turns up, and the
whole neighborhood arms to hunt down the killer-dog. At this
point, however, Plaxy manages to get "compassionate leave,"
and returns to track him down before they do—baiting him
with torn scraps of a familiar shirt impregnated with her even
more familiar aroma, calling him with certain inhuman cadences he has taught her, haunting the places they had once
frequented in the surrounding hills. Finally, she gets close
enough to lure him, calling him by name and saying her own:

> . . . but when she was within a few paces he backed, growl-
> ing, away from her. . . . His tail under his belly trembled with
> recognition and love, but his teeth were still bared . . . . Every
> time she advanced, he backed and growled . . . . She covered
> her face with her hands and threw herself on the ground sob-
> bing. The sight of her impotent distress evidently worked the
> miracle . . . for Sirius crept forward, crying with the strife of
> love and fear, till at last he reached out and kissed the back of
> her neck . . . . While she continued to lie still, fearing that
> any movement might scare him away, he nuzzled under her
> face. She turned over and let his warm tongue caress her cheeks
> and lips. Though his breath was foul as a wild beast's and the
> thought of his recent human killing revolted her, she made no
> resistance. At last he spoke. "Plaxy! Plaxy! Plaxy!" He nosed
> into the open neck of her shirt. Then she dared put her arms
> around him.

Though she has actually tasted the beast in him, knowing
him for the murderer of her own kind, she hopes still to domesticate him, dreams the fairy-tale dream that love is enough,
that it is again possible, always possible to "go home."

> "Soon it will be dark enough to go home," she said, "home
> to Tan-y-Voel, my dog, and a great big meal. I'm hungry as

hell. Are you?" He said nothing for a moment; then, "Yester-
day, I ate a part of a man." He must have felt her shudder.
"Oh," he said, "I was savage. And shall be again, unless you
hold me tight with your love."

Though he, too, apparently, still believes in love, he knows
that there is no home for him in the world of the living. Indeed, he has already told her, "The spirit in me needs the
world of men, and the wolf in me needs the wild. I could only
be at home in a sort of Alice-in-Wonderland world, where I
could have my cake and eat it." But, of course, death is that
Wonderland, the dark underground which only young girls
can enter in dreams and leave again with impunity; and Sirius
is delivered to it by a shot out of the darkness, as Plaxy is
attempting to convince him that there is someplace else for
him to go.

Even after he has been mortally wounded, she pleads with
him still, "but, my darling . . . we must get you home before
daylight . . ."; to which he answers, "Dying—stay—Plaxy—
dear," then, "Dying—is very—cold," and at last, "Plaxy-Sir-
ius—worth while." Nothing remains for her, she thinks at first,
except to embrace him and bestow on him a final kiss. Then
she realizes that she must also recognize the reality and inevitability of his death, which she does by singing over his lifeless body a wordless dirge of his own composing, in which,
she realizes, he had predicted and praised his own bitter end.
Only at that point is she ready for her humbler, happier ending: marriage and begetting and useful work in the world of
men. But this Stapledon does not tell us, having already forecast it more than once; and he is able to close, therefore, on a
note of sustained pathos the only passage in all his work which
has ever moved me to tears.

How different Stapledon's tragic version of the myth of the
Animal Groom is from the standard fairy-tale version with its
domestic eucatastrophe. Not only does it end in a premature
death rather than a lifelong marriage, but its male protagonist
is at the close more rather than less bestial. The loving embrace which traditionally redeems him, moreover, occurs not
just once but over and over, each time in vain; and clearly can
only end after a ceremonial hunt which defines him as a beast

in death and forever after. In all of these respects. *Sirius* is more like the more popular twentieth-century travesty of the traditional tale, *King Kong*, in which the discrepancy of "bride" and "groom" is exaggerated until the terror and pathos of their misalliance verges on the ridiculous. Yet, as the recent remake of that film attests, the dream of a love transcending ultimate miscegenation dies hard. In *Sirius*, however, it is ironically undercut from the start; existing as it does chiefly in the ever-hopeful heart of its heroine, but not in the head of its hero, much less that of the narrator of their foredoomed tale.

One of the things that foredooms it, it is suggested, is the very nature of that heroine, who, however vestigially romantic, enters the scene, as is appropriate to her time and place, already devirginated. Indeed, we cannot help suspecting that, unlike her virginal forerunners, she wants it both ways, i.e., desires the Beast both for the possibilities of sublimation she senses in him, and for his sheer murderous beastliness. If she is at all "innocent" in this regard, she is ambiguously so—like prenubile, sexually unawakened girls who fall in love with stallions not in spite of, but precisely because of their dimly sensed phallic menace. And she resembles them, too, in her desire to domesticate her animal lover without quite humanizing him.

In any case, Stapledon's recension of the archetypal story cannot be interpreted as the orthodox Freudian, Bruno Bettelheim, interprets its older prototypes in *The Uses of Enchantment*; arguing that they teach their child audience "that eventually there comes a time when we must learn about what we have not known before—or, to put it psychoanalytically, to undo the repression of sex. What we had experienced as dangerous, loathsome, something to be shunned, must change its appearance so that it is experienced as truly beautiful. It is love which permits this to happen." Then he adds, aware of the sexual bias of such tales, that "at least in the Western tradition . . . only the male aspects of sex are beastly." Though we can continue to retell the old versions of "Beauty and the Beast" in the nursery even in our own time, perhaps (both *Sirius* and *King Kong* would seem to indicate) it is impossible to reimagine it for a contemporary adult audience without in some fundamental way subverting its significance. Moreover, this would be especially true for an author like Stapledon, who considers himself emancipated from the sexual taboos of his ancestors and is bent on portraying a heroine who is herself sexually "liberated."

Yet certain elements in Stapledon's novel are transmitted unchanged from the original tale—along with their implicit meanings. Plaxy is, for instance, like all of her maiden prototypes, the youngest child in her family, and like them she consummates her monstrous marriage in a lonely and ambiguously idyllic setting far from the place where she has grown up. But most strikingly of all, in her case, as in all the others as summarized by Bruno Bettelheim: "It is the father who causes the heroine to join the Beast; she does it because of her love for or obedience to her father. . . ." Stapledon, in fact, goes out of his way to emphasize this point in the commentary of his narrator, Robert, who asks, for intance, after Plaxy has made her final decision to live alone with Sirius, "Does it not seem probable that the underlying motive of this decision was the identification of Sirius with her father?" He feels obliged to add that "Plaxy herself, now my wife, scorns this explanation." But in the very first chapter he has told us of the letters she had written him about her "marriage" to Sirius, in which she herself spoke of her union as "a strange duty" connected with "her father's work."

Clearly, the one significance of the myth which Stapledon found still relevant to his own situation, is the suggestion implicit in this narrative detail that—once more in the words of Bettelheim: "For the girl to love her male partner fully, she must be able to transfer her earlier, infantile attachment to her father. She can do this if he, despite hesitation, agrees to her doing so. . . ." Yet though Stapledon, who quite obviously has in *Sirius* projected upon her his erotic fantasies about his own daughter, permits Plaxy to end up in the arms of her Animal Groom, indeed to belong to him in "spirit" forever, he is less blithe about her being able to do so in the flesh and unscathed than were the anonymous authors of "Beauty and the Beast." Across the ending of his novel, therefore, falls the shadow of another archetypal tale, best known to us perhaps in the story of Romeo and Juliet, which reflects the darker side of his own Oedipal ambivalence: the father's unwillingness to turn his beloved girl child over to one too different in kind from him.

And who is not in some sense "too different" in the unconscious of a father—because of family origin, class, race, religion, nationality, or, inevitably, age? Only those, it turns out, who are too *close* for comfort, and thus raise the specter of incest, which in "giving away" his daughter the father seeks to exorcise. Between the threat of exogamy and the menace of endogamy, there is little psychic space; and Sirius represents both at once, being, in one sense, Plaxy's "brother" and, in another, a creature of an impassively alien species. Small wonder, then, that the myth of the Tabooed or Forbidden Love inhibits the eucatastrophe in Stapledon's novel. Traditionally, however, there is one place in which such impossible unions can be consummated, if the love that binds the unfortunate pair proves as strong as Law itself, but the way to that place is death, mutual and simultaneous. Here once more *Sirius* (and *King Kong*, too) subvert the mythic pattern in a lopsided *Liebestod*, quite different in its implications from the full thanatic unions which give a common archetypal resonance to stories otherwise as different from each other as *Pyramus and Thisbe*, *Tristan and Isolde*, *Antony and Cleopatra*, *Romeo and Juliet*—or, for that matter, James Fenimore Cooper's *The Last of the Mohicans* and Herman Melville's *Pierre*.

It is the girl who survives in *Sirius*, taking in the flesh an all-too-human second husband, though avowing herself eternally bound in "spirit" to the Animal Groom, who has been magically translated like Cupid in Apuleius' *The Golden Ass*, though not into a god but a ghost; which is to say, the dream or myth he was before Plaxy had projected it onto his bestial self. Even so, it is possible to imagine a posthumous union, if the surviving bride is similarly metamorphosed. Stapledon, however, does not portray Plaxy as joining her ghostly lover on the other side, as Catherine joins Heathcliff in *Wuthering Heights*. There is, indeed, in *Sirius* one spirit who is described as having, perhaps, returned from the dead: Plaxy's mother, who appears to the "man-dog" or seems to, telling him with maddening ambiguity, "Don't *believe* I still exist, for that would be false to your intellect; but don't refuse the *feeling* of my presence in the universe, for that would be blind." But there is no indication that Sirius ever manifests himself even so ambiguously to Plaxy. Only the more cryptic hint in the novel's last sentence that he, as Plaxy entones his requiem, has been translated into the Heavens, reincorporated into the undying Morning Star after whom he was named: "As she sang, red dawn filled the eastern sky, and soon the sun's bright finger set fire to Sirius."

A Man Divided was, on its appearance in 1950, the least noticed of all Stapledon's fictions. Indeed, it was not even mentioned in the London Times obituary which appeared shortly thereafter. At that point, his reputation as a novelist had already begun to fade with the general reading public and only a handful of aficionados were aware of his classic status as a writer of science fiction. Most of those who knew of him at all tended to think of him as a second- or third-rank "celebrity," occasionally called out of obscurity to adorn the speaker's list at Communist-sponsored meetings. But how he had become such a celebrity they did not know. Nor did this last of his novels do much to redeem his reputation, seeming to the few who read it then (as it does to the even fewer who read it now) a rather tired book, incoherent, confused—and more than a little dull. Besides, it is not even science fiction; lacking the futurist thrust, the cosmic scope, and even the Wellsian vision of the End of Man, which characterize Stapledon's more successful books.

To be sure, as its title indicates, it is concerned still with the problem of the sundered self, the conflict between the lower and higher elements in human personality, which Stapledon had managed to treat in more or less orthodox science-fiction fashion in Last and First Men, Odd John, and Sirius. But this time he renders it in the "low mimetic mode," demanding of the reader the belief proper to a realistic portrayal of everyday life, rather than the poetic suspension of disbelief appropriate to a prophetic myth. To be sure, A Man Divided insofar as it is a story of a single man possessed turn and turn about by two souls, the grosser of which finally takes over completely, reminds us of Robert Louis Stevenson's haunting symbolist fantasy Dr. Jekyll and Mr. Hyde.

In Stapledon's novel, however, Victor Cadogan-Smith/Vic

Smith is not like Jekyll/Hyde produced in a laboratory by an experimenter who seems more black magician than real scientist. He is a product of "nature," with a psychological etiology rather than experimental physical origin; and his story therefore resembles a case history of "multiple personality" or manic depression, rather than a nightmare expressing the dark ambivalence common to us all. Stapledon's novel is in some sense also an "allegory," a rather perfunctorily fictionalized version of a generalization to be found throughout his work: in *Philosophy and Living*, for instance, and in *Sirius*, where the man-dog reflecting on the "tyrant species," observes, "They were cunning brutes . . . but not nearly so consistently intelligent as he had thought. They were always slipping back into sub-human dullness. . . ." But in this respect, too, it differs, to its disadvantage, from *Dr. Jekyll and Mr. Hyde*, which came to its author in a series of cryptic images, and therefore resists all reductive efforts to interpret it.

In any event, if *A Man Divided* is in one respect something less than *Dr. Jekyll and Mr. Hyde*, in another it is something more. Not only is it a study of psychic splitting, but it is also a didactic essay on a variety of subjects ranging from education to the occult, an autobiography, a love story, and a meditation on growing old. In fact, the autobiographical elements in *A Man Divided* seem most to have intrigued those who have deigned to pay it attention at all; especially the descriptions of experiences attributed to Victor though much like Stapledon's own in shipping offices or as a teacher for the Workers Educational Association and the British Armed Forces. Even more intriguing, though more problematical, are references to the protagonist's extramarital love affairs, his difficulties with his wife and children, his dabbling in radical politics and "spiritualism," his flirtation with suicide. Nonetheless, it is all finally baffling rather than illuminating, since what Stapledon gives with one hand, he takes away with the other. That is to say, Victor Cadogan-Smith, as if deliberately to confuse us, is made four years younger than Stapledon, is given three children instead of two, an aristocratic background rather different from his author's, a military career utterly different (he volunteers for service, becoming an officer and a war hero); and in the end, he dies by his own hand. We are presented, that is to say, with an odd commingling of actual reminiscences and fantasies based, presumably, on what Stapledon wished or feared he might have done: none of it irrelevant as spiritual autobiography, perhaps, but the whole misleading as a factual account of his life.

Furthermore, even in what are apparently the most direct transcriptions from life, Stapledon tends to move too quickly from specifics to generalities, rehashes of essays already published in the magazines to which he contributed, or sketches for what would have seemed more appropriate in their pages. For instance, shortly after Maggie, Victor's great love, has entered the scene, we learn of her conversation with her great-aunt Abigail, a "witch," who on her deathbed tells her, "You will find, Maggie dear, that you can be strong both in the old wisdom and in the new wisdom, about which I know nothing but that the two clashing wisdoms are at the bottom one." This turns out, however, to be a summary of Stapledon's article "Conflict of Wisdoms," in which he had urged the synthesis of the occultist and scientific world views, so that due allegiance could be paid to the "spirit" and the "paranormal."

At least in this case, out of respect to the fictional integrity of his tale, Stapledon is brief. He confines his editorial aside to a few sentences rather than the nearly ten pages he devotes later on to an intrusive essay or perhaps better, harangue, on Workers Education. Presumably spoken by Victor in his "wide-awake" condition to his confidant, the book's provincial, lower-class narrator, that harangue includes—along with some teacher's room anecdotes—reflections, political, and pedagogical, ranging from such pertinent professional observations as:

> . . . the really first-class people, are (quite rightly) so intent on research, and so hard pressed with teaching and administration in the university, that they don't take on extra-mural work and do it whole-heartedly . . . . So the job has to be done largely by people who, though they may be first-class human beings, are not quite first-class academically; because no matter how intelligent they may be, their hearts are not wholly devoted to academic study and research.

to incredibly doltish "Stalinist" clichés, like Vic's response to the narrator's objection that "compulsory" adult education will never work, since "*real* education could never be compulsory":

> "That's an over-simplification. The stalwarts in our movement insist on it, but I'm beginning to doubt it. We shall have to change our minds in the end, otherwise we shall never catch the people who need it most. Of course, when they *are* compelled, we shall have to find out how to make them glad they were compelled. People will put up with compulsion all right if the aim of the compulsion is manifestly a good one . . . . Think how much compulsion is accepted in Russia, for the sake of the new revolutionary state."

There are, moreover, other equally long, and often more tedious, passages in which, abandoning the pretense of fiction almost completely, Stapledon lectures us through his "enlightened" mouthpiece, as if we were not readers in quest of diversion and delight, but extramural students swotting for a certificate. It seems finally, as if only his love story can keep him within the bounds of the "novelistic"; which is to say, keep him true to the promptings of his imagination rather than the demands of his political commitments, as the Jekyll and Hyde aspect of his tale cannot. Yet at first, Maggie appears to be part of that mythic paradigm in which an abused female has traditionally played an essential role. So she seems also to be assimilated into the allegory; representing the way in which each of the two Victors—who elsewhere are shown confronting war and peace, the church, the family, the intellectuals, and the "comrades"—respond to Woman and Love.

But Maggie refuses to remain a symbolic woman. Indeed, from the moment we catch our first glimpse of her, we begin to forget the novel's allegorical intent. She is realized so vividly and particularly that it is impossible to think of her as representing anything except herself:

> . . . She was a well-built wench, certainly, but . . . her shape was somehow rather unfinished, rather like a statue in the rough . . . . And as to her face! I should have advised the sculptor to begin again on fresh stone. The eyes were very wide apart, and of a curious dark grey . . . . Strange eyes, certainly, with lashes and eyebrows of an unusual red-brown. The hair, too, was rust-red . . . . But the nose! The sculptor must have broken the first nose and tried to do something with the stump. It was broad and flat, merely a place where a large

nose might have been. The mouth was fantastically wide and full. The sculptor had evidently been frightened of having another accident, so he had left a great deal of space to play about with . . . .

"She reminds me of a hippopotamus," says the narrator, through whose eyes we have been seeing her. No doubt, he is jealous of her strange charm, by which Victor has clearly been captured; since up to that point he had been, as it were, Victor's only true love. Both as somnolent snob and fully awakened spirit, Victor has had sex with girls and has even courted, indeed almost married one of them. But ever since their days together as Oxford undergraduates, it had been to his friend alone to whom, in his waking state, Victor had poured out his heart; though by the same token, he had bullied and scorned him whenever he lapsed into the surly torpor of his second state. Quite like a wife, we cannot help thinking. Yet however dear he may have been to Victor, for the reader that narrator remains disconcertingly dim; so that we scarcely remember his name (it is Harry Tomlinson), much less what he looks like (he is short and dark, while Victor is tall and blond). He seems sometimes, indeed, less person or even persona than a narrative device—someone after all has to tell the story—or a symbol: *l'homme moyen*, who serves as a foil for both the superhuman and sub-human aspects of his friend.

Yet, however sketchily, Harry is somehow *there* until Maggie's entry, after which he seems utterly to disappear, except as a voice and an ear. Indeed, all the characters of the novel fade in her dazzling, ugly-beautiful light: not just minor figures like Victor's father, the young woman he nearly marries, the three children he eventually begets, even both Victors then, except in relation to her. What moves us in *A Man Divided*, what alone we find hard to forget when all the rest has slipped from our memory is her story, her image. This is true in part, I think, because only she among the book's personages seems to come not from the top of Stapledon's head, but from his deep psyche. She has the hallucinatory vividness of an obsessive dream; and, indeed, we are told that long before Victor had encountered her as a waitress in a London restaurant, he had dreamed her as a child, a poor Shetland fisherman's daughter.

In the novel, the dream proves true, the shadowy figure at its center appears in the flesh and is provided with a whole life history, including amatory misadventures with a lumpen sadist and a Negro sailor. It is, moreover, rendered so specifically and in such detail that I find myself wondering whether Maggie was not drawn from life. Years after Stapledon's death, when Mrs. Stapledon was asked by Harvey Satty whether she was the model for certain female characters in her husband's books, including the maternal figures in *Odd John* and *Sirius*—and Maggie, she acknowledged her relationship to the first two. But of Maggie she said, "I don't think she resembled me very closely, but I think we had the same sort of . . . accommodating attitude." It is only, however, when she has become a long-time wife and mother, that Maggie is presented as essentially "accommodating" rather than as disturbingly problematical. And in any case, she is carefully distinguished from Agnes Stapledon, who, after all, was Olaf's kin and social peer, by her humble origins as well as by her grotesque physical appearance. If there was a model for her in his life, it must have been, I am inclined to believe, one of those premarital or extramarital loves whom Stapledon so tantalizingly hints at—or seems to—everywhere in his work. But perhaps she was only a dream-figure, who had never materialized in actuality and whom he felt obliged therefore to evoke in fiction as he sensed his own death approaching.

Unlike Pax, at any rate, and more like Panther, in *Last Men in London*, the anonymous Neptunian woman in *Far Future Calling*, and certain of the female mutants in *Odd John*, Maggie evokes the mystery not of Maternity but of erotic Ugliness. Frequently, throughout his *oeuvre*, Stapledon expresses his impatience with the limited notions of feminine beauty imposed on us by modern movies and the art of Ancient Greece; and occasionally he suggests, as he does again here, that one test of an "advanced" spirit is its ability to recognize the loveliness of what the conventional world finds merely hideous. Looked at from the outside, however, Stapledon's erotic response to the repulsive and the freakish seems to verge on the pathological—like his identification of supreme moments of "awakening" with the suffering or infliction of pain, which may, in fact, be part of the same syndrome. Certainly in this novel, the second is as nearly omnipresent as the first.

Victor's first awareness of the enlightened self within him comes with his schoolboy experiences of being beaten by a sadistic master and his own brutal chivying of a helpless fellow student. Moreover, his clearest vision of the rightness of the cosmos and the universality of spirit, imperceptible to his doltish alter ego, occurs after he has destroyed a nest of German soldiers (we are back again to his favorite war, World War I), finally shooting one down in cold blood:

> ". . . I must tell you of the other waking I had during the war . . . . We were very heavily shelled, and had a lot of casualties . . . . Presently the Boches came at us from their trench, and in our reduced state we hadn't an earthly . . . the survivors, *en masse*, gave up resisting, and made off down a communication trench. My morale then broke too, and I followed them, helter-skelter . . . . When I woke, I was already mixed up with the others again, stampeding; and the surprise of waking was so startling that I came to a standstill and laughed . . . . I felt a sort of lofty pity for us all, but I was utterly remote and detached . . . . This happened in a flash, and was mixed up with thoughts of Socrates and Jesus Christ and the problem of good and evil . . . .
>
> ". . . I had to do something to assert the integrity of the universal in us. I took the German boys completely by surprise, poor devils, and pitched a handgrenade at them. It was a messy business. One of them was still able to cause trouble when I ran in, but I put a bullet in his face with my pistol. As I did it, I felt a strong friendliness toward him . . . .
>
> ". . . it was as though the little ordinary 'I' woke to be the universal 'I' for a few minutes. I woke to be something more than Victor, even the awakened Victor . . . ."

It is an odd sort of experience for a long-time pacifist, only reluctantly converted to the advocacy of limited violence by a second World War. But the vision which he attributes to the formidable front-line fighter he never was is very like those he had assigned to such characters in his earlier novels as the ambivalent war-resister Paul and the superdog Sirius. What eventually becomes of Maggie, however, is unique in his work. She does not remain like the latter a beast to the end, though one with visions; but, without transcendent illumination becomes fully human: being translated from an ambivalently desired "hippopotamus" to a beloved wife, transmogrified from the Beast to Beauty. So at least Harry sees her relationship with the fully "awakened" Victor:

With the true Victor she attained that passionate friendship
between equals which is the fullest expression of love; though
(she insisted) it was only through his powerful influence on
her that she was able to rise to be in a manner his equal. To
her he seemed always godlike . . . . He had raised her, formed
her spirit. For him and with him she had become more than
herself. In fact he was Eros to her Psyche . . . .

If the allusion to Apuleius suggests that in *A Man Divided*
Stapledon is once more possessed by the myth of "Beauty and
the Beast," it also indicates that this time he is fully conscious
of the fact, as he was not in *Sirius*. It is possible that at the
urging of his friend, E. V. Rieu, he may have been reading a
translation of *The Golden Ass*, which appeared almost simultaneously with his last novel in the Penguin Classics series.
But Stapledon is, in any case, playing games with that archetypal story; doubling it to begin with, as if to signify that in
marriage the female as well as the male yearns for metamor-
phosis in the embrace of the other. If the "true Victor," which
is to say, the "god" present in any "groom," can elevate Maggie to his own level; the other Victor, which is to say the bestial and the juvenile which coexist with the divine in him,
seeks from her a similar upward transformation.

But as the fable develops, it becomes clear that at this point
in his life Stapledon believes that the magic of conjugal love
works only one way. Though early in the book, Victor had
spoken of how when his own unaided efforts are not enough
to keep the best in him alive, it is Maggie's "witchcraft" which
does the job, those powers eventually prove insufficient. As
he grows older, he wakes to full awareness less and less often
and for briefer and briefer periods, which he fears will shrink
to nothing at all. Nor is he comforted by the fact that his doltish
alter ego has during that time begun to try to remake himself
in his image. Unlike the "true Victor," however, that somnolent "brother" cannot remember his other life, but must learn
from secondhand sources—chiefly the writings of the "awakened Victor" and Maggie's imperfect recollections—the nature
of the "god" who shares his body.

In the end, therefore, he becomes not a merging of the two
selves, which Stapledon seems to think both impossible and
undesirable, but a pathetic counterfeit. Though he manages

finally to teach, somewhat inadequately, the "true Victor's" classes and to write essays which reproduce, rather obtusely, his brilliant insights, this leaves him with feelings of inadequacy and guilt. Even when he succeeds in living lovingly with the family he can never quite believe is *his*, no longer brutally alienating his son nor shrinking from the "hideousness" of his wife's animal sexuality, he knows that this is not enough. In terms of the myth once more, he has been metamorphosed from a beast (throughout the text, he is constantly compared to the supercilious, vicious and incorrigibly stupid camel) not into an incarnate deity of love nor even a humanly beautiful bridegroom, but only a terrified baby. When finally, after years of locking her bedroom door against him, Maggie takes him into her bed, it is, therefore, Harry tells us, "not with the exultation or surrender to a god, but almost as if she had given her breast to her baby, with a kind of ardent compassion."

Indeed, the doltish Victor at one point boasts of this, assuring the narrator that though he is well aware that "I can never be to her what my 'brother' is . . . I could give her *something* which he could not give, or not in the same degree, namely a man to mother." If this seems rather like what we gather from the frame story of *Star Maker*, the "Interludes" in *Death into Life* and (more obliquely) the domestic scenes in *Odd John* and *Sirius* was Stapledon's view of his relationship to his own wife, what he then goes on to say is even more so:

> ". . . because I have had an ideal imposed on me, by outside influences, and I haven't the strength (or the effective will) to live up to it, deep in my heart I *hate* the things I love. And so I keep queering my own pitch with sudden acts of resentfulness and cruelty, hurting or insulting the very things I love; hurting Maggie, just because she's too good for me, and because she was forced on me by my other self . . . . And in all this I am not exceptional at all. I am just what the plain man is. O God, how I hate myself sometimes; and him, and everything. I hate the bad things for being bad and the good things for being good."

Even what should have saved him, the aging dolt believes—his occasional "supernormal insights" and the symbiotic union with his wife—have served only to exacerbate his

feelings of impotence and guilt. Nor has the great world around
him, he insists, fared much better than he, threatening indeed
to destroy itself, and thereby the hope of a fairer future. Furthermore, as he walks with Harry and explains all this, Victor's aging body buckles in the blustery weather and his nerve
fails him. "The fact is," he says, "life is getting me down, and
any little thing can take the lid off hell. Everything is so bleak
and hopeless, everything. And I do everything in such a
second-class blindfold way. Fancy never having got beyond
being a journeyman in adult education after all these years!
. . . And now of course the growing old." But at this point,
we become uncomfortably aware of the man behind the mask;
that other sixty-year-old teacher of extramural classes, Olaf
Stapledon, berating himself and condemning the society in
which he lives in much the same terms—though from a public
platform rather than on a lonely moor. How then to tell the
author from the character who cries, "It's *not* finding its soul
. . . . It's damning itself. Within fifty years time it will probably have wiped itself off the planet with atomic warfare."

Though in all of his earlier books there are moments of
apocalyptic despair, never before has he struck this note of
muted melancholy. Nor have any of his characters, however
they may have been tempted to take their own lives, actually
committed suicide. Victor, however, not merely cries out, "To
me the whole of contemporary existence begins to seem like
the last and dullest scene of a rather tiresome play. I want to
get away and go to sleep"; but he does indeed die by his own
hand—taking, of course, his better half with him. Yet Stapledon did not follow his example (though he was dead of a heart
attack before the end of the year in which this book appeared).
Nor does he allow Victor's worse half to have the final word.
He closes instead with a posthumous letter from the "true Victor," answering point by point his "brother's" case against the
world. I find this rebuttal rather unconvincing, however; in
part because its rhetoric seems forced and tired, but most of
all because there is in it nothing which seems new or surprising for a reader of Stapledon's other novels.

"To hell with the poor Dolt's death-wish," he begins by
saying, "where indeed it belongs. My wish is wholly for life,
life eternal, not just for my own individuality . . . but for the

spirit . . . inherent in the lives of all ephemeral individuals."
Then he continues by confronting the threat of World War III,
which Stapledon himself addressed under the auspices of the
Waldorf conference of intellectuals:

> "Out of the horror of our contemporary world, out of our
> sense of doom, our doltish nightmare, comes a new hope of
> true waking . . . and at least the *possibility* of a new world.
> Strange glorious changes are striving for birth . . . .
> "But let us for the sake of argument suppose that the very
> worst does happen, and that within a quarter of a century, or
> a quarter of a year, mankind destroys itself . . . what then?
> Were those who foresaw it fools to remain alive, vainly striv-
> ing against it? No! Even the destruction of a living world is
> worth living through, however painful; if one . . . can see the
> disaster as an episode in the perennial struggle of the spirit in
> the unnumerable successive hosts of individuals in all the
> worlds . . . ."

What *is* a little new and surprising, perhaps, is that through
the "awakened" Victor, Stapledon finally faces up to the problem of personal immortality. It had, in fact, haunted him from
the start, but customarily he had dealt with in metaphorical
disguise as the End of Man or the End of Everything:

> " . . . Maybe death is simply the complete ending of us;
> and if so, let us be grateful for eternal sleep. Maybe we go on
> from aeon to aeon in subsequent temporal lives . . . for the
> progressive fashioning of our individual souls . . . . Maybe
> we wake in some completely *other* temporal and spatial (or
> non-spatial) system of existence, made . . . of something in-
> conceivable to us. Or again, maybe at death we are gathered
> up at once into eternity . . . ."

"But," he interrupts himself, "I still haven't said what I wanted
to say." And what he wanted to say turns out to be, after all
this high-level speculation, reminiscent of Socrates in the
*Apology*, almost absurdly anti-climactic, though also truly pathetic in one somehow aware of the imminence of his own
death:

> " . . . If I do survive, I shall do my best to make some sort
> of contact with Maggie, and with you, too, Harry, you old
> sceptic. So, both of you, please keep an ear open for the tele-
> phone bell, so to speak. I may have something important to
> say . . . ."

# AFTERWORD

Whether Victor ever contacted Maggie or Harry from the "other side," we have no way of knowing. We do have, however, a posthumous message from Olaf Stapledon himself in the form of an incomplete manuscript, lovingly edited by his wife. It is addressed, however, neither to her nor to his long-time confidant E. V. Rieu, only to the numinous presence which true believers call "God" but which he refers to simply as "you." Published in 1954 under the title of *The Opening of the Eyes*, this after-the-last work is a kind of prayer or psalm, whose opening strophe, "The Shock of Vision," begins, "At last I have seen you!/My mind's star, my heart's heart!," and ends, "It is enough that I have seen you. Help me be faithful to you in the utmost of my power." His prayer is answered immediately by an inner voice which is not his own; and he cries triumphantly, "You, who will not let me call you God, have said in my heart, 'I am, and you are mine. Even your sin is mine.'"

But his vision and the euphoria it has engendered are soon threatened, as that voice evokes for him the recent death in intolerable pain of a "saintly" friend; and he is moved to protest, "if you are for me a God of love, you are equally . . . a God of ruthless power, scorning tenderness." Finally, indeed, his contemplation of the mystery of unmerited suffering plunges him into something much like what mystics have traditionally dubbed "the dark night of the soul": the exacerbated agony of those who have attained ultimate illumination and lost it. "The vacuum is complete in the belljar of my soul," he writes. "The little bird that breathed the air of your presence lies dead . . . the vacuum itself is hell, the dumb and frightening presence of sheer nothingness . . . it creeps into the soul. It licks and looses and dissolves the firmest tissues of the soul."

Yet the ineffable "you" returns once more, this time demanding that Stapledon describe what he has seen, bearing witness if only to himself. And the prayer becomes a meditation and confession, in which Stapledon recounts his own spiritual odyssey from the moment he watched the seals from the cliff and conceived *Last and First Men*:

> Long ago (it was while I was scrambling on a rugged coast, where great waves broke in blossom on the rocks) I had a sudden fantasy of man's whole future, aeon upon aeon of strange vicissitudes and gallant endeavours in world after world, seeking a glory never clearly conceived, often betrayed, but little by little revealed. The seeming was you, and the glory was you. Since then, year after year, I have tried to create in words symbols of that vision. The labour was you; and you were the splendour which those crude symbols failed to manifest.

But, as the passage itself confesses, we have heard all he has to say before; so that I at least feel dismayed to be told it all again—wondering what compels him beyond the old man's need to rehearse the story of his life to whomever will listen, again and again and again.

Beginning in 1946 with the "Interludes" of *Death into Life* (one of which in its original form evoked his earliest memory of himself as a baby leaving "a wet patch on the knee of a doting visitor in a Victorian drawing-room") and the autobiographical passages in his last book-length essay *Youth and Tomorrow*, and climaxing in *A Man Divided*, he had more and more shamelessly used his work as an occasion for reminiscence. Similarly, he had turned a 1948 address to the British Interplanetary Society into a resumé of all his earlier theoretical work. To be sure, in *The Opening of the Eyes*, he recaptures a splendor of rhetoric and a precision of language absent from his books ever since *Darkness and the Light*. He uses it, however, only to treat again his lifelong flirtation with the Christian Church ("I can neither go in with the faithful nor boldly turn back to join the triumphant forces of the Godless . . ."); his wrestling with the "scientific" view of man as an insignificant animal doomed to extinction; his ambivalent response to the utopian "Religion of Progress"; and especially his obsession with Russian communism and the World Revolution.

Before he is through, Stapledon has managed to touch on every topic that has ever concerned him, from entropy and the social role of the arts to the relative nature of time and the mounting evidence for the validity of "paranormal" experiences; even rehearsing once more his advocacy of conjugal love with extramarital privileges. Indeed, one of the oddest passages of the book occurs toward its close, when in a penultimate conversation with his "disbelieved-in God," Stapledon confesses that "alas, through loving you I fatally love not one nor two but every potential sweet companion whom I meet. For each of them is you." To this "you" answers ("Dare I believe, great daimon," Stapledon asks parenthetically, "that your answer conceals a smile?"), "If you love them all strictly as symbols of celestial beauty, you cannot have too many. But if so, you must be nearer sainthood than your behaviour declares."

No, sooner is this uncharacteristically humorous colloquy over, however, than Stapledon feels the "daimon" withdraw, leaving him once more "a frightened minnow." Indeed, this remains the pattern, throughout; as the inveterately twi-minded "I," unsure whether the presence or absence of the terrible "You" is more intolerable, prays sometimes, "Possess me . . . so strongly that I shall never again fall from you, never sink back into the nightmare that was formerly I," and sometimes, "Give me at least unawareness of you. Give me oblivion. Let me at last escape into annihilation." But the ambivalence is hardly new, being indeed the hallmark of Stapledon's work. Finally, it is difficult to grant that there is *anything* substantially different in *The Opening of the Eyes* from what Stapledon has already written about himself, his world, or the numinous power he elsewhere calls, "the Star Maker," "the Whole," "the Dark-Light," or "the Other." Yet he himself in-

sists throughout that its occasion was a unique vision, vouchsafed to him only when he was "very old" and prescient
somehow of his imminent death.

A small controversy, therefore, continues to this day over
whether his posthumously published essay represents an unprecedented breakthrough on Stapledon's part into certainty,
peace, and at-oneness with the Creator of All, or only a reca-
pitulation of the dialectic interplay of faith and doubt which
had characterized his thinking from the start. E. V. Rieu in his
preface contends on the basis of his reading of the text, as well
as a conversation he had with Stapledon a year or so before
he died, that he "had come to terms with reality; and comprehension had been added to acceptance. There was a note of
serenity in his bearing . . . . " Quoting these words in 1963,
in an article titled "Olaf Stapledon: Cosmic Philosopher," Sam
Moskowitz raised the ante a little, stating point-blank, "He had
accepted God. He had admitted the Cosmic Mind at last."

But to this, Agnes Stapledon objected strongly, telling
Harvey Satty that she had been "a bit upset" by Moskowitz's
conclusion; since though it was "very similar" to Rieu's in the
preface to which she had earlier given her blessing, "Moskowitz took it a step further, which made it seem less acceptable."
She appears also to have complained to Moskowitz himself;
this time, however, out of courtesy perhaps, shifting the burden of the blame to Rieu. So, anyhow, her comments which
Moskowitz cites in his later piece, "Olaf Stapledon: The Man
and his Work," first published in *Fantasy Commentator* for
Winter 1978-79, suggest. "It is much too simple and final,"
she writes. "I hope Olaf was as serene in his thinking as Rieu
believed him to be—but if he was serene I don't believe it was
because 'comprehension had been added to acceptance.' I believe, rather, that he had come to terms with reality by preparing himself to surrender the struggle to comprehend . . . . "

Indeed, the very passage which Moskowitz quotes in support of his, and presumably Rieu's, position seems to me in
its non-commital caginess ("perhaps," "disbelieved-in," "illusion," "pretense," and "fiction" are strange words for an
unequivocal declaration of faith) to sustain Mrs. Stapledon's
demurral:

Is this perhaps hell's most exquisite refinement, that one
should be haunted by the ever-present ghost of a disbelieved-
in God . . . . Illusion though you are, I prefer to act in the
pretense of your reality, rather than from stark nothingness.
Without the fiction of your existence, I am no more than a
reflex animal and the world is dust.

She protested also against Moskowitz's unqualified assertion that her husband "had renounced Communism and socialism," asserting that Olaf "had never been a member of the
Communist Party, but he continued to admire some things
about the Communist philosophy, just as he continued to de-
test some attitudes and actions of the party members. He never
abandoned the socialist ideal in which he included all that
was best in Communism . . . . "

But Moskowitz apparently clung to his opinion on this
subject, wanting, needing to do so, perhaps, because he had
been present at the Communist-sponsored meeting for peace
in Newark, New Jersey, in the context of which Stapledon's
prized ambivalence seemed something closer to duplicity. In
support of his position, he cites in his second article a passage
from A Man Divided, describing Victor's break with the comrades after they had asked him to lie on their behalf, and one
from The Opening of the Eyes, in which Stapledon declares,
"If one must reject the comrades, it is because they work for a
world-wide revolution. For the world revolution, a painful social change, is the only hope. But what sort of revolution do
the comrades desire, and by what methods do they work for
it?" Yet the quotation from the novel is, even if we presume
it to express the author's as well as the character's point of
view, equivocal at the best; while the extract from The Opening of the Eyes represents just one stage in a long, complex
argument with himself which constitutes the crux, the very
center, of Stapledon's last book.

To understand the real import, then, of his presumably final disavowal of communism, we must put it back into context; realizing first of all that it appears at the very beginning
of the forty-first section of the fifty-three into which the work
is divided. The whole section, called "Rejection of the Comrades," is itself an introduction to a developing argument
which climaxes three sections later, when under the heading

"Desertion of the World," Stapledon writes in a passage, the last two sentences of which Moskowitz had quoted in his earlier piece:

> . . . I will not any longer meddle in the mad world's corruption. I will keep myself clean for you. With wholesome disgust I spurn the world, I spurn the flesh, I spurn beauty, I spurn love. Above all I spurn the subtle lure that snares the comrades, the call of brotherhood in the Revolution, and in mankind's seeming progress! There can be no progress but the lonely climbing of each solitary soul toward you.

In light of this, it is clear that Stapledon's rejection of communism arises from his resolve to transcend all earthly allegiances, rather than a political change of heart. Indeed, the "comrades" represent for him the noblest of all temptations and therefore the most difficult to resist. He had indicated this much earlier, writing in Section 38, as his vision and his faith in himself faltered, "Not your voice, fictitious daimon, but only the voice of the comrades, can speak to me with authority . . . . The comrades insistently call me. Their contempt for my hesitation and squeamishness undermines me . . . ." Nor is his rejection of them final, since scarcely has he declared it than the voice of the "daimon" speaking from his heart suggests that this decision, like his resolve to foreswear the pleasures of the flesh, may have been prompted merely by "a vulgar itch for spiritual superiority."

"Discipline you surely need," that inner voice goes on to tell him, "but for the world's sake, not your own desired salvation. Here at least you may learn from the comrades, who know well, in their way, that salvation is not for any lone individual but for the community." Moreover, as Stapledon's prayer, which has become a meditation then a confession without ceasing ever to be a prayer, draws to a close, the apocalyptic view of society which possesses him is rather like the one being propagated by the "comrades" in that time of the Cold War:

> Between rich and poor, masters and servants, leaders and led, employers and workers, there can be no trust, no friendliness. And now between the embattled halves of the world, with their conflicting gospels, each half-true, half-false, the final war begins.

In the qualifying phrase "half-true, half-false," however, Stapledon betrays the growing skepticism, which by under-cutting the claims of both sides, is leading him nearer and nearer to total despair; and which he resolves not in some newfound serenity, but in the desperate hope beyond hope in which he had sought refuge before. Indeed, the words in which he describes his final attitude echo the concluding paragraph of *Last and First Men* written two decades earlier:

> And even if by some miracle mankind achieves a happier state, what then? Sooner or later, some unimportant astronom-ical event will casually destroy us. Or may you not at any mo-ment project upon us out of your supramundane sphere some immaterial and inconceivable fiat to annihilate our universe?
>
> And no matter what catastrophe destroys us, it will be no accident but the intended climax of your music.
>
> And in all other worlds in all your galaxies, the upshot no doubt will be the same. Sparks and hints of joy are everywhere turned to grief.

This time, however, the last word is "grief"; and though there are two sections on free will and necessity which follow, it marks the real end of the meditation, insofar as it ends at all. Stapledon left *The Opening of the Eyes* unfinished, I am tempted to believe, not just because death intervened, but be-cause it is essentially unfinishable—like his *oeuvre* as a whole destined never to achieve closure. As his bipolar titles have all along declared, *Last and First Men*, *Darkness and the Light*, *Saints and Revolutionaries*, *Philosophy and Living*, *A Story Between Jest and Earnest*, *A Fantasy of Love and Discord*, Sta-pledon was a man divided, in whose imagination thesis and antithesis forever aspired toward a synthesis they could never attain.

# CHRONOLOGY

1886 Born on May 10 in Wallasey, Merseyside, England, to William Clibbett Stapledon and Emmaline Miller.

1886–92 Lives in Port Said, Egypt.

1893–99 Attends Abbotsholme School, Uttotexter, Derbyshire.

? B.A. and M.A. in History, Balliol College, Oxford.

1910–11 Master at Manchester Grammar School.

1911–13 Works for Blue Funnel Line in Liverpool and Port Said.

1913–15 Teaches for Workers Educational Association and also extension courses for the University of Liverpool.

1915–19 Serves with Friends Ambulance Unit in France.

1919 Marries Agnes Zena Miller on July 16 at Friends Meeting House, Reigate, Surrey.

1920 Ph.D., Philosophy, University of Liverpool.

1920–40 Lives at 7 Grovesnor Avenue, West Kirby.

1920 Takes up lecturing again for Workers Educational Association and teaches extension courses in psychology, philosophy, and industrial history. Daughter Mary born on May 30.

1923 Son John David born on November 6.

1930 Publishes his first novel, *Last and First Men*, whose mythic universe and philosophical themes were to be the basis of all his later fiction.

1932 Death of father. Publishes *Last Man in London*, considered a sequel to *Last and First Men*.

1935 Death of mother. *Odd John* published.

1937 Publishes *Star Maker*, extending to its limits the macrohistory of *Last and First Men*.

1939 A full-time member of the University of Liverpool staff.

1942 Returns to fiction, after five years of non-fiction works, with *Darkness and the Light*.

1944 *Sirius* published.

1949 Only British delegate at the Cultural and Scientific Conference for World Peace held at the Waldorf-Astoria, New York City.

1950 Last work, *A Man Divided*, published. Dies on September 6.

# CHECKLIST OF WORKS
# BY OLAF STAPLEDON


## Books

*Latter-Day Psalms*. Liverpool: Henry Young, 1914. (non-fiction)

*A Modern Theory of Ethics: A Study of the Relations of Ethics and Psychology*. London: Methuen, 1929. (non-fiction)

*Last and First Men: A Story of the Near and Far Future*. London: Methuen, 1930. (fiction)

*Last Men in London*. London: Methuen, 1932. (fiction)

*Waking World*. London: Methuen, 1934. (non-fiction)

*Odd John: A Story Between Jest and Earnest*. London: Methuen, 1935. (fiction)

*Star Maker*. London: Methuen, 1937. (fiction)

*New Hope for Britain*. London: Methuen, 1939. (non-fiction)

*Saints and Revolutionaries*. London: Methuen, 1939. (non-fiction)

*Philosophy and Living*. Harmondsworth: Penguin Books, 1939. (non-fiction)

*Beyond the "Isms."* London: Secker and Warburg, 1942. (non-fiction)

*Darkness and the Light*. London: Methuen, 1942. (fiction)

*Old Man in New World*. London: Allen and Unwin, 1944. (fiction)

*Sirius: A Fantasy of Love and Discord*. London: Secker and Warburg, 1944. (fiction)

*The Seven Pillars of Peace*. London: Commonwealth, 1944. (non-fiction)

*Death into Life*. London: Methuen, 1946. (fiction)

*Youth and Tomorrow*. London: St. Botolph, 1946. (non-fiction)

*The Flames: A Fantasy*. London: Secker and Warburg, 1947. (fiction)

*A Man Divided*. London: Methuen, 1950. (fiction)

*The Opening of the Eyes*. Ed. A. Z. Stapledon. Preface by E. V. Rieu. London: Methuen, 1954. (fiction, posthumous)

*"Nebula maker."* Hayes Middlesex: Bran's Head Books, Ltd., 1976. (fiction, posthumous)

*Far Future Calling: Uncollected Science Fiction and Fantasies*. Ed. Sam Moskowitz. Philadelphia: Oswald Train, 1979. (fiction, posthumous)

Selected Articles

"Experiences in the Friends' Ambulance Unit." *We Did Not Fight: Experiences of War Resisters*, ed. Julian Bell. London: Cobden-Sanderson, 1935. Pp. 359–74.

"A World of Sound." *Hotch-Potch*, ed. John Brophy. Liverpool: Council of the Royal Liverpool Children's Hospital, 1936. Pp. 243–51. (fiction)

"Science, Art and Society." *The London Mercury* 38 (Oct. 1938), pp. 521–28.

"The Claims of Politics." *Scrutiny* 8 (Sept. 1939), pp. 151–56.

"Escapism in Literature." *Scrutiny* 8 (Dec. 1939), pp. 299–308.

"Tradition and Innovation To-day." *Scrutiny* 9 (June 1940), pp. 33–45.

"Literature and the Unity of Man." *Writers in Freedom: A Symposium*, ed. Hermon Ould. London, New York, Melbourne: Hutchinson & Co., 1941. Pp. 113–19.

"Sketch-Map of Human Nature." *Philosophy: The Journal of the British Institute of Philosophy* 17 (July 1942), pp. 210–30.

"The Great Certainty." *In Search of Faith: A Symposium*, ed. Ernest W. Martin. London: Lindsay Drummond, 1943. Pp. 37–59.

"What Are 'Spiritual' Values?" *Freedom of Expression: A Symposium*, ed. Hermon Ould. London, New York, Melbourne: Hutchinson International Authors, 1944. Pp. 16–26.

"The Core." *The Windmill*. London: William Heinemann, Ltd., 1945. Pp. 112–18. (fiction)

"Skepticism and the Modern World." *World Review*, pp. 55–59.

"Reconstruction in Holland." *Contemporary Review* 169 (Feb. 1946), pp. 71–76.

"The Religious Approach." *The Present Question*, ed. H. Westmann. London: Chapman & Hall, 1947. Pp. 108–23.

"Data for a World View: The Human Situation and Natural Science." *Enquiry* 1 (1948), pp. 13–18.

"Data for a World View: Paranormal Experiences." *Enquiry* 1 (1948), pp. 13–18.

"Interplanetary Man." *Journal of the British Interplanetary Society* 7 (1948), pp. 213–33.

"The Meaning of Spirit." *Here and Now: Miscellany*, eds. Peter Albery and Sylvia Read. London: Falcon Press, 1949. Pp. 72–82.

"Conflict of Wisdoms." *Enquiry* 2 (1949), pp. 24–29.

# SELECT LIST OF WORKS
## ABOUT OLAF STAPLEDON

Bailey, K. V., "A Prized Harmony: Myth, Symbol and Dialectic in the Novels of Olaf Stapledon," in *Foundation: The Review of Science Fiction* (Jan. 1979, no. 15), ed. Malcolm Edwards (London, 1979).

Coates, J. B., "Olaf Stapledon," in *Ten Modern Prophets* (1944).

Davenport, Basil, "The Vision of Olaf Stapledon," introduction to *To the End of Time* (1953).

Gillings, Walter H., "Men of the Space Age," *Fantasy Review* (Dec. 1948–Jan. 1949). Reports the content of Stapledon's extemporaneous speech at the October 9, 1948, meeting of the British Interplanetary Society. This is not the same as his prepared speech which was printed in the *Journal of the British Interplanetary Society* (Nov. 1948).

———, "The Philosopher of Fantasy," *Scientifiction* (June 1937).

Kunitz, Stanley J., and Howard Haycraft, eds., biographical sketch, in *Twentieth Century Authors* (1942).

Martin, E. W., "Between the Devil and the Deep Sea: The Philosophy of Olaf Stapledon," in *The Pleasure Bond*, ed. Malcolm Elwin (1947).

Michel, John B., "The Philosophical Novels of Olaf Stapledon," *The Alchemist* (Summer 1940).

Moskowitz, Sam, ed., *Far Future Calling: Uncollected Science Fiction and Fantasies of Olaf Stapledon* (Philadelphia: Oswald Train, 1979).

Moskowitz, Sam, "The Flames; a Fantasy," *Fantasy Commentator* 2 (Winter 1947–48).

———, "Olaf Stapledon: Cosmic Philosopher," introduction to *Darkness and the Light* (Westport, Ct: Hyperion Press, 1974).

———, "Peace and Olaf Stapledon," limited-edition brochure of 112 copies (1952). An abridgement, "Bold Man in New World," appeared in *Shangri-La* (Oct. 1949).

Smith, Curtis C., introduction to *To the End of Time* (Boston: Gregg Press, G. K. Hall & Co., 1975).

————, "Olaf Stapledon: Saint and Revolutionary," *Extrapolation: A Journal of Science Fiction and Fantasy* (Dec. 1971), pp. 5–15.

————, "Olaf Stapledon's Dispassionate Objectivity," in *Voices for the Future*, Vol. 1 of *Essays of Major Science Fiction Writers*, ed. Thomas D. Claresan (Bowling Green, Ohio: Bowling Green University, Popular Press, 1976).

"Un Utopiste au XX Siecle, W. Olaf Stapledon, (I) Les Themes Scientifiques, (II) La Fiction Litteraire," *Caliban* 2, 3 (1967).

Versins, Pierre, ed., *Encyclopedie de L'Utopie des Voyages Extraordinaires et de la Science Fiction* (Lausanne: L'Age d'Homme, 1972), pp. 829–34.

"The Worlds of Olaf Stapledon: Myth or Fiction?" (*Mosaic* XIII, nos. 3–4), in *Other Worlds: Fantasy and Science Fiction Since 1939*, special issue, ed. John J. Teunissen (Winnipeg: University of Manitoba, 1980).

# INDEX